Kids of All Ages

BIG BOOK of Bible Crafts

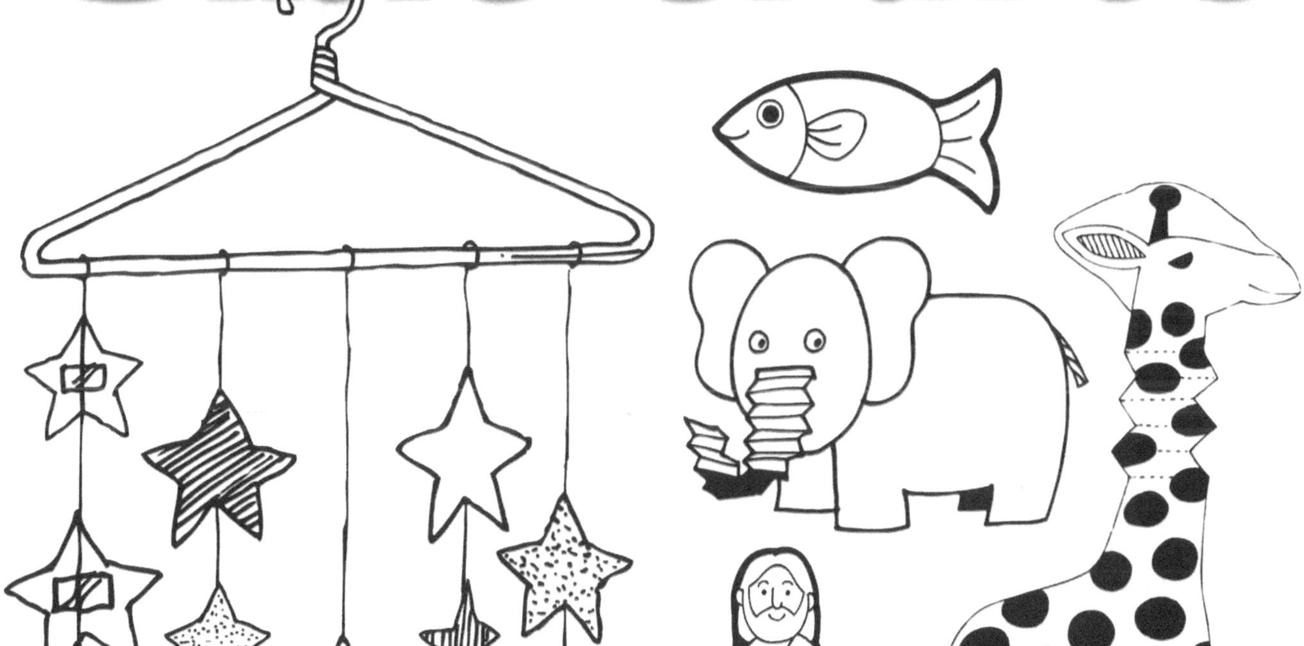

DAVID C COOK
transforming lives together

BIG BOOK OF BIBLE CRAFTS FOR KIDS OF ALL AGES
Published by David C Cook
4050 Lee Vance Drive
Colorado Springs, CO 80918 U.S.A.

Integrity Music Limited, a Division of David C Cook
Brighton, East Sussex BN1 2RE, England

ISBN 978-0-8307-7239-1

The content included in this book was originally published in *Bible Crafts & More Ages 3–6* by Standard Publishing in 2005 © Standard Publishing, ISBN 978-0-7847-1784-4; *Really Big Book of Cool Crafts for Kids* by Gospel Light in 2005 © Gospel Light, ISBN 978-0-8307-3847-2; *The Big Book of Bible Crafts* by Gospel Light in 2000 © Gospel Light, ISBN 978-0-8307-2573-1; and *Hot Crafts for Cool Kids for Ages 9–11* by David C Cook in 2009 © David C Cook, ISBN 978-1-4347-6722-6.

Cover Design: James Hershberger
Illustrators: Lynne Davis, Chizuko Yasuda, Marilee Harrald-Pilz,
Kriseida Vallejo, Sandy Flewelling

Printed in the United States of America

6 7 8 9 10 11 12 13 14 15

081524

Contents

Section Two: Grades 1–6

Old Testament

New Testament

Bible Verse Crafts

Helping children memorize God's Word can be especially fun when combined with a craft that the children take home. Choose from these crafts to teach specific Bible verses.

How to Use This Book

The activities in *Big Book of Bible Crafts for Kids of All Ages* can be done in any order and easily fit into any curriculum. Simply use the Contents pages to match a project with the lesson you're teaching. The crafts can also be used at home to teach and reinforce Bible stories and lessons.

The book is divided into two sections—crafts for young children (preschool and kindergarten) and crafts for elementary children (grades 1–6). In each section, the Bible-related crafts are arranged in biblical order. Crafts based on stories from the life of Jesus are arranged in chronological order.

For each craft, you will find:

Materials

The materials you will need to gather for the craft are listed in this section. Most projects use only basic materials, along with some items easily found at craft, hardware, or discount stores.

As you prepare for the number of children doing the craft, remember to have extra pieces in case of mistakes or lost pieces. Replenish basic supplies, such as glue, scissors, markers, etc., as needed.

Before Class

This section provides instructions for any preparations you need to do. In addition to copying patterns, precutting materials, etc., make up a sample of each project to be sure the directions are fully understood and potential problems are avoided.

Simplification and Enrichment Ideas

Tips have been added to some crafts to help you adapt the crafts for children with varying skill levels. You can adapt a craft for younger age levels by utilizing the simplification ideas. Use the enrichment ideas to challenge older kids to go a step further with their crafts.

Instructions for Children

Step-by-step instructions are given for what the children are to do. As children create their crafts, look for times when you can talk about the ways God shows His love to us. Ask open-ended questions. Listen with interest to the answers and give the children opportunities to ask questions of their own.

Talk About

The projects in this book include thought-provoking, age-appropriate questions and conversations that can help you enhance craft times. The conversations for a project may relate to a Bible story, a biblical principle, or a Scripture verse. It may include interesting facts related to the craft. Share these conversation suggestions with other adult helpers so they can use them with individual children or small groups. Always have a Bible open to the proper passage when reviewing a Bible story or reinforcing a specific verse.

Tips

Crafts are an excellent way for children to express their creativity while they build relationships with others. When children are focused on using their hands to create a project, they are often more relaxed and willing to talk or listen than they might be in formal classroom settings. Following a few helpful tips can make craft times successful for everyone!

Select and Adapt

Children may become discouraged when a project is too difficult for them. Finding the right projects increases the likelihood children will be successful and satisfied with their finished products. Begin your selection by focusing on crafts designed for the ages of your children, but don't ignore projects for older or younger ages. Remember that elementary-age children enjoy many of the projects geared for preschool and kindergarten children. And younger children are always interested in doing "big kid" things. Plan on working along with the children, helping with tasks they can't handle alone.

Feel free to alter the craft materials and instructions in this book to suit your children's needs. Adapt crafts for younger or older children by using the simplification or enrichment ideas provided.

Plan for including children with special needs. Discuss with parents or caregivers the kinds of crafts their children can be successful at doing. Provide adaptive scissors and large crayons that can be held with the whole fist. Bingo daubers work great for adding color to a project! Be aware of a child's sensitivity to various textures and smells. Watch for signs of frustration and provide less-structured projects for the child—modeling dough, collage materials, etc.

Be Prepared

If you are planning to use crafts with a child at home, here are some helpful tips:

- Start with projects that call for materials you have around the house. Make a list of items you do not have so you can gather them.
- If certain materials seem too difficult to obtain, a little thought can usually lead to appropriate substitutions. Often your creative twist ends up being an improvement over the original plan.

If you are planning to lead a group of children in doing craft projects, keep these hints in mind:

- Choose projects that allow children to work with a variety of materials.
- Make a sample of each project to be sure you understand the instructions so you can avoid potential problems.
- For a larger group, you may want to adapt some projects by simplifying procedures or varying the materials required.

- Plan your project selections far enough in advance to allow time to gather all needed supplies. Many items can be acquired as donations from individuals or businesses, if you plan ahead and make your needs known.

Encourage and Show Interest

Encourage creativity in each child! Always remember that for a child, the process of creating is more important than what the final product may look like to an adult. Provide a variety of materials with which children may work so they may make creative choices on their own. Don't insist that children "stay inside the lines" or make their projects "look just like the sample."

Show an interest in the unique way each child approaches a project. Avoid the temptation to say, "That's cute." Instead, affirm the choices the child has made during the process. ("I see you like to paint with blue." "You really used lots of circles.") Treat each child's work as a masterpiece. The comments you give a child today can affect the way that child views art in the future, so be positive. Being creative is part of being made in the image of God, the ultimate creator!

Be sure to encourage students to personalize their crafts. Listen carefully so you can bounce off students' comments or ideas as they work. Sometimes spontaneous discussion is the most meaningful.

Make It a Message

Many projects can easily become crafts with a message. Invite older children to create slogans or poetry they may print on their projects. Print out the words younger children dictate to you. Print on a whiteboard or piece of paper words to be written on a craft, allowing children to copy what you have written. Provide copies of an appropriate poem, thought, or Bible verse for children to attach to their crafts.

Make It Fun

Don't forget that craft time should be a relaxed and fun time. If the unexpected happens, keep your sense of humor and encourage kids to enjoy the process and the interaction of the group.

Leading a Child to Christ

One of the greatest privileges of serving in children's ministry is to help guide children to become members of God's family. Pray and ask God to prepare the kids you know to understand and receive the good news about Jesus. Ask God to give you the sensitivity and wisdom to communicate effectively and to be aware as opportunities occur.

When talking with children about salvation, use words and phrases they understand; never assume kids understand a concept just because they can repeat certain words. Avoid symbolic terms that will confuse literal-minded thinkers. As you watch and pray, you will see kids developing relationships with God.

Here are some questions you can ask and things you can discuss with a child who is interested in accepting Jesus as their Lord and Savior. Encourage the child to look up and read the Bible verses along with you.
Read John 3:16. **Why did God send Jesus to earth?** (God loved us so much that He wants us to have eternal life with Him.)

First John 3:1 says that God wants us to be His children. But sin, doing wrong, separates us from God. Read Romans 6:23. **What do you think should happen to us when we sin?** (die) **But what is God's gift to us?** (eternal life in Jesus)

Jesus willingly died on the cross to take the punishment for our sins. Read 1 Corinthians 15:3. **But Jesus didn't stay in the tomb. After three days, He came back to life! Jesus died so that we can live forever in heaven with Him.**

Are you sorry for the wrong things that you've done? If you are, what should you do? Read 1 John 1:9. **Our sins are wiped away when we're truly sorry for what we've done and when we turn to God.**

Read Ephesians 2:8. **How are we saved?** (by God's grace, through faith) **Christian faith is a lifelong adventure here on earth. With Jesus as Lord of our lives, we build a life of submitting to God, following Jesus, and keeping in step with the Spirit.**

At this point, continue to talk with the child about accepting Jesus as Lord and Savior. Include what your church teaches about how this happens. If you have any questions about salvation, talk with your pastor or children's ministry leader.

God wants every person to accept the free gift of eternal life that He's offering. What do you need to do about this?

Craft Recipes

Flubber

- 3 c. warm water
- 2 c. white glue
- 3 tsp. borax
- food coloring *(optional)*

Mix 1½ cups warm water and the white glue in a bowl. In a second bowl, mix 1½ cups warm water and the borax. If adding food coloring, add it to the water and borax mixture, one drop at a time.

Pour the borax mixture into the glue mixture. Use a metal spoon to lift and turn the mixture until only a teaspoon of liquid remains. Pour off the excess liquid. Store the mixture in an airtight container.

Goop

- ½ c. cornstarch
- ¼ c. water
- food coloring (or tempera powder)

Mix the cornstarch, water, and food coloring. Pour the mixture onto a tray or into bowls. Allow the children to explore! Store the mixture in an airtight container.

Modeling Dough

- 2 c. flour
- 1 c. salt
- ½ tbsp. cream of tartar
- ¼ c. cornstarch
- small drop of oil
- 1 c. cold water
- food coloring (or dry flavored gelatin)

Mix the flour, salt, cream of tartar, cornstarch, and oil. Knead the dough and slowly add cold water until the dough is soft and forms a ball. Divide the dough into smaller portions and add food coloring, one drop at a time. Store the prepared dough in airtight containers.

Putty

- ⅓ c. laundry starch
- 1 c. white glue
- food coloring, scented oil or extract *(optional)*

Pour the starch into a bowl. Mix in the food coloring and scented oil or extract, if desired. Slowly pour the glue into the starch, stirring the mixture as the glue is added. The mixture should begin to clump together.

Let the mixture rest three to five minutes. Then pour it onto a cookie sheet or countertop and knead several minutes. If the mixture is sticky, add a small amount of starch. The putty should not stick to fingers or playing surface. Store in an airtight container in the refrigerator.

Sugar Dough

- 2 c. sugar
- 3 c. flour
- 1 c. water
- food coloring, scented extract *(optional)*

Mix the sugar, flour, and water together. Stir in a few drops of food coloring to color the dough, if desired. Add a few drops of scented extract to make it smell nice. Knead the dough until it is smooth. Store in an airtight container.

Textured Paint

- 2 c. gray (or desired color) tempera paint
- ½ c. grit or sand
- 4 tbsp. white glue

Mix all the ingredients together. Store in an airtight container.

Section One

Preschool–Kindergarten

Crafts for Young Children

Remember these guiding principles as you work on any craft with young children:

- The process the child goes through is more important than the finished product.
- Don't override the child's delight of experimenting with color and texture.
- Avoid the temptation to do the project for the child or to improve on a child's efforts.
- If you have a child who seems frustrated with some of the limitations of working on a structured craft, the frustration may be a signal that the child needs an opportunity to work with more basic, less-structured materials: blank paper and paints, play dough, abstract collage shapes and objects that can be glued onto surfaces such as paper or cardboard.

Using Glue

Purchase glue in large containers (up to one-gallon size). Since preschoolers have difficulty using glue bottles effectively, you may want to try one of the following procedures:

- Pour small amounts of glue into several shallow containers (such as margarine tubs or the bottoms of soda bottles).
- Dilute glue by mixing a little water into each container.
- Have children use paintbrushes to spread glue on their projects.

Cutting with Scissors

- Provide blunt-tip scissors for the children to use when cutting is required for a craft.
- Remember some of the children in your class may be left-handed. Have two or three pairs of left-handed scissors available.
- Precut fabric, felt, or ribbon for younger children.

"Things God Made" Book

Materials

- craft foam in various colors
- wide-tip permanent marker
- resealable plastic bags (5 per child)
- flat nature items (leaves, flowers, small pebbles, several per child)
- craft glue
- scissors
- stapler
- ruler

Before Class

Cut the craft foam into 7" x 12" rectangles, one for each. Cut a variety of small craft foam triangles and squares, about 1" in size. Lay five resealable bags directly on top of one another with openings facing the same direction. Staple the bags together at the bottom, opposite of the openings (sketch a).

Instructions for Children

- Fold the 7" x 12" foam piece in half to make a book cover. Use a marker to print "Things God Made" on the front cover.
- Lay the bags inside the folded cover with the stapled edges along the fold. Staple all layers together along the fold (sketch b).
- Glue foam shapes around the edge of the front cover to make a border (sketch c).
- Select and place nature items in the bags.

Enrichment Idea

Take children on a nature walk to collect items for their books.

Talk About

We can learn about God by looking at the wonderful things He has made. What is one of your favorite things that God made? We can also learn about God by listening to the stories from the Bible.

a.

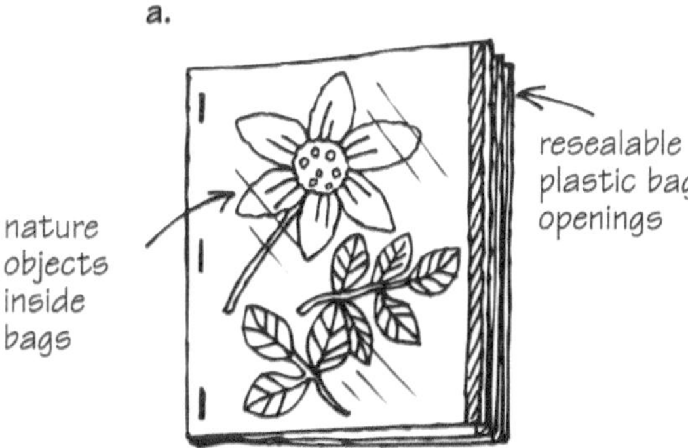

b.

c.

Hot Air Balloon Mobile

Materials

- mobile patterns (pp. 15–16)
- white card stock
- old sponges
- acrylic paint in a variety of colors (including light blue, yellow, and orange)
- pencil
- ruler
- scissors
- hole punch
- string
- newspapers
- shallow containers
- plastic clothes hangers (preferably child-size, 1 per child)
- paint shirts
- wet wipes
- spring clothespins *(optional)*

Before Class

Copy the mobile patterns onto the card stock and cut out the pieces. You will need one balloon, one sun, and two clouds for each child. Cut sets of four strings in various lengths from 5" to 12" (one set for each child). Punch a hole at the top center of each mobile piece. Cover the work area with newspaper. Pour the paint into shallow containers. Cut the sponges into 2" squares. Dampen the sponges.

Simplification Idea

Show young children how to pinch a sponge square in a clothespin. They can grasp the clothespin with the whole fist and then dab the sponge into the paint to lightly paint the desired area.

Instructions for Children

- Use the light-blue paint to sponge paint one side of each cloud. Use the yellow and orange paint to sponge paint one side of the sun. Use a variety of colors to sponge paint one side of the hot air balloon. Let all the pieces dry. Then slip a string through the punched hole in each piece. Tie the pieces to a hanger (see sketch).

Enrichment Idea

When dry to touch, allow the children to turn their pieces over and sponge paint the opposite sides. Allow time for all the pieces to dry.

Talk About

If you were on a hot air balloon ride, would you like to fly above the clouds, in the clouds, or below the clouds? What do you think you would see in a cloud? What might you see above the clouds? Below the clouds? Genesis 1 says God made the sky on day 1. He made the sun on day 4. Children can hang their mobiles at home as reminders that God made the world.

Vegetable Print Napkin

Materials

- muslin
- fabric paint in various colors
- various firm vegetables (carrots, potatoes, celery, etc.)
- paring knife
- fabric scissors
- ruler
- disposable plastic plates
- water
- newspaper
- wet wipes
- paint shirts

Before Class

Wash and dry the muslin to preshrink before cutting. Cut the muslin into 12" squares, one for each child. Wash and dry the vegetables, then cut the vegetables into pieces suitable to be held by small hands. Form stamps by carving a simple shape into the flat edge of each vegetable piece, or use the shape of the vegetable itself. Cover the work area with newspaper. Pour or squeeze paint onto plastic plates.

Instructions for Children

- Dip a vegetable stamp into paint and then press the stamp onto a cloth square. Repeat, dipping the stamps into paint for each print you want to make. Try using a variety of shapes and paint colors.

- Allow the paint to dry completely. This may take up to four hours.

- Children may use the finished squares as dinner napkins.

Enrichment Idea

Provide several pieces of cloth for each child. Allow the children to make sets of four napkins to give as gifts to their families.

Talk About

On day 3, God made vegetable plants and trees that produce fruit. What are your favorite vegetables to eat? Which fruits are sweet to taste? We can thank God for providing good food to eat.

Crawling Creatures Bug Jar

Materials

- circle pattern (p. 19)
- fine-mesh screen material
- colored tissue paper
- black and green permanent markers
- hammer and nail (or drill and drill bit)
- chenille wires
- empty plastic jars (with mouth 2¾" wide)
- standard-size mason jar canning bands
- craft glue
- scissors
- ruler
- damp paper towels
- twist ties *(optional)*

Before Class

With a permanent marker, trace the circle pattern onto the screen material and cut out. Using craft glue, glue a screen to the inside of a mason jar band and let dry. Prepare one jar lid for each child. Use a hammer and nail to make two small holes opposite each other near the top of each jar (sketch a). Cut colored tissue paper into 2" squares (approximately eight for each child).

Instructions for Children

- Use a green permanent marker to draw grass around the bottom of the jar (sketch b).
- Crumple tissue squares to form flowers. Glue the flowers to the grass on the jar (sketch b). Use a damp paper towel to wipe off any extra glue.
- With a teacher's help, poke the ends of a chenille wire through the holes in each side of the jar to make a handle. Bend the ends inside the jar to keep the wire from slipping out.
- Use a permanent marker to print "Bugs" on the side of the jar (sketch c).
- Screw on a prepared lid.

Enrichment Idea

Older children may enjoy using tissue paper and twist ties to make butterflies and spiders (see sketches). To make a butterfly: Place a twist tie around the middle of a piece of tissue paper. Twist the tie together several times. Curl the tips of the tie to make the antennae. To make a spider: Cut two twist ties in half. Twist the four pieces together in the middle and bend them to make legs. Crumple a piece of tissue paper for the body. Crumple a small piece for the head and glue it to the body. Glue the body to the legs. Glue the butterfly and spider to the outside of a jar or place them inside the jar.

Talk About

The Bible tells us God made every living creature, including bugs! What kinds of bugs do you like? You can collect some bugs and put them in your jar. Be sure to provide leaves and water for the bugs. Screw on the lid so the bugs don't escape! After you watch them for a while, take the bugs outside and let them go. Then catch some more bugs!

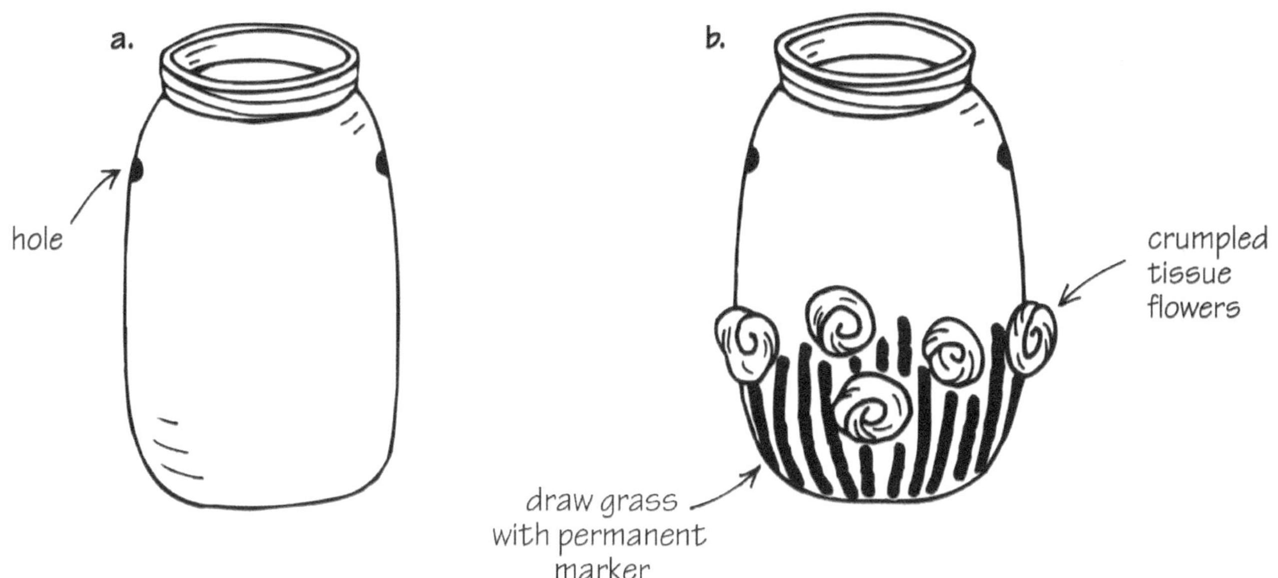
a.
hole
b.
crumpled
tissue
flowers
draw grass
with permanent
marker

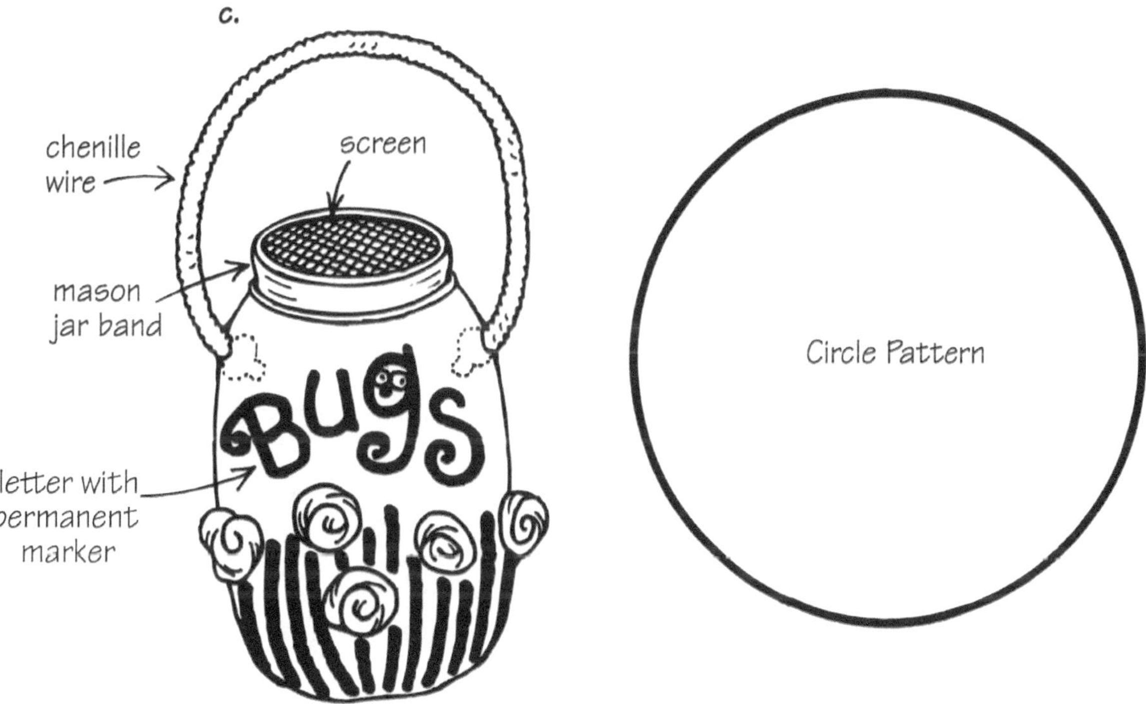
c.
chenille
wire
screen
mason
jar band
Bugs
letter with
permanent
marker
Circle Pattern

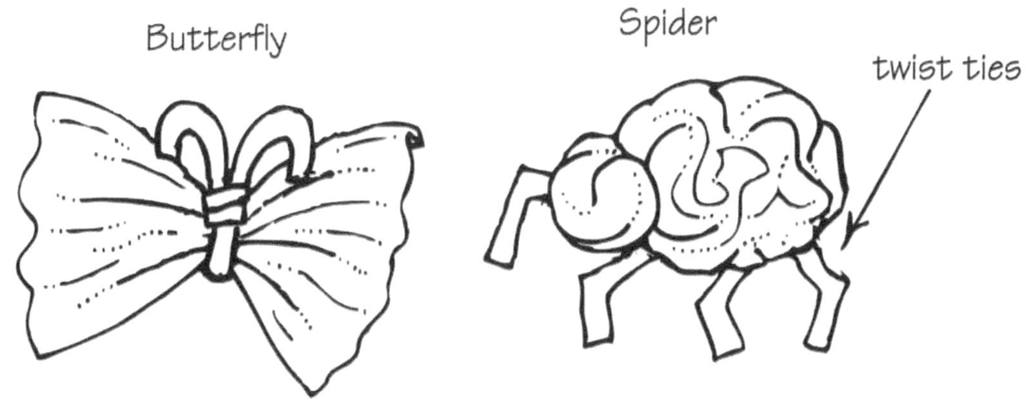
Butterfly
Spider
twist ties

Long-Neck Giraffe

Materials

- giraffe pattern (p. 21)
- brown yarn
- wood spring clothespins (2 per child)
- yellow card stock
- brown crayons (or washable markers)
- glue
- scissors
- ruler
- tape

Talk About

The Bible tells us God made all kinds of wonderful animals on day 6. God created giraffes to have long necks. Why do you think God made their necks so long? (to eat leaves at the top of tall trees) **What animals did God make that have long noses?** (elephants, aardvarks)

Before Class

Copy the giraffe pattern onto the card stock. Cut yarn into 2½" lengths. You will need one giraffe and one piece of yarn for each child.

Simplification Idea

Cut out the giraffes for younger children.

Instructions for Children

- Color brown spots on the giraffe's body and neck.
- Cut out the giraffe.
- Tape a piece of yarn in place for a tail.
- With a teacher's help, fold the giraffe's neck accordion-style (see sketch).
- Clip two clothespins onto the bottom of the giraffe's body to make legs.

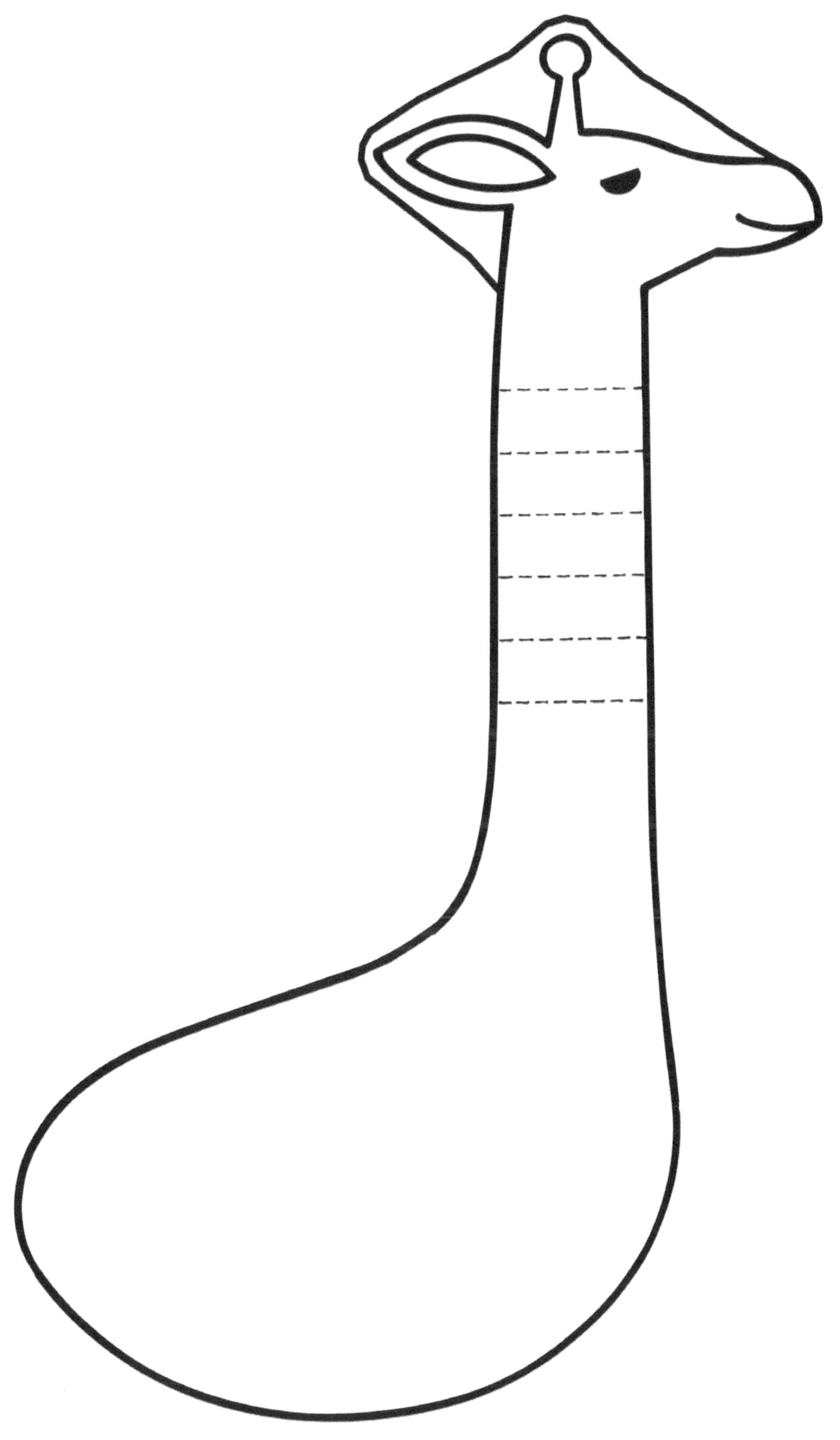

Paw-Print Bookmark

Materials

- paw-print patterns (p. 23)
- felt
- yarn
- ruler
- lightweight cardboard
- card stock
- pencils
- scissors
- washable markers
- glue

Before Class

Trace the paw-print patterns onto cardboard. Cut out the cardboard pieces, making one of each pattern for every two or three children. Cut yarn into 10" lengths, one for each child.

Simplification Idea

For younger children, copy the paw-print patterns onto card stock and cut out the shapes. Make a set of four matching paw prints for each child. Cut out felt shapes to be added to the paw prints.

Instructions for Children

- Choose one pattern and trace it onto the card stock four times. Cut out the four prints.
- Cut shapes from felt for paw pads and toenails or hooves. Glue the felt pieces onto two of the cutout paw prints (sketch a).
- With a marker, print "Thank You," on the third print and "God!" on the fourth print (sketch b).
- Spread glue on the backs of the two lettered prints. Place one end of a length of yarn on each glued print.
- Press the two decorated prints on top of the two glued prints, sealing in the yarn.

Talk About

People sometimes identify animals by looking at paw prints left in the dirt or snow. Have you ever seen a path of paw prints? What kind of animal do you think left those prints? Place your bookmark in your Bible and remember to thank God for the different kinds of animals He made.

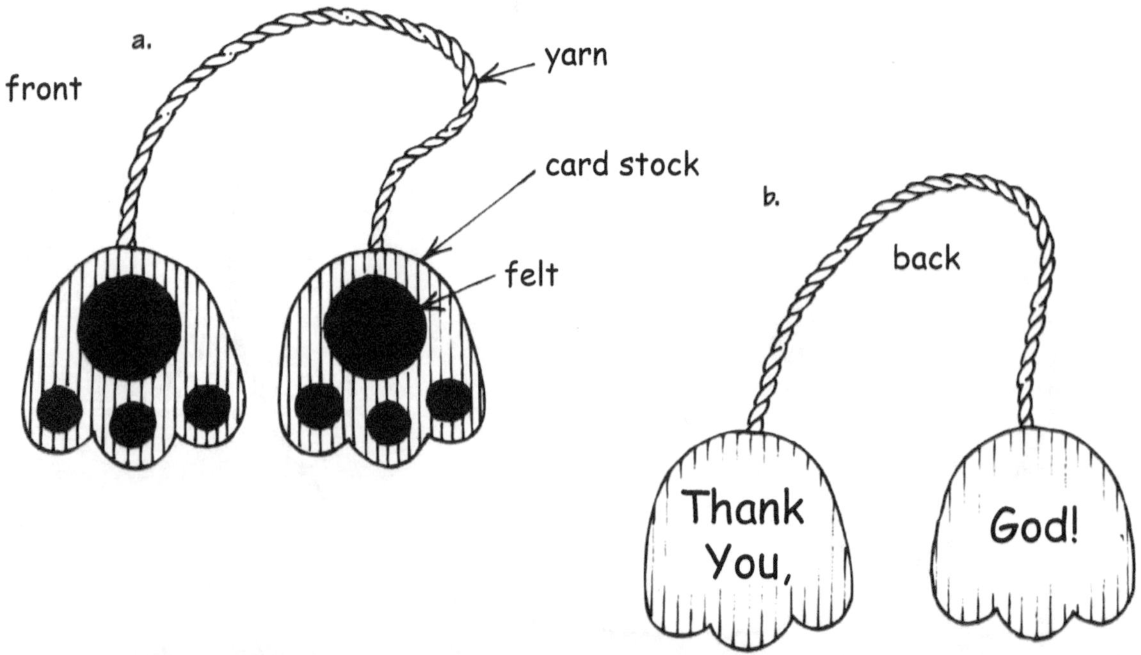

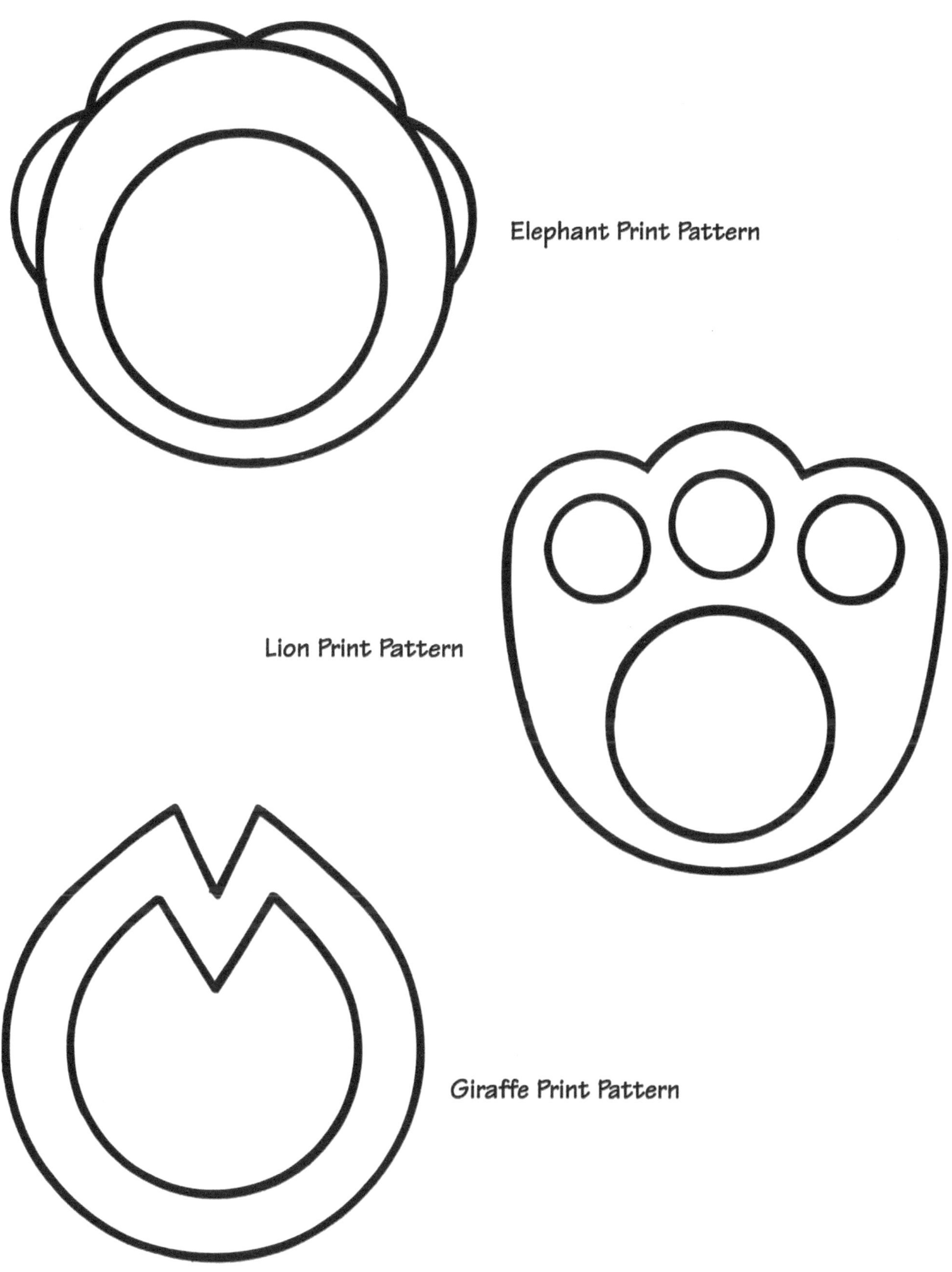
Elephant Print Pattern
Lion Print Pattern
Giraffe Print Pattern

Garden of Eden Picture

Materials

- large sheets of black construction paper
- chalk in various colors (including brown, green, and blue)
- aerosol hair spray
- scissors
- animal crackers
- green netting
- blue foil wrapping paper
- small twigs
- cotton balls
- sand
- several plastic spoons
- shallow containers
- craft glue
- paintbrushes
- utility knife

Before Class

Cut the netting and foil paper into a variety of small shapes to be used as treetops and bodies of water. Pour the sand into shallow containers. Place a spoon in each container of sand. Cut the twigs into 2" to 3" lengths. Place the animal crackers, cotton balls, and twigs in separate containers.

Instructions for Children

- Use chalk to color the background for a garden picture on a sheet of black construction paper. Color a blue sky, brown dirt, and green grass.
- When completed, the teacher will set the chalk by spraying the picture with hair spray in a well-ventilated area. Allow a few minutes for the hair spray to dry.
- Glue on the small twigs for tree trunks and green netting for foliage. Glue on pieces of blue foil paper for water and cotton balls for clouds.
- Brush a light coat of glue onto the brown chalk areas and sprinkle sand over the glue. With a teacher's help, pour any excess sand back into the container.
- Glue a few animal crackers onto the picture.

Talk About

What animals did you put in your Garden of Eden picture? God made all the animals. What other things did God create?

Handprint Banner

Materials

- felt in a variety of colors (including white)
- sewing machine and thread (or craft glue)
- scissors
- ruler
- straight pins
- yarn
- tempera paint in a variety of colors
- squeeze bottles of fabric paint
- plastic-coated paper plates
- newspaper
- plastic drinking straws (1 per child)
- wet wipes
- paint shirts
- acrylic jewels and sequins *(optional)*

Before Class

Cut the white felt into 7" x 9" rectangles, one for each child. Cut the colored felt into 4½" x 6" rectangles, one for each child. Cut each colored rectangle into two triangles by cutting in half diagonally (sketch a). Lay the short sides of the triangles over the bottom edge of the white banner rectangle, overlapping in the center and making the outer edges of the triangle even with the banner (sketch b). Pin in place. Machine stitch the triangles to the banner. Fold over 1" at the top of the banner. Cut four equally spaced ⅛" slits in the fold (sketch b). Cut the yarn into one 28" length and four 12" lengths for each child. Cover the work area with newspaper. Pour the paint onto paper plates.

Instructions for Children

- Weave the straw through the slits in the banner (sketch c).

- With a teacher's help, tie an end of the long length of yarn onto each end of the straw. Tie two short lengths of yarn onto each end of the straw for tassels.

- Dip one hand into the paint on the paper plate. Place your hand in the center of felt banner, creating your handprint.

- Clean your hands with wet wipes.

- Print your name on the banner with fabric paint. Allow the banner to dry overnight.

Enrichment Idea

Have the children decorate the triangle pieces at the bottom of their banners. The children can use fabric paint, or they can glue on small felt shapes, acrylic jewels, and sequins.

Talk About

Each banner is different because the banners have our handprints on them. God made each person special with unique features and abilities. We can thank God for making us special.

"God Made Me" Mirror

Materials

- mirror patterns (p. 27)
- card stock
- aluminum foil (or silver-coated card stock)
- yarn
- washable markers
- glue
- hole punch
- pencil
- ruler
- scissors
- assorted decorative materials *(optional)*

Before Class

Copy the mirror back and front patterns onto card stock and cut them out, one back and one front for each. Cut out the center circle on the mirror front. Cut the aluminum foil into 2½" squares, one for each. Cut the yarn into 2' lengths, one length for each.

Instructions for Children

- Use markers to decorate one side of both pieces of the mirror.
- Glue a foil square, shiny side up, onto the undecorated side of the mirror back piece (sketch a).
- Spread glue on the undecorated side of the mirror front piece. Then place the glued side down onto the mirror back, with the foil showing through the frame (sketch b).
- With a teacher's help, punch a hole near the bottom of the handle. Thread yarn through the hole and tie the ends in a knot.

Enrichment Idea

Provide a variety of decorative craft materials (stickers, jewels, buttons, sequins, etc.). Children can choose materials to decorate their mirrors.

Talk About

Who do you see in your mirror? What color of eyes do you have? What color is your hair? God made people on day 6. The Bible tells us in Genesis 1:31: "God saw all that he had made, and it was very good." I'm glad God made you—you!

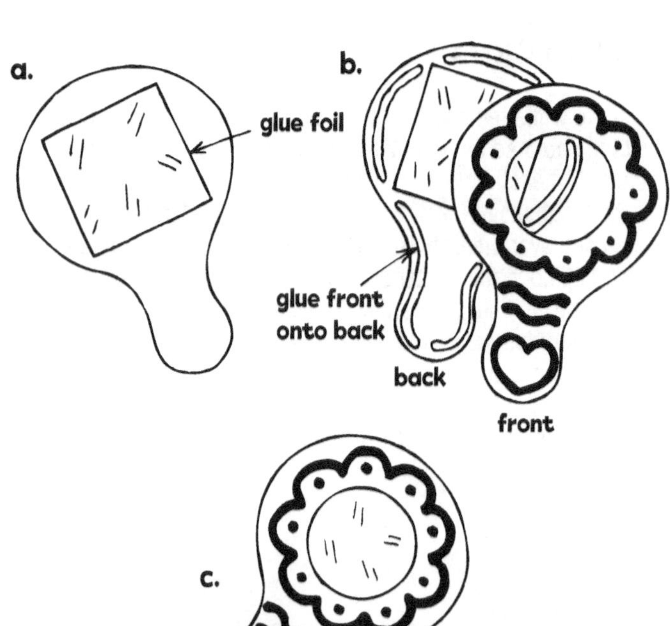

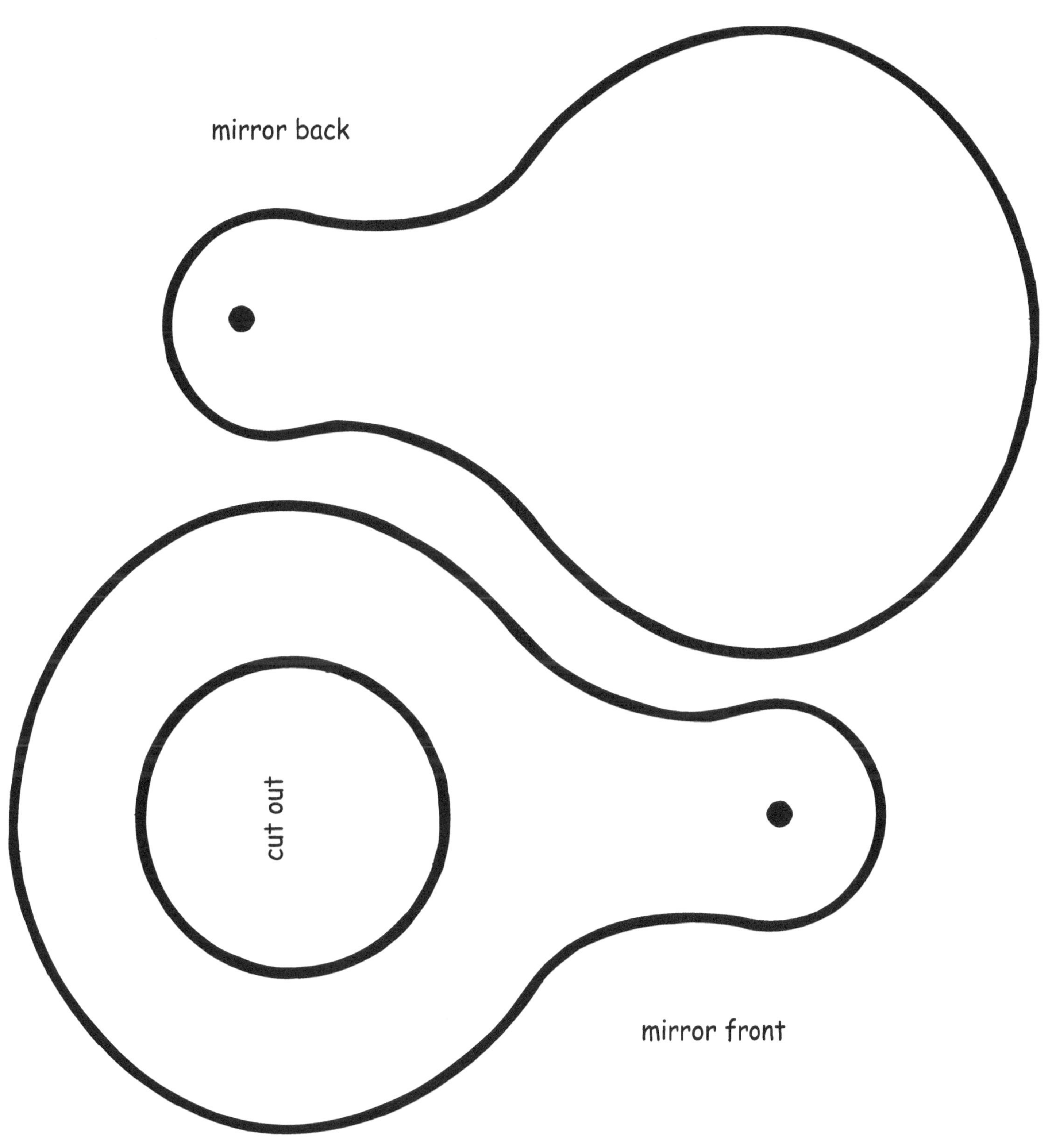
mirror back
cut out
mirror front

Personalized T-Shirt

Materials

- T-shirt pattern (p. 29)
- card stock
- marker
- scissors
- felt (or fabric or precut letters)
- crayons
- glue

Before Class

Copy the T-shirt pattern onto card stock, one for each. Cut out letters from felt or fabric for the name of each child (or collect precut letters). Have extra fabric, felt, or precut letters for names of visitors.

Instructions for Children

- Use crayons to decorate a shirt.

- Glue the letters of your name onto the shirt. (A teacher may assist by putting a small dot of glue on each letter and handing the letters, one at a time, to the child.)

Talk About

Who were the first people God made? (Adam and Eve) **Who made you?** (God) **God made you, ___** (child's name)**. And God made you, ___** (child's name). Do this for each child. **Thank You, God, for making each of these children.**

God Made Me

Noah's Flood Hat

Materials

- weather patterns (p. 31)
- white card stock
- sturdy, white 10" paper plates (1 per child)
- ruler
- pencil
- utility knife
- blue curling ribbon
- ¼" silver Mylar ribbon (found with gift wrapping supplies)
- scissors
- crayons
- flower stickers
- silver glitter
- glue
- tape (or stapler and staples)
- cotton balls

Before Class

Copy the weather patterns onto card stock, one page for each child. Cut out the patterns, one set for each child. Using a ruler and pencil, divide the bottom of paper plates into eight even wedges (sketch a). With a utility knife, cut the wedges apart along the pencil lines, leaving a 1" to 2" uncut rim (sketch a). Cut curling ribbon and Mylar ribbon into 18" lengths—four lengths of blue ribbon and four lengths of Mylar ribbon for each child.

Instructions for Children

- Lay the prepared paper plate upside down. Color the cut portion of the plate blue for the sky. Then color the rim of the plate green for grassy hills (sketch b). Add flower stickers (or draw flowers) onto the grass. Color the raindrops blue and the sun yellow.

- Prepare the weather pieces: Add glue and silver glitter on the white lightning bolt. Color the rainbow. Glue cotton balls onto the clouds.

- Lay the paper plate on the table with the colored side up. Bend the blue sky wedges up (sketch c). Tape the rainbow, sun, lightning bolt, and clouds to the bent-up wedges.

- Tape a raindrop to one end of each blue ribbon. With a teacher's help, tape the raindrop ribbons and lengths of Mylar ribbon to the rim, alternating around the sides and back of the hat.

Talk About

Noah and his family experienced rain, sunshine, and a rainbow! Our world needs all kinds of weather. Why do we need rain? (It provides water to drink. Rain fills lakes and oceans.) **Why do we need sun?** (It keeps us warm, gives us light, and makes plants grow.) **We can trust God to be with us in all kinds of weather!**

God's Promise Cloud

Materials

- sun and cloud patterns (pp. 33–34)
- crepe-paper streamers in 6 rainbow colors (red, orange, yellow, green, blue, and purple)
- yarn
- light-blue crayons
- yellow copy paper
- 11" x 17" white copy paper (or butcher paper)
- scissors
- ruler
- glue
- hole punch
- paper towels
- stapler and staples

Before Class

Copy the sun pattern onto yellow copy paper and cut out one sun for each child. Set a printer to enlarge the cloud pattern to approximately 175 percent, and print copies on 11" x 17" white paper. Cut out two clouds for each child. (Or draw large identical cloud patterns on butcher paper and cut out.) Cut crepe-paper streamers into 18" lengths, one length of each color for each child. Cut yarn into 16" lengths, one length for each child.

Instructions for Children

- Lay two paper clouds back to back so the shapes match. Then color the front of each cloud with a light-blue crayon.

- Lay one cloud with the colored side down onto the work surface. Put a drop of glue on one end of each crepe-paper streamer and attach the streamers across the bottom of the cloud in rainbow order: red, orange, yellow, green, blue, and purple (sketch a).

- Lay the second cloud, colored side up, on top of the cloud with the streamers. Make sure the edges are even. With a teacher's help, staple the clouds together around the edges, leaving a 6" opening near one end (sketch b).

- Scrunch two or three paper towels, and gently stuff them into the opening. Then staple the opening closed.

- Glue the paper sun onto the top corner of the cloud. Then punch two holes near the top of the cloud, about 4" apart. Thread yarn through the holes, and tie a knot at the ends for hanging (sketch c).

Talk About

Hang your cloud near an open window to see the streamers flutter in the breeze. When have you seen a real rainbow? Allow the children to share. **God puts rainbows in the sky to remind us that He loves us and will never send another flood to cover the entire earth.**

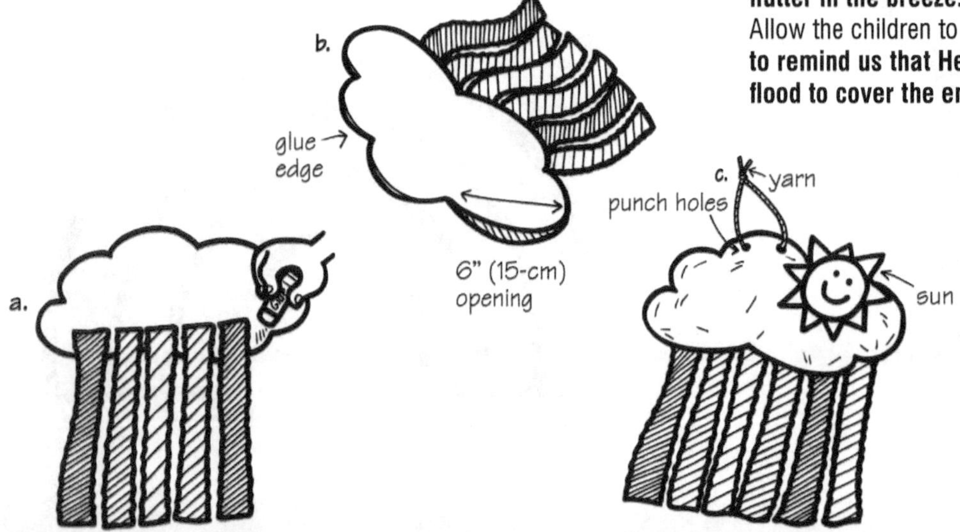

"God Cares" Wreath

Materials

- paper plates
- scissors
- black permanent marker
- yarn
- ruler
- crayons
- washable markers
- decorative stickers
- glitter paint
- self-sticking bows in rainbow colors
- hole punch

Before Class

Cut the center out of a paper plate to make a wreath (see sketch). Prepare one for each child. Print "God Cares" across the top of each wreath. Cut 8" lengths of yarn, one for each child.

Instructions for Children

- Use crayons or washable markers, stickers, and glitter paint to decorate a wreath. Try to include as many colors of the rainbow as possible: red, orange, yellow, green, blue, and purple.

- Choose one or more bows to stick onto the wreath.

- Punch a hole at the top of the paper plate wreath. Thread yarn through the hole and tie a knot at the ends for hanging.

Talk About

How did God care for Noah? (God told Noah how to build an ark and what to take onto the ark. God kept Noah and his family safe inside the ark during the flood.) **How does God care for you? Where will you hang your wreath to help you remember that God cares?** Encourage the children to think of places to hang their wreaths at home (on a door, a doorknob, or a wall) as a reminder that God cares for them.

Abraham and Lot Finger Puppets

Materials

- Abraham and Lot finger puppet patterns (p. 37)
- white card stock
- fabric scissors
- utility knife
- colorful yarn (or ½"-wide ribbon)
- crayons
- glue

Before Class

Copy the finger puppets onto card stock. Cut out one set per child. Using a utility knife, carefully cut out the finger holes. Cut a variety of 1½" lengths of yarn, cutting enough for each child to choose two lengths in favorite colors.

Instructions for Children

- Color a set of puppets. Remember that Abraham was older than his nephew Lot.
- Choose and glue a yarn belt on each puppet.
- Put your fingers through the holes to make legs for the puppets. Practice making the puppets walk slow and fast. Make the puppets bend their knees to kneel in prayer to God.

Enrichment Idea

Older children may enjoy creating puppet plays, acting out various scenes from the story of Abraham and Lot. The Bible characters could travel together, talk about their flocks and herds and tents, and go separate directions to avoid arguing over the land.

Talk About

Where did God say Abraham should go? ("To the land I will show you.") **Have you ever walked a long way? How far did you walk? Who went with you? Did you use a map? These finger puppets remind us of the long journey made by Abraham and Lot and their families. Abraham listened to and obeyed God. We can obey God too.**

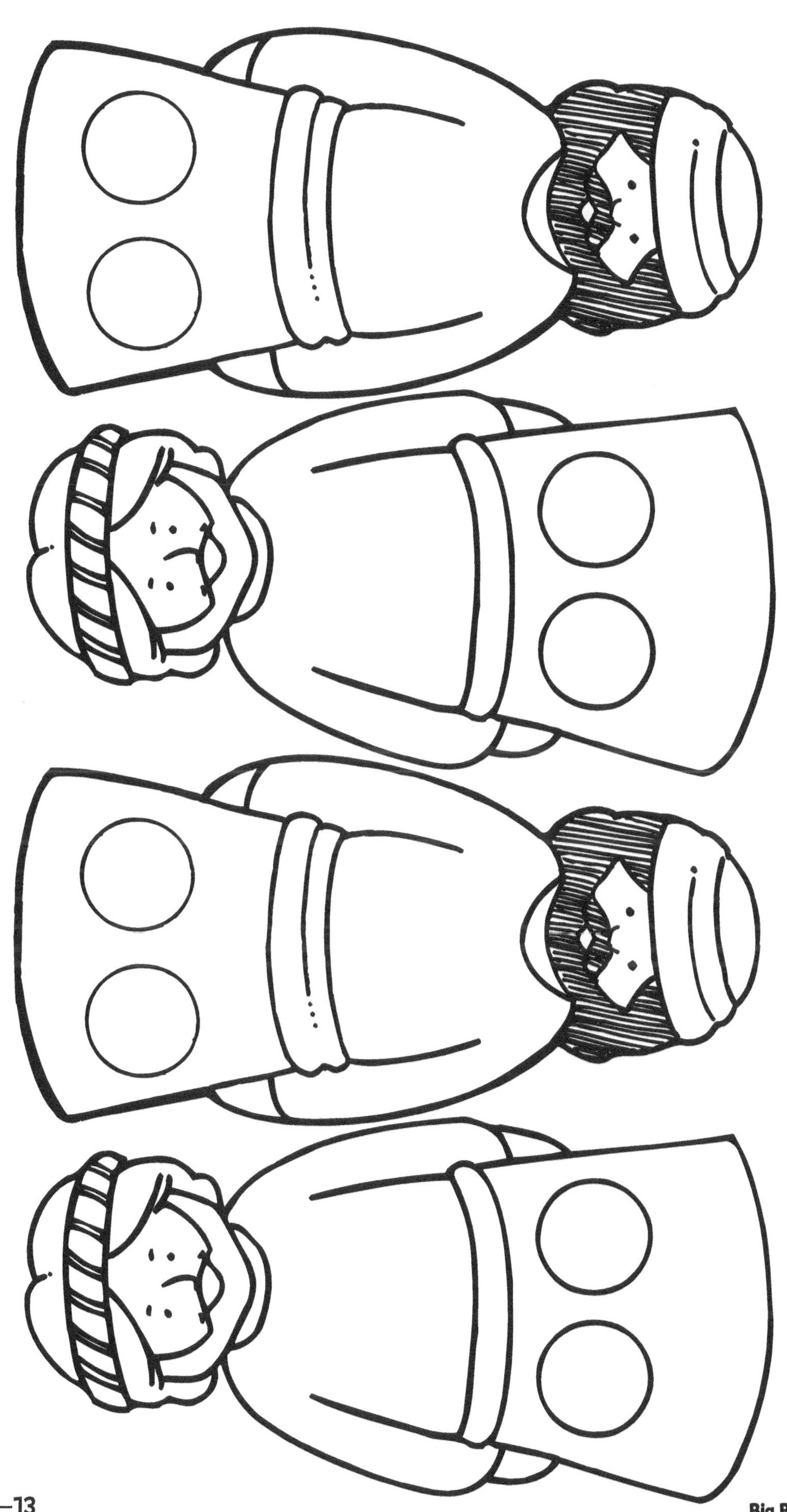

"Count the Stars" Mobile

Materials

- star patterns (p. 39)
- sand
- string
- child-size plastic clothes hanger (1 per child)
- yellow card stock
- ruler
- scissors
- glue
- glitter crayons (or glitter markers)
- tape
- small shallow containers
- large shallow box

Before Class

Copy the star patterns onto card stock, two pages per child. For each child, cut three 18" lengths and two 30" lengths of string. Tie one end of each length of yarn onto the bottom bar of a clothes hanger, alternating the lengths. Trim the ends, if needed. Pour sand into small shallow containers.

Simplification Idea

Cut out the stars for younger children. Each child will need ten stars.

Instructions for Children

- Cut out a set of ten stars.
- Color some stars with glitter crayons.
- On other stars, dot with glue and then sprinkle with sand. Shake the excess sand into the large shallow box.
- With a teacher's help, tape the backs of the stars to the free ends of the strings (see sketch). Tape one, two, or three stars on each string.

Talk About

How many stars do you think there are in the sky? Let children guess. **Scientists have learned that there are too many stars to count! God promised Abraham he would have as many children, grandchildren, great-grandchildren, and great-great grandchildren as there are stars in the sky! God kept His promise. This mobile can remind you that God keeps His promises!**

Family Faces

Materials

- house pattern (p. 41)
- white card stock
- magazines (or catalogs and sale flyers) with pictures of people
- scissors
- crayons
- glue
- plain paper
- washable markers

Instructions for Children

- Color and cut out a house.
- Choose a picture to represent each person in your family. Glue those pictures onto your house. Or you can draw pictures on squares of paper and glue the drawings to your house.
- With a teacher's help, print "__________'s (your name) Family" onto the house.

Before Class

Copy the house pattern onto the card stock, one for each child. Find magazines that show pictures of people of all ages—men, women, boys, girls. Be sure the pictures include a variety of ethnicities. Or find and print images of people from the Internet. Cut 2" squares of paper.

Talk About

The Bible tells us that Abraham and his wife Sarah waited a long time to have a baby. They were happy when their son Isaac was born. Who gives us our families? (God) **Who is in your family? We can thank God for our families.**

Simplification Idea

Precut the houses and pictures of people.

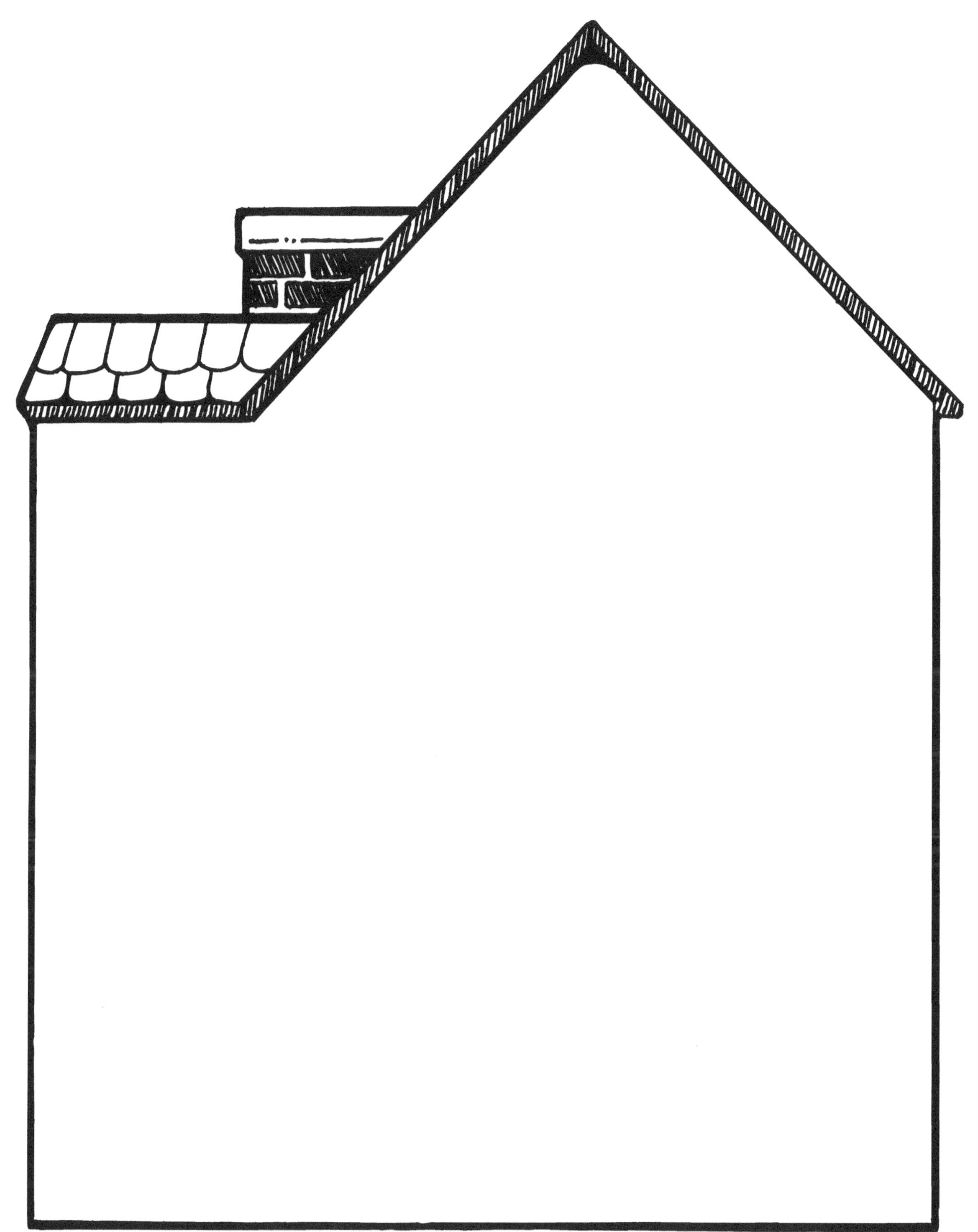

Joseph Stick Puppet

Materials

- Joseph puppet and coat pattern (p. 43)
- white card stock
- scissors
- colored pencils (or crayons)
- small pieces of colorful fabric
- washable markers
- glue
- jumbo craft sticks (1 per child)
- tape

Before Class

Copy the Joseph puppet and coat pattern onto white card stock, one puppet and coat for each child.

Simplification Idea

Precut the puppets and fabric pieces.

Instructions for Children

- Color the hair, headband, arms, hands, legs, and shoes of the Joseph puppet.
- Cut out the puppet.
- Using a marker, trace the coat pattern onto a piece of colorful fabric. With the teacher's help, cut out the coat. Glue the coat to the puppet. If desired, glue on other scraps of fabric to decorate the coat.
- Tape a craft stick to the back of the puppet.
- Use the puppet to tell about God's care.

Enrichment Idea

Older children may enjoy using their puppets to tell Joseph's story in first person. Example: "Hello. My name is Joseph. I have 12 brothers. My father loves all of us, but I am his favorite son."

Talk About

How did God take care of Joseph? (gave him a loving father, protected him when his brothers were jealous of him, kept him safe in Egypt) **When has God helped you do something that was difficult? We can trust God to care for us and be with us wherever we are.**

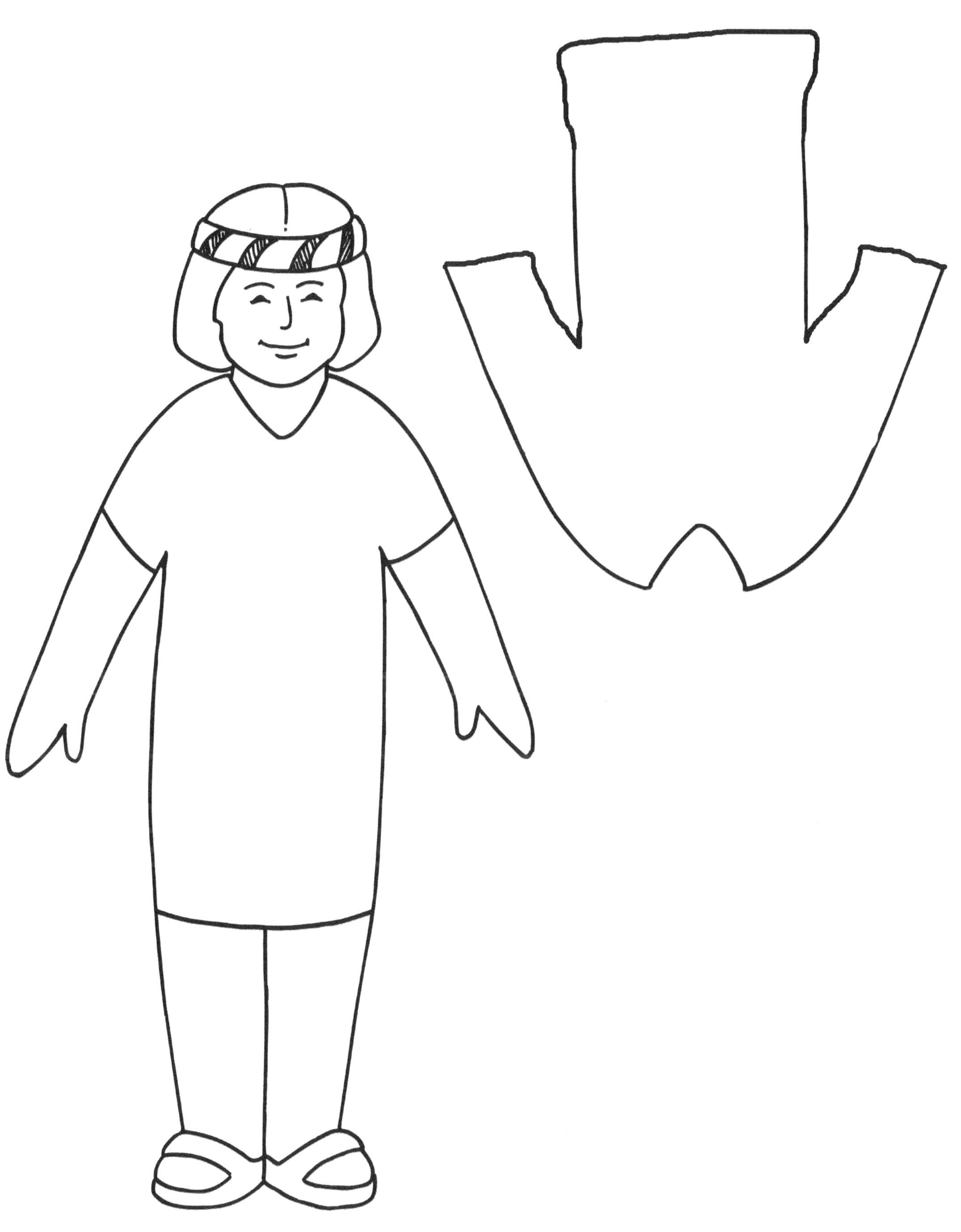

Baby Moses in a Basket

Materials

- tan or light-brown felt
- ruler
- scissors
- fine-tip black permanent marker
- toilet paper tubes
- construction paper
- white baby socks (1 per child)
- fiberfill stuffing
- small rubber bands
- brown markers
- raffia (or straw)
- craft glue

Before Class

For each child, cut a 1½" circle of felt and draw a baby's face on the circle, using the fine-tip marker. Prepare a "basket" for each child: Cut a ½" strip out of a toilet paper tube (sketch a). Then cut a 1" x 13" piece of construction paper and glue it around the upper edges and ends of the paper tube (sketch b).

Instructions for Children

- Fill a baby sock with stuffing—almost to the top. With a teacher's help, secure a rubber band around the top of the sock (sketch c).
- Glue a felt face onto the sock directly under the rubber band (sketch d). Then fold the top of the sock over to make a cap (sketch e).
- Color the sides of a prepared toilet paper tube, making it look like a basket.
- Glue pieces of raffia inside the basket. After the glue has dried, place "baby Moses" in his basket.

Talk About

Miriam lived with her family in the country of Egypt. The king of Egypt did not believe in God. He wanted to kill all the baby boys who were born to God's people. Miriam's mother decided to hide her baby boy. She put the baby in a little basket-boat and placed it on the river. Miriam stayed to watch over her baby brother. God helped Miriam to be brave and help her family. Have you ever done anything brave? How do you help your family?

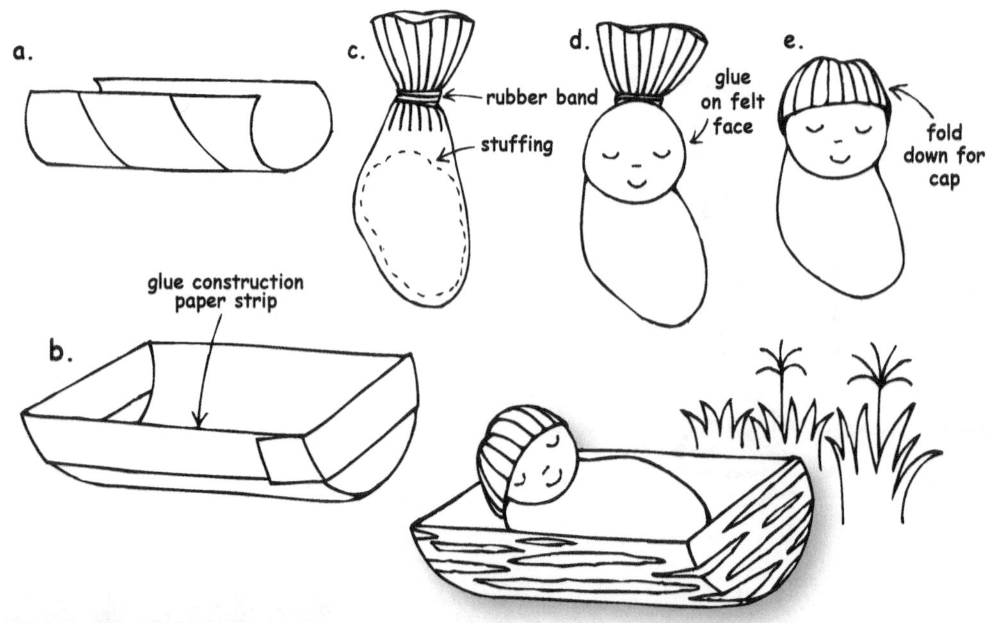

Salty Sea Jar

Materials

- table salt
- green and blue powdered tempera paint
- 16-oz. plastic food containers with lids
- measuring cup and spoon
- 4-oz. clear jars with lids (1 per child)
- spoons
- cotton balls
- craft glue

Before Class

Pour one cup of salt into a plastic food container. In two other containers, mix one cup of salt with one teaspoon of powdered tempera, one for each color. (Note: three cups [24 ounces] of salt will fill six 4-ounce jars.) Prepare three containers of salt (white, green, and blue) for every six children in your class.

Instructions for Children

- With a spoon, layer green salt in the bottom of a jar (sketch a).
- Add a blue layer of salt.
- Add a white layer of salt.
- Repeat the layering until the jar is filled.
- Tap the jar lightly to let the salt settle. Then place several cotton balls on top of the salt.
- With a teacher's help, squeeze glue around the inside of a jar lid and tightly screw it onto the jar (sketch b).

Enrichment Idea

Have the children assist in mixing the tempera and salt. You can measure the ingredients into containers, snap on lids, and then allow the children to shake the mixture to color the salt.

Talk About

Have you ever felt trapped in a bad situation? What happened? Allow the children to share. **When Moses and the Israelites left Egypt, God told them to set up camp by the Red Sea. Pharaoh thought the people were trapped and couldn't go anywhere, so he ordered his army to go after the Israelites. But God sent a great wind to blow back the water of the sea. Moses and the people of Israel crossed the sea on a dry path. When we look at our Salty Sea Jars, we can thank God because He is powerful. He can help us.**

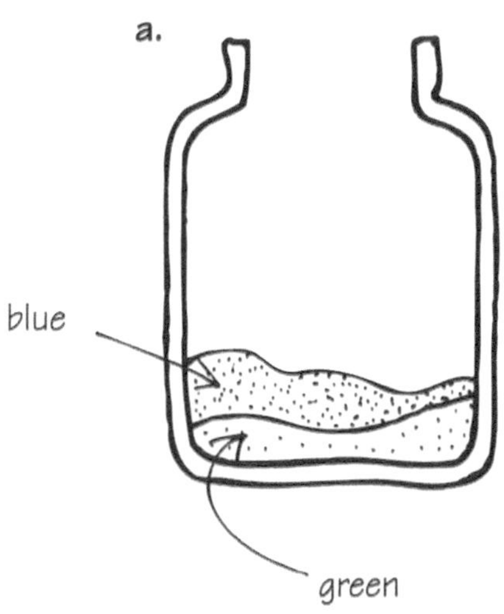

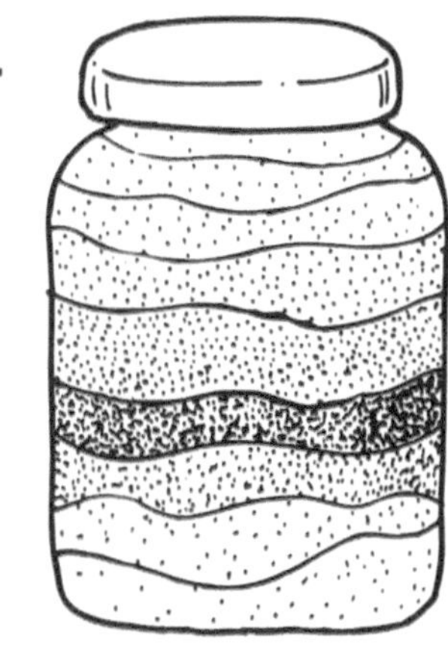

"Part the Water" Picture

Materials

- 8½" x 11" sheets of white and blue card stock
- ruler
- pencil
- brown and orange construction paper
- scissors
- tan acrylic paint
- sponges
- spring clothespins
- hole punch
- yarn
- shallow containers
- water
- newspaper
- colored dot stickers
- markers
- glue
- paint shirts
- brown crayons, happy face stickers or Bible character stickers of Moses and the Israelites *(optional)*

Before Class

Using a pencil, draw a line horizontally across the center of each sheet of white card stock, one for each child (sketch a). Measure and cut a sheet of blue card stock into four pieces. Each child will need two 4¼" x 5½" pieces (sketch b). Cut the brown construction paper into a wavy mountain range shape, approximately 2" x 11", one for each child (sketch c). Cut orange construction paper into 1½" circles, one per child. Dampen sponges and cut them into small squares, one for each child. Clip a clothespin to each sponge. Cover the work area with newspaper. Pour paint into shallow containers.

Simplification Idea

In place of sponge painting, use crayons to color the bottom half of the white card stock. Use happy face stickers or Bible character stickers for Moses and the Israelites.

Instructions for Children

- Using tan paint, sponge paint the bottom half of the white card stock (sketch d). Allow the paint to dry.
- Glue the mountain range above the tan section on the card stock. Glue the orange sun above the mountains (sketch e).
- Stick dot stickers in the middle of the tan section to represent the Israelites crossing the Red Sea on dry ground (sketch e). Draw faces on the dots with markers.
- Lay two pieces of blue paper on top of the scene you created so that the blue papers are covering the tan section with the sticker faces. With a teacher's help, punch two evenly spaced holes along both sides of the blue pieces (sketch f).
- Insert yarn through the holes on one side of the picture and tie a knot to secure. (Be sure the yarn is loose enough to open and close the blue piece.) Repeat this process for the opposite edge of the picture.
- Open and close the blue pieces to show how God parted the Red Sea and allowed the Israelites to cross on dry ground (sketch g).

Talk About

When they were at the Red Sea, how did God help the Israelites escape from the Egyptian army? (God sent a big wind that divided the sea waters. Then the people could walk across to the other side on dry land.) **When has God helped you? What did He do?**

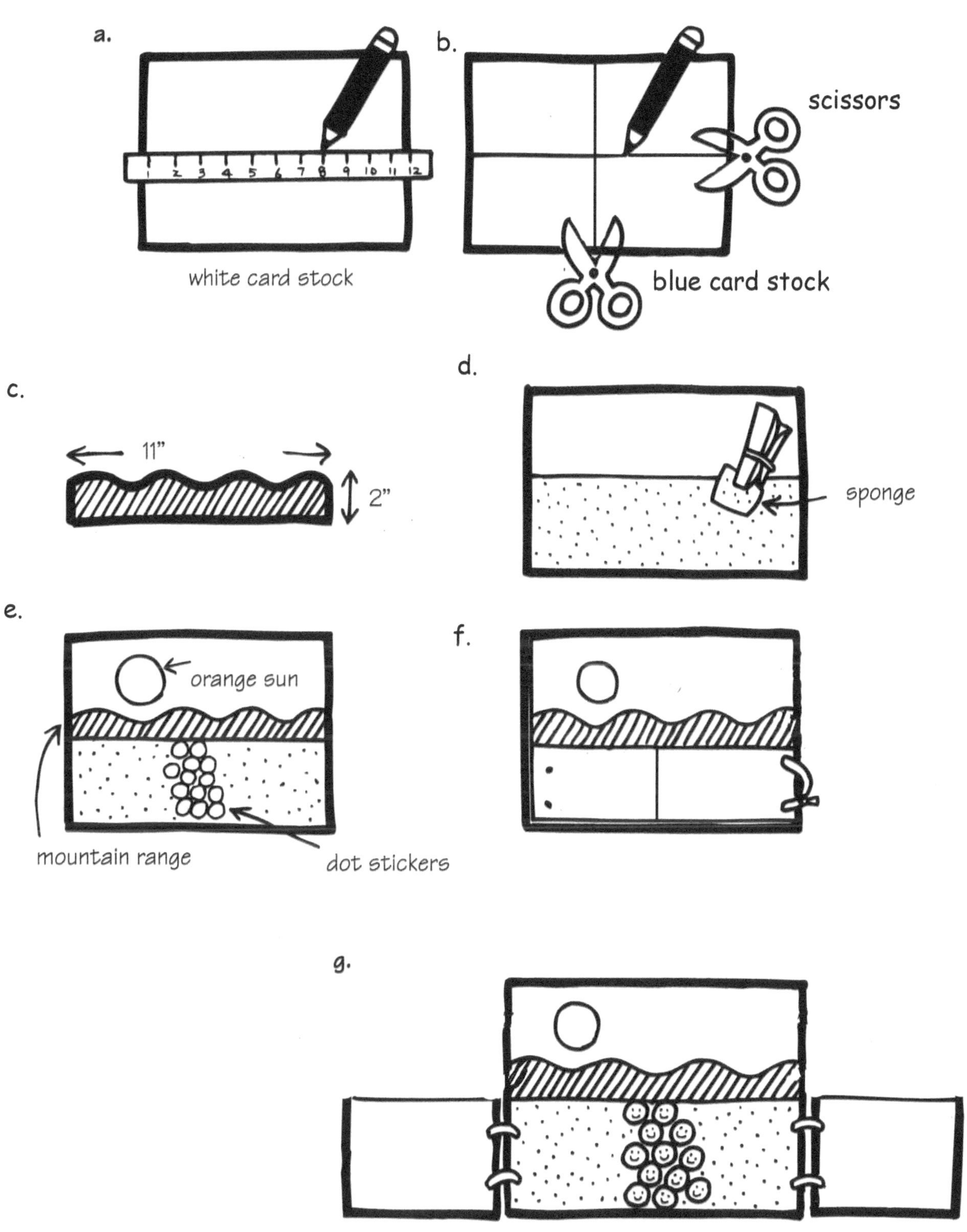
a.
1 2 3 4 5 6 7 8 9 10 11 12
white card stock
b.
scissors
blue card stock
c.
11"
2"
d.
sponge
e.
orange sun
mountain range
dot stickers
f.
g.

"Sing to the Lord" Maracas

Materials

- Bible
- ½" dowels
- saw
- knife
- ruler
- duct tape
- empty 6-oz. juice boxes (1 per child)
- solid-colored duct tape
- dried beans
- colored dot stickers (or permanent markers)

Before Class

Cut dowels into 6½" lengths—one for each child. Cover the top and sides of each juice box with duct tape. Use a knife to poke a hole slightly smaller than ½" in the bottom of each box (sketch a).

Instructions for Children

- Place several dried beans inside the box through the hole in the bottom of the box.

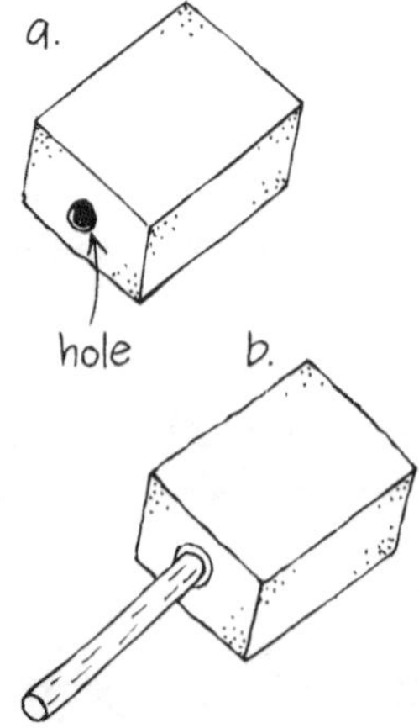

- Push one end of the dowel into the hole. With a teacher's help, secure the dowel to the box, using duct tape.
- Use dot stickers to decorate box.
- Hold the dowel and shake the maraca to create your own rhythm.

Enrichment Ideas

- Bring in actual maracas to show to the children.
- Play an instrumental recording of a praise song and have the children play along.

Talk About

God saved Moses and the Israelites from the Egyptian army that was chasing them. After they had safely crossed the Red Sea on dry ground, Moses and the people made up a song and sang to God. Moses' sister and the other women played instruments as they sang. The people sang about God's strength. They sang about His great love. Read aloud Exodus 15:1 from a Bible. **If you were to make up a song to sing to God, what would your song be about?** Let the children make up a song and play their maracas as they sing to God.

Desert Sand Painting

Materials

- glue
- small shallow containers
- water
- sand
- large shallow container
- newspapers
- brown construction paper
- orange and yellow crayons (or yellow construction paper and scissors)
- paintbrushes
- plastic spoons

Before Class

Pour glue into small shallow containers. Dilute the glue with a small amount of water so it will spread easily with a paintbrush. Prepare a container of glue for every two to three children. Pour sand into a large shallow container. Cover the work area with newspaper.

Instructions for Children

- Near the top of the brown paper, use orange and yellow crayons to draw and color a sun (sketch a).
- Use a paintbrush to paint glue on the bottom half of the paper, making mountains and the desert ground.
- Place your picture in the large shallow box. Use a spoon to sprinkle sand over the glue.
- Carefully shake the extra sand from your picture into the large container (sketch b). Lay the picture flat to dry.

Talk About

Have you ever seen a desert? Was the ground grassy or dry? Allow children to share. **A desert is hot and dry. Moses and the Israelites lived in a desert for a long, long time. Even though sometimes the people disobeyed God, God still loved and took care of them. He sent food for them to eat. He gave them water to drink. How does God take care of you?**

"God's Army" Helmet

Materials

- army helmet and feathers patterns (p. 51)
- white (or light-gray) card stock
- scissors
- ruler
- crayons (or washable markers)
- tape

Before Class

Copy the helmet and feathers patterns onto card stock, one for each child. Cut 1" x 11½" strips of card stock for each child.

Instructions for Children

- Color and cut out an army helmet.

- With a teacher's help, tape one end of a strip of card stock to one side of the helmet. Size the helmet to fit your head and tape the other end of the strip to the other side of the helmet.

- Color and cut out the feathers piece. Fan the feathers by cutting along the dotted lines. Tape the feathers piece onto the back side at the top of the helmet (see sketch).

Talk About

The Israelite people were being treated badly. They needed God's help. God told Gideon to take an army of only 300 soldiers to fight against a really big enemy army. Gideon obeyed God, and the 300 soldiers obeyed Gideon. With God's help, Gideon's army won the battle. God wants us to obey Him. Who do you obey? How can you obey God?

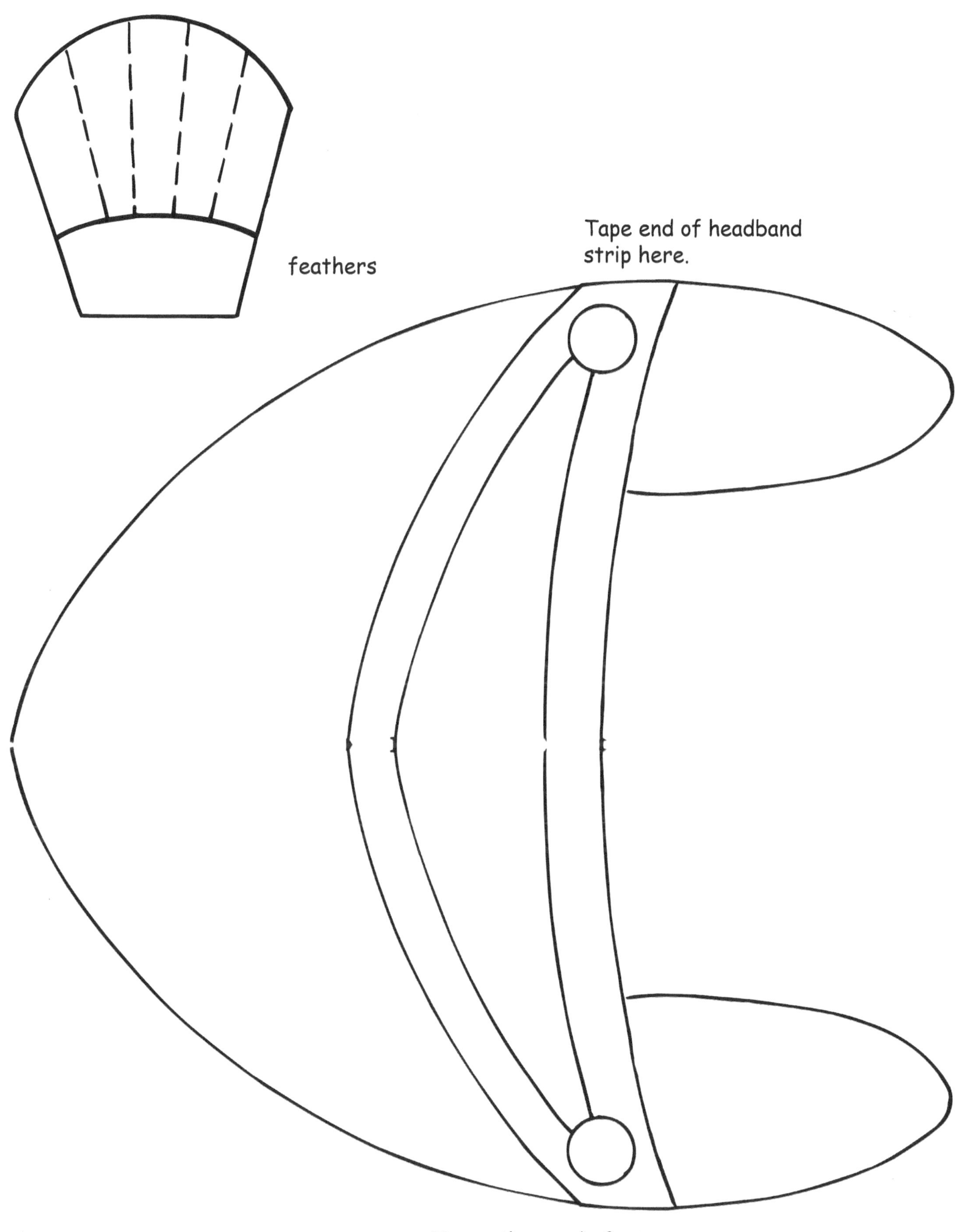
feathers
Tape end of headband strip here.
Tape other end of headband strip here

Gideon's Torch

Materials

- tissue paper (red, yellow, and orange)
- ruler
- scissors
- glue
- shallow containers
- gold or other metallic-colored crayons or markers
- black construction paper (1 sheet per child)
- tape

Before Class

Cut the tissue paper into 12" squares, four to five squares for each child. Pour small amounts of glue into shallow containers.

Instructions for Children

- Decorate a sheet of black paper with gold or metallic-colored crayons or markers.
- With a teacher's help, roll the paper (colored side out) into a narrow cone shape. Tape the open edge in place (sketch a).
- To make tissue flames, place a crayon in the center of a tissue square. Gather the tissue around the end of a crayon. Remove the crayon and pinch the gathered end of the tissue together (sketch b).
- Dip the pinched end of the tissue paper flame into a container of glue. Then push the flame down into the paper torch (sketch c). Repeat this step to make additional flames (sketch d).
- Allow the glue to dry.

Talk About

In Bible times, people used candles or fire to see at night. God told Gideon to have his army hide torches under clay jars so the enemy wouldn't see them sneaking up. When Gideon's army blew trumpets and broke their jars, the sound and lights surprised the enemy soldiers so much that they ran away. God helped Gideon and his army to win the battle without fighting! Has God ever helped you in a surprising way? What happened? Encourage the children to hold up their torches as they share some experiences.

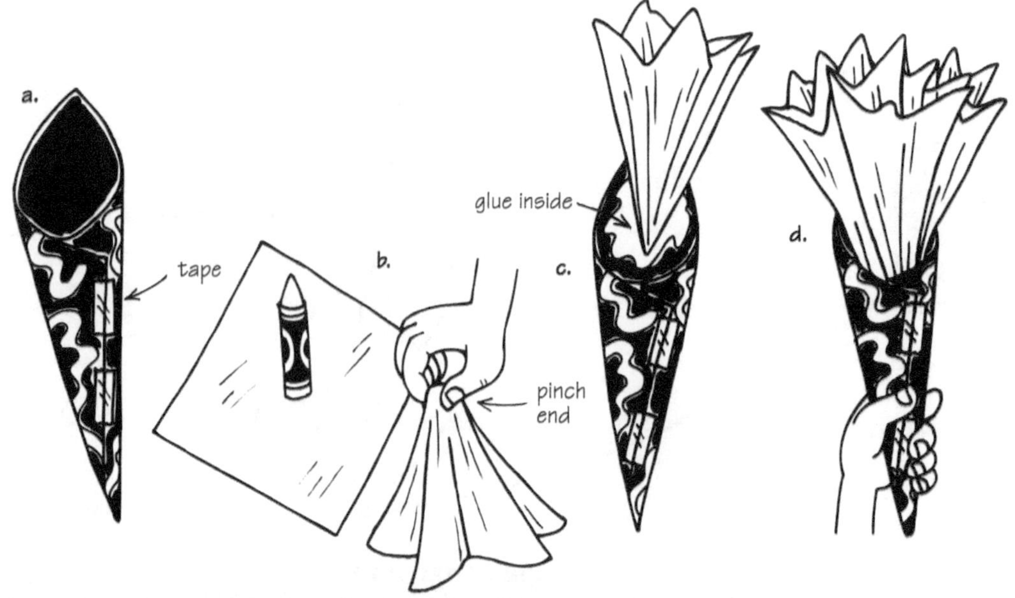

"I Am God's Helper" Necklace

Materials

- pendant pattern
- white card stock
- hole punch
- scissors
- ruler
- yarn
- glue
- colorful plastic drinking straws
- crayons
- star stickers *(optional)*

Before Class

Copy the pendant pattern onto white card stock and cut out. Punch two holes in the top of each pendant where indicated. Prepare a pendant for each child. Cut 24" lengths of yarn, one for each child. Dip the ends of the yarn in glue and allow them to dry. Cut straws into various lengths.

Instructions for Children

- Color the pendant. Then string the pendant onto a length of yarn. Add several pieces of plastic straw on each side of the pendant to form a necklace.
- With a teacher's help, tie the ends of the yarn together at an appropriate length to make a necklace.

Enrichment Ideas

- Ask children to tell or act out ways they can be helpers at home, at church, or at other places they go.
- Place star stickers on the children's pendants as they pick up toys, put away supplies, or help in other ways around the classroom.

Talk About

How old were you when you started to help clean your room or do chores around your house? What did you do to help? Allow time for the children to share. **When Samuel was a young child, his mother took him to the place where people came to worship God. Samuel helped Eli the priest to take care of God's special place of worship. What can we do to take care of our classroom or church building?**

David's Harp

Materials

- harp pattern (p. 55)
- corrugated cardboard
- pencil
- heavy-duty scissors
- ruler
- drinking straws
- tape
- 3" rubber bands (5 per child)
- washable markers

Before Class

Trace the harp pattern onto cardboard and cut it out. Prepare a cardboard harp for each child. Cut straws into 4" pieces, one for each child.

Instructions for Children

- Use markers to color and decorate the cardboard piece.
- Tape a straw piece across the harp, 1" from the top edge.
- Stretch five rubber bands around the cardboard and over the straw to make harp strings (see sketch). Tape the rubber bands in place on the back of the harp so they won't pop off.
- When completed, gently pluck the strings to play music like David!

Talk About

What are some songs you like to sing? Encourage children to share. **There are lots of songs we can sing to God. When we sing songs to God, we are praising Him. To praise someone is to say how good he or she is. David liked to sing and praise God with his harp. David played a harp (or lyre) to make a king feel better too!**

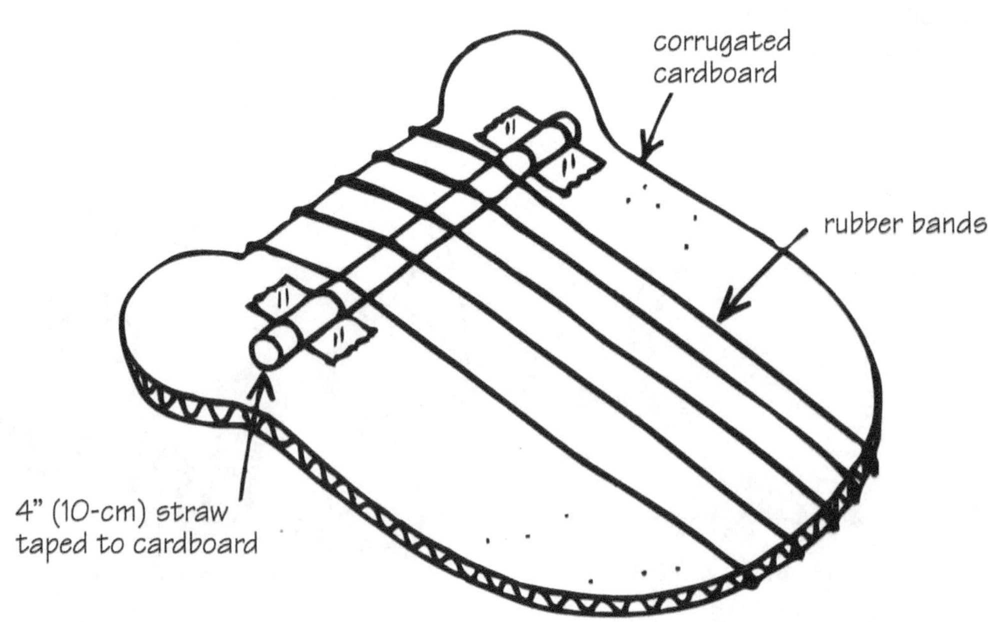

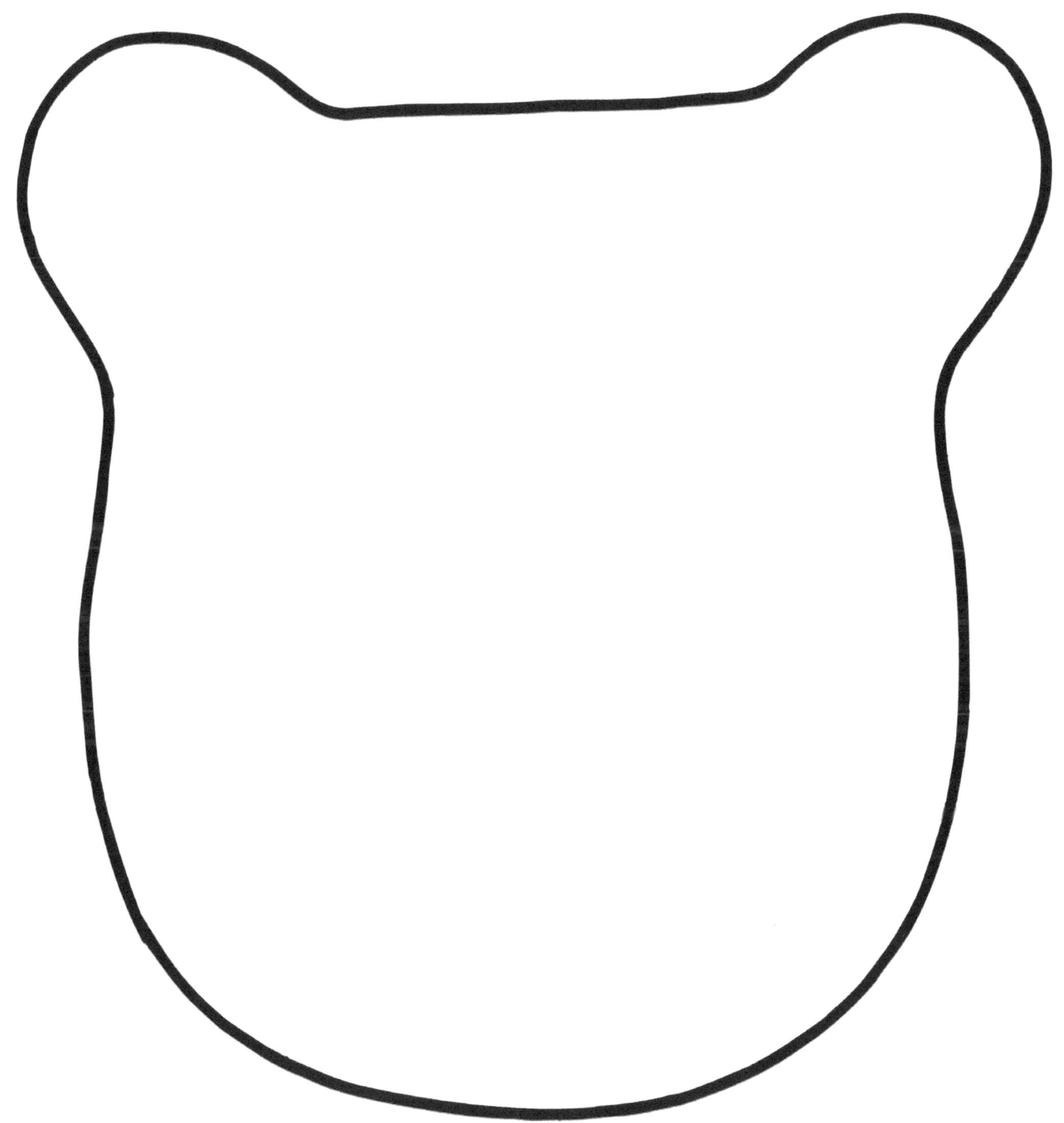

Fuzzy Lamb

Materials

- ear pattern
- pencils
- white felt
- scissors
- black chenille wires
- ruler
- 9" white paper plates (1 per child)
- cotton balls
- black medium-size pom-poms (1 per child)
- wiggle eyes (2 per child)
- small shallow containers
- glue
- paintbrushes
- newspapers (or parchment paper)

Before Class

Trace the ear pattern onto white felt. Cut out two ears for each child. Cut chenille wires into 4" lengths, one for each child. Draw lines around the rim of the plates at 1" intervals. Pour glue into small shallow containers. Cover the work area with newspaper.

Simplification Idea

Younger children may have difficulty cutting and curling the fringe on the paper plate. You can do this step for them before class.

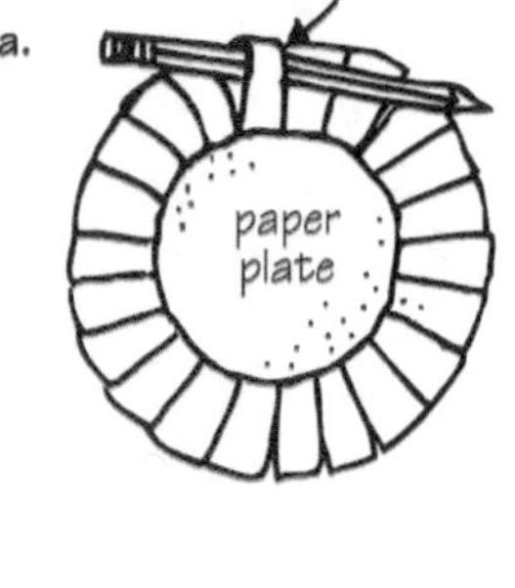

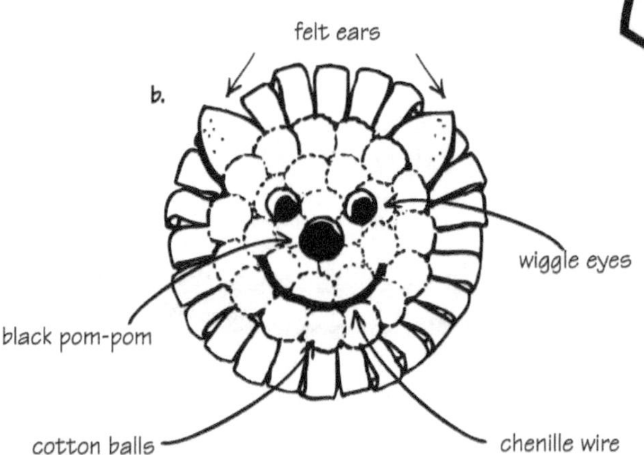

Instructions for Children

- Cut on the lines around the rim of a paper plate. Using a pencil, curl back the paper-plate fringe (sketch a).
- Glue one felt ear to each side of the plate edge.
- Paint glue on the front center of the plate and then push cotton balls onto the glue.
- Glue on a black pom-pom for the nose, a chenille wire piece for the mouth, and two wiggle eyes to complete the lamb's face (sketch b).

Talk About

David took care of his father's flock of sheep. Do you have an animal to take care of? What do you feed the animal? What other ways do you care for the animal? Allow time for children to share. **God helped David when he needed to protect the sheep from a lion and a bear. God has power to help and protect you from harm too.**

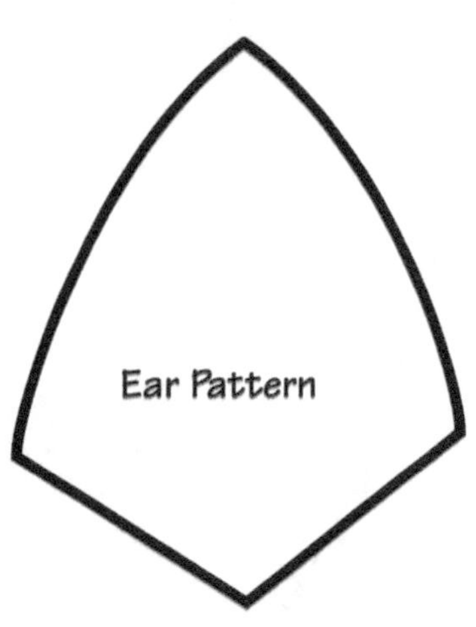

“We Love Him” Singing Shaker

Materials

- small plastic containers with lids that can be taped shut (small drink bottles, margarine tubs, etc.)
- 2” x 4” labels
- permanent markers
- dried beans or rice
- funnels (or construction paper and tape)
- strapping tape (or electrical tape or duct tape)
- heart or musical note stickers
- whiteboard and dry-erase marker

Before Class

Be sure the plastic containers are clean and dry. If funnels are not available, create funnels by rolling sheets of construction paper into funnel shapes and taping the open edges closed. Print “We Love Him” on a whiteboard.

Simplification Idea

- You may want to prepare the labels for younger children.

Instructions for Children

- Print “We Love Him” on a label and attach the label to the side of a container.
- Using a funnel, pour a handful of beans or rice in the container.
- Place the lid on the container and tape it shut.
- Decorate the container, using stickers and markers.

Talk About

After God saved David’s life, David wrote and sang a song to God. David sang, “The Lord is my rock, my fortress and my deliverer.... The Lord lives! Praise be to my Rock!” (2 Samuel 22:2, 47). What songs do we sing to God? Help the children name songs they know about God (or make up a song that can be sung to a familiar tune). Lead the children in singing a song to God while playing their shakers.

Worker's Apron

Materials

- tool patterns (p. 59)
- colored card stock
- muslin fabric
- ruler
- fabric scissors
- sewing machine and thread
- ¼" ribbon
- safety pins (1 per child)
- scissors
- crayons (or washable markers)
- jumbo craft sticks (4 per child)
- glue
- fabric markers in various colors

Before Class

Copy the tool patterns onto card stock, one set of tools for each child. Make a tool apron for each child, following these instructions: Use fabric scissors to cut a 10" x 12" piece of muslin. Sew a ½" hem around both short sides and one long side of the fabric (sketch a). Fold up the hemmed long side of the fabric to make a 4" pocket (sketch b). Sew the pocket edges along the 4" sides, then stitch down the middle of the pocket to make two smaller pockets. Turn the apron over and fold down the top edge of the apron ½"; sew along the bottom edge to make a casing. Fasten a safety pin to one end of a 3' length of ribbon and thread it through the casing (sketch c).

Simplification Idea

For younger children, cut out the tools before class.

Instructions for Children

- Color the tools as desired. Cut out the tools.
- Glue a craft stick to the back of each tool to make it sturdy (sketch d).
- Decorate an apron, using fabric markers (sketch e).
- Put the tools in the apron pockets. With a teacher's help, tie the apron around the waist.

Talk About

Many people helped to build God's temple. Some workers cut the stones for the steps. Woodcutters cut down trees for the walls. Metalworkers made beautiful furnishings out of gold and bronze. Everyone worked together. What jobs do you do with your family? What tools do you use? (dust cloth, broom, rake, etc.) **What jobs could we do together at our church building?**

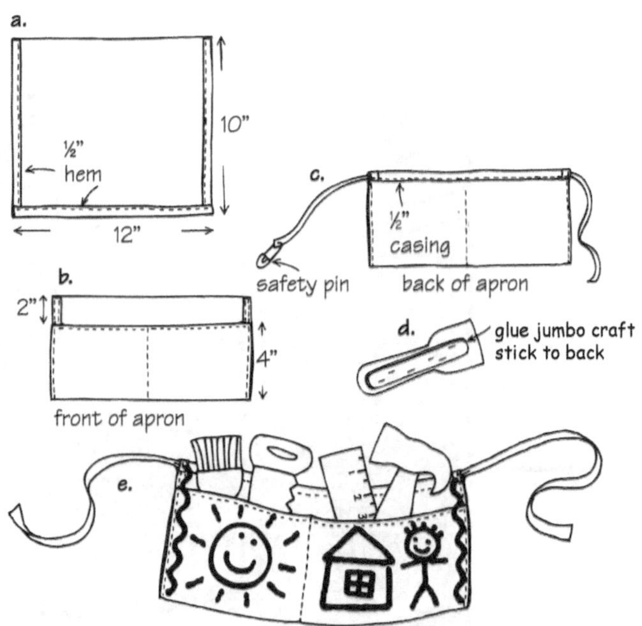

1
2
3
4
5
6

Raven Puppet

Materials

- copy of the raven pattern (p. 61)
- black construction paper
- white colored pencil (or crayon)
- scissors
- craft glue
- drinking straws (1 per child)
- tape
- wiggle eyes (2 per child)
- small pieces of bread
- black feathers *(optional)*

Before Class

Fold a sheet of black construction paper in half. Cut out the raven pattern, and place it on the fold of the construction paper (sketch a). With a white pencil, trace the outline of the bird onto the black paper. Cut out the bird (sketch a). Prepare a raven for each child.

Instructions for Children

- Fold down the wings of the raven to make them stick out (sketch b).
- Glue the bird's body together (sketch b). Don't glue the wings closed.
- Tape a drinking straw to the middle of the body, under a wing.
- Glue one wiggle eye on each side of the head.
- Glue a small piece of bread to the raven's beak.
- When the glue is dry, hold onto the straw and move it up and down to make the raven "fly"!

Enrichment Idea

If black feathers are available, older kids will enjoy gluing them onto the wings.

Talk About

What happens if there is no rain for a long time? (Nothing grows. Streams dry up.) **Where Elijah lived, it hadn't rained for a long time, so there was little food and water. But God took care of Elijah. God helped Elijah find a stream that had water to drink. And God sent ravens to give Elijah food. How does God take care of you?**

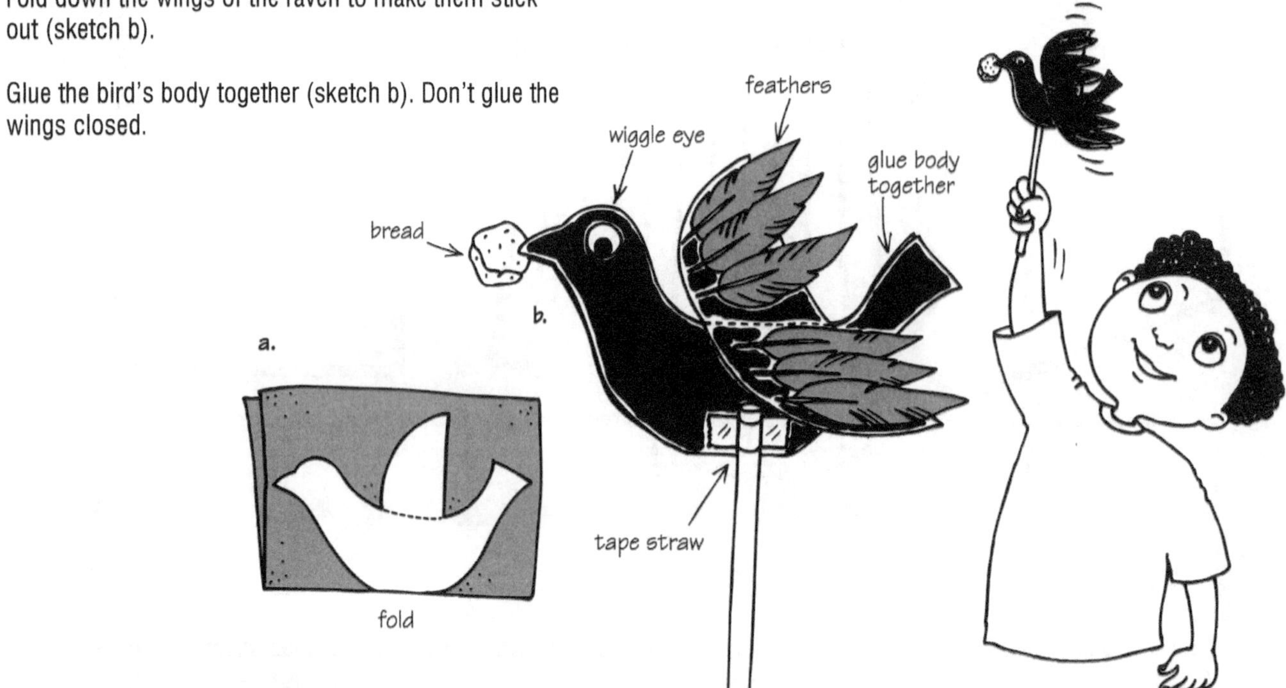

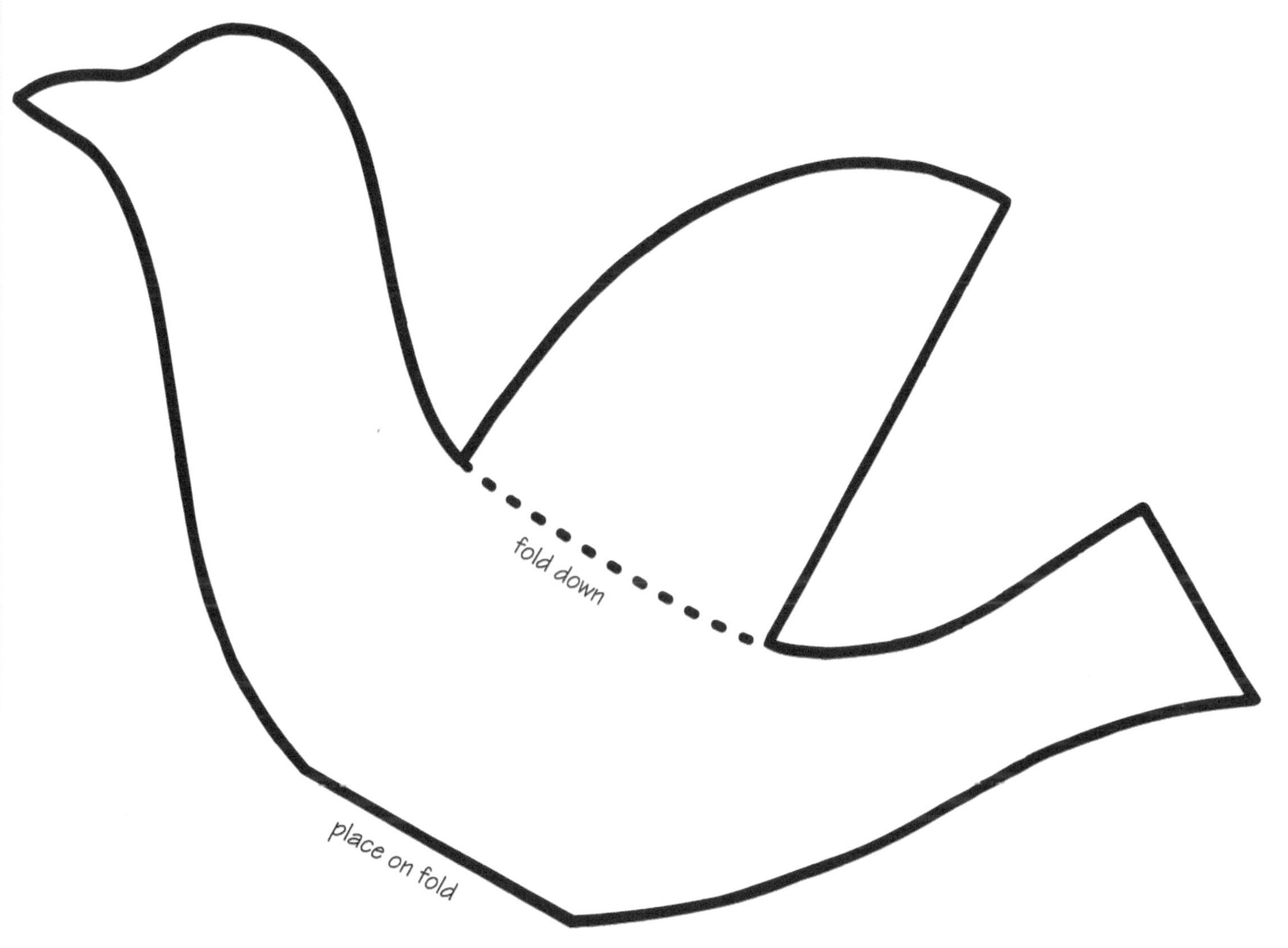
fold down
place on fold

King's Scepter

Materials

- gold wrapping paper
- yellow cellophane wrap
- ruler
- scissors
- paper towel tubes (1 per child)
- glue
- small shallow containers
- paintbrushes
- permanent markers
- decorative stickers (stars, hearts, etc.)
- white copy paper
- tape
- newspapers

Before Class

Cut 6½" x 11" pieces of gold wrapping paper, one for each child. Cut 6" squares of yellow cellophane, one for each child. Pour glue into small shallow containers. If desired, dilute the glue with a little water so it spreads easily. Cover the work area with newspaper.

Instructions for Children

- Brush a thin coat of glue onto the back of a piece of gold wrapping paper. With a teacher's help, wrap the glued paper around a paper towel tube.
- Decorate the wrapped tube, using markers and stickers.
- Crumple a sheet of white paper into a tight ball. With a teacher's help, cover the paper ball with a piece of yellow cellophane wrap. Tape the ball to the top of the decorated paper tube.

Talk About

In Bible times, kings used scepters to point and give orders. A king would also hold out his scepter if he agreed to see someone who came to talk to him. Queen Esther wanted to help her people. Before she went to see the king, Esther prayed. God helped Esther be brave—and the king held out his scepter! When can you ask God to help you be brave? Hold out a scepter to indicate each child's turn to share.

"Praise!" Pipes

Materials

- poster board
- ruler
- scissors
- drinking straws
- yarn
- hole punches
- glitter markers
- crayons
- craft glue
- whiteboard and dry-erase marker
- double-sided mounting tape *(optional)*

Before Class

Cut poster board into 1" x 6" strips, two for each child. Cut straws into the following lengths: 7", 6", 5", 4", 3", and 2", one length of each size for each child. Cut yarn into 2½' lengths, one for each child. Print "Praise!" on a whiteboard.

Simplification Idea

Using double-sided mounting tape can make this project go faster, eliminating the mess of glue and drying time.

Instructions for Children

- Punch holes on both ends of one poster board strip near the corners (sketch a).
- Thread the ends of a piece of yarn through the punched holes. Tie knots to secure the ends.
- Decorate one side of the strip with glitter markers and crayons. Print your name or "Praise!" on the strip (sketch b). Set aside this strip.
- Squeeze a line of craft glue lengthwise along the center of the other poster board strip.
- Evenly space the straws on the glued strip in graduating order. Make sure the top ends of the straws are even and extend about 1" above the edge of the strip (sketch c).
- Squeeze another line of glue over the straws. Carefully place the decorated strip on top of the straws. Align the edges of the top poster board strip with the bottom strip (sketch d). Allow the glue to dry.
- Play the Praise Pipes by placing your mouth about 1" above the straws then blowing gently. Do not blow directly into the straws. Blow air along the even ends of pipes to make different tones!

Talk About

What instrument do you know how to play? What instrument would you like to learn to play? Allow children to share. **David and other musicians wrote many songs to praise God. They played instruments as they sang to God.** Read Psalm 150 to children. **Let's blow across the tops of our pipes and praise God!**

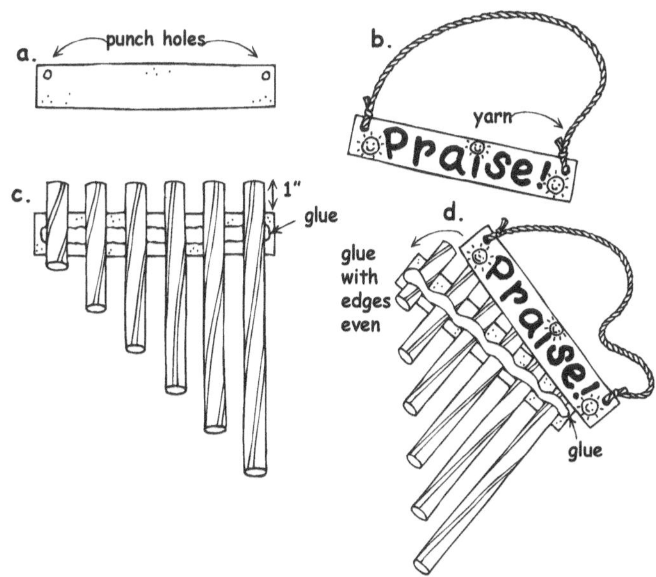

"Three Men in a Fire" Puppets

Materials

- fabric scraps
- ruler
- fabric scissors
- yellow card stock
- pinking shears
- orange and red markers (or crayons)
- tape
- jumbo craft sticks (3 per child)
- small wiggle eyes (6 per child)
- mini pom-poms (3 per child)
- craft glue

Before Class

Cut fabric scraps into 2" squares, three for each child. Cut card stock into 7" squares. Fold the squares in half diagonally. Using pinking shears, cut the square into two equal triangles (sketch a). Cut one triangle for each child.

Simplification Idea

Draw the eyes and noses instead of using wiggle eyes and pom-poms.

Instructions for Children

- Using orange and red markers, draw flames on one side of a yellow triangle.
- Fold the paper into a cone shape (sketch b). Tape the edges closed on the back side.
- To make Shadrach, Meshach, and Abednego puppets, glue two wiggle eyes onto each of the three craft sticks (sketch c). Glue on pom-poms for noses. Allow the glue to dry.
- Use markers to draw hair, headbands, and other features on the figures.
- Wrap and glue fabric squares around the puppets to make clothes.
- Place the puppets into the cone pocket to show Shadrach, Meshach, and Abednego in the fiery furnace (sketch d).

Talk About

How did Shadrach, Meshach, and Abednego obey God? (They worshipped only God. They wouldn't bow down to the king's statue.) **How did God save the three men from the fiery furnace?** (He sent a heavenly being into the fire to protect them.) **How can we show our love to God?** (Pray to Him. Learn about Him from the Bible. Be kind and loving to other people.)

a.

7"

7"

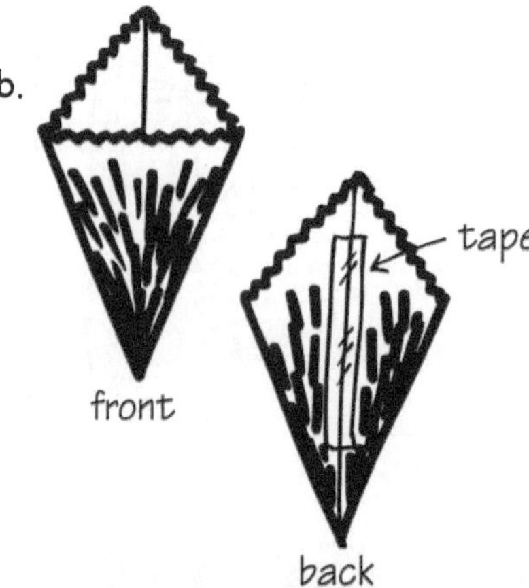

c.

pom-pom

wiggle eyes

Fiery Furnace Shades

Materials

- poster board
- yarn
- ruler
- scissors
- markers in a variety of colors
- hole punch

Before Class

Cut poster board into 2" x 6" rectangles, one for each child. Fold each poster board rectangle in half (sketch a), and cut off all four corners (sketch b). Starting at the folded edge, cut a ¼" slit in the middle of the poster board, stopping 1" before the opposite edge (sketch c). Cut string into 18" inch lengths, two for each child.

Instructions for Children

- Open the poster board shades.
- Punch holes in opposite sides of the shades (sketch d).
- Use markers to decorate the shades.
- Thread a piece of yarn through each hole, and tie a knot to secure each end.
- With a teacher's help, tie the yarn around your head to wear the shades.

Talk About

People sometimes wear sunglasses (or "shades") to protect their eyes from the glare of bright lights. Shadrach, Meshach, and Abednego could have used some sunglasses when they were thrown into a fiery furnace! But God protected them. When they came out of the furnace, their clothes didn't even smell like smoke! When has God protected you? Encourage children to wear their shades as they share stories of God's protection.

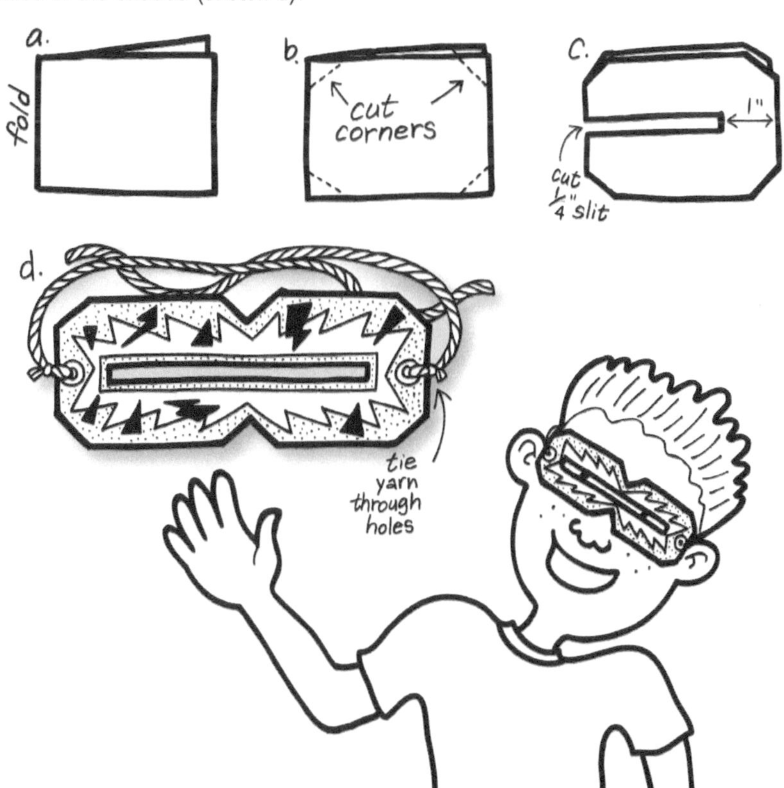

Lion Puzzle Magnet

Materials

- lion pattern (p. 67)
- small jigsaw-puzzle pieces
- brown spray paint and orange spray paint
- newspaper
- yellow card stock
- adhesive-backed magnet tape
- scissors
- ruler
- 7 mm wiggle eyes (2 per child)
- craft glue
- small shallow containers
- paintbrushes

Before Class

In a well-ventilated area, place puzzle pieces on newspaper and spray-paint the puzzle pieces orange and brown, approximately 12 pieces for each child. Copy the lion pattern onto yellow card stock and cut out, one per child. Cut magnet tape into 3" lengths, one for each child. Cut triangular tips off some puzzle pieces to use for each lion tail, one tip for each child (sketch a). Pour craft glue into shallow containers.

Instructions for Children

- Glue wiggle eyes onto a lion's face.
- Use a paintbrush to spread a small amount of glue to the back of each puzzle piece. Glue the pieces around the face of the lion to make a mane.
- Glue a triangular tip on the end of the tail (sketch b).
- When the glue is dry, attach a magnet to the back of the lion.

Talk About

Lions are very strong and powerful animals. But God is more powerful than the strongest lion. God kept Daniel safe in the lions' den, and God will keep you safe too. He gives you people who take care of you. Who are some of the people that care for you? What do they do to keep you safe? Encourage children to share. Be sure to include community helpers, such as police officers and firefighters.

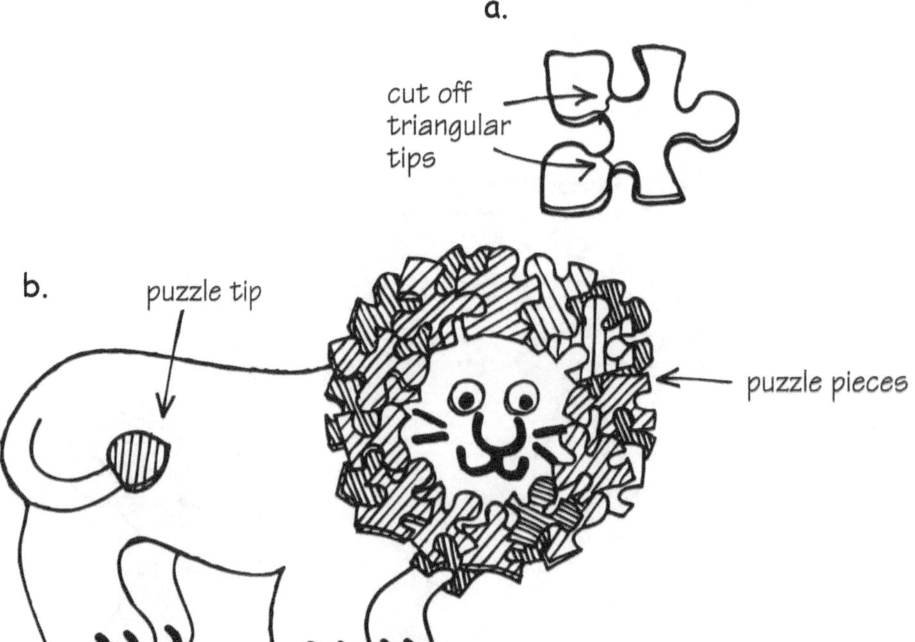

Prayer Spinner

Materials

- arrow pattern
- two colors of card stock
- scissors
- straight pin (or pointed scissors)
- store ads and magazines
- paper fasteners (1 per child)
- markers
- glue sticks

Before Class

Cut 8" circles out of one color of the card stock. Using the pattern, cut arrows from the second color of card stock. Use a pin or tip of a pair of scissors to put small holes in the center of the circles and in the ends of the arrows. Prepare a circle and arrow for each child. Gather store ads and magazines that picture things children can pray for or thank God for (families, nature and food items, other children, etc.)

Simplification Idea

Precut pictures that children can choose from to create their prayer spinners.

Instructions for Children

- Look through store ads and magazines and choose a few pictures of things you can pray for or thank God for. Cut out the pictures.

- Glue the pictures around the edges of a circle.

- If a specific picture cannot be found, draw that picture on the circle.

- With a teacher's help, push a paper fastener through the hole in the arrow and then through the hole in the circle. Spread the ends of the paper fastener on the back of the circle.

Talk About

Why was Daniel thrown into a den of lions? (Daniel prayed to God, even though he knew the king had signed a law that said the people were to pray only to the king.) **Daniel knew he was making the right choice when he chose to pray to God. We can make right choices and pray to God too. Point your arrow to something you can pray about. What will you say to God?** Encourage the children to share. Then pray together.

Jonah Shaker

Materials

- Jonah and fish patterns
- white or blue plastic (or foam) disposable plates
- scissors
- clear plastic beverage bottles with caps (1 per child)
- permanent markers
- plastic fish-shaped confetti
- shallow containers
- pitcher
- water
- blue food coloring
- blue electrical tape
- small fish or seashell stickers

Before Class

Trace the patterns onto plastic plates and cut them out, one Jonah and one fish for each child. Fill a pitcher with water. Put confetti into shallow containers.

Simplification Idea

Clear plastic energy drink bottles may have wider mouths that will make it easier for inserting objects into the bottle.

Instructions for Children

- Use permanent markers to decorate a plastic fish and a Jonah figure.
- Gently bend the fish and Jonah figure to fit through the bottle opening and push them into the bottle.
- Drop several confetti fish into the bottle.
- With a teacher's help, fill the bottle with water, stopping about 1" from the top.
- To make the seawater, put a few drops of blue food coloring into the bottle.
- Put the cap on the bottle and twist it tightly closed. Wrap a piece of tape around the bottle cap to secure it (sketch a).
- Shake the bottle to mix the food coloring with the water.
- Put a few stickers on the outside of the bottle.
- Tip the bottle back and forth to see Jonah and the fish swim under the sea.

Talk About

Have you ever run away from home? How did you feel? Allow the children to share. **Even though Jonah ran away and didn't obey God, God loved Jonah and took care of him. God loves you too. What are some ways God takes care of you?**

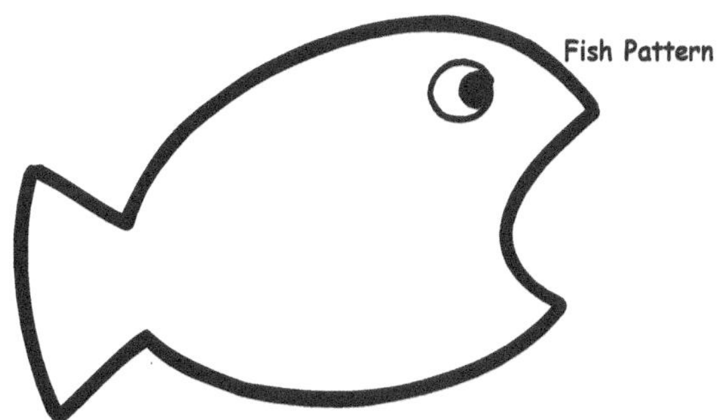

Spouting Whale

Materials

- whale patterns (p. 71)
- white card stock
- scissors
- hole punch
- tempera paints (black, gray, light blue, and green)
- shallow containers
- small sponge pieces
- spring clothespins
- newspaper
- paper fasteners (2 per child)
- medium-size wiggle eyes (1 per child)
- glue

Before Class

Copy the whale pieces onto card stock and cut out the pieces, one set for each child. With a hole punch, punch holes in each whale piece where indicated. Cover the work area with newspaper. Pour paint into shallow containers. Clip clothespins to sponge pieces to use as handles.

Instructions for Children

- Sponge black paint onto the whale body and tail. Then sponge gray paint on top of the black paint.
- Sponge blue and green paint on the water spout.
- Allow the paint to dry.
- Using paper fasteners, attach the tail and water spout to the whale (see sketch).
- Glue on a wiggle eye above the whale's mouth.
- Wiggle the whale's tail. Make the water spout move forward and backward!

Talk About

The Bible says a big fish swallowed Jonah. It could have been a whale. Have you ever seen a real whale? God made whales with something special—a blowhole on top of their heads. When a whale comes up out of the water, it blows air and water out of the blow hole. The water spouts out like a water sprinkler! God protected Jonah inside the fish. God protects you too!

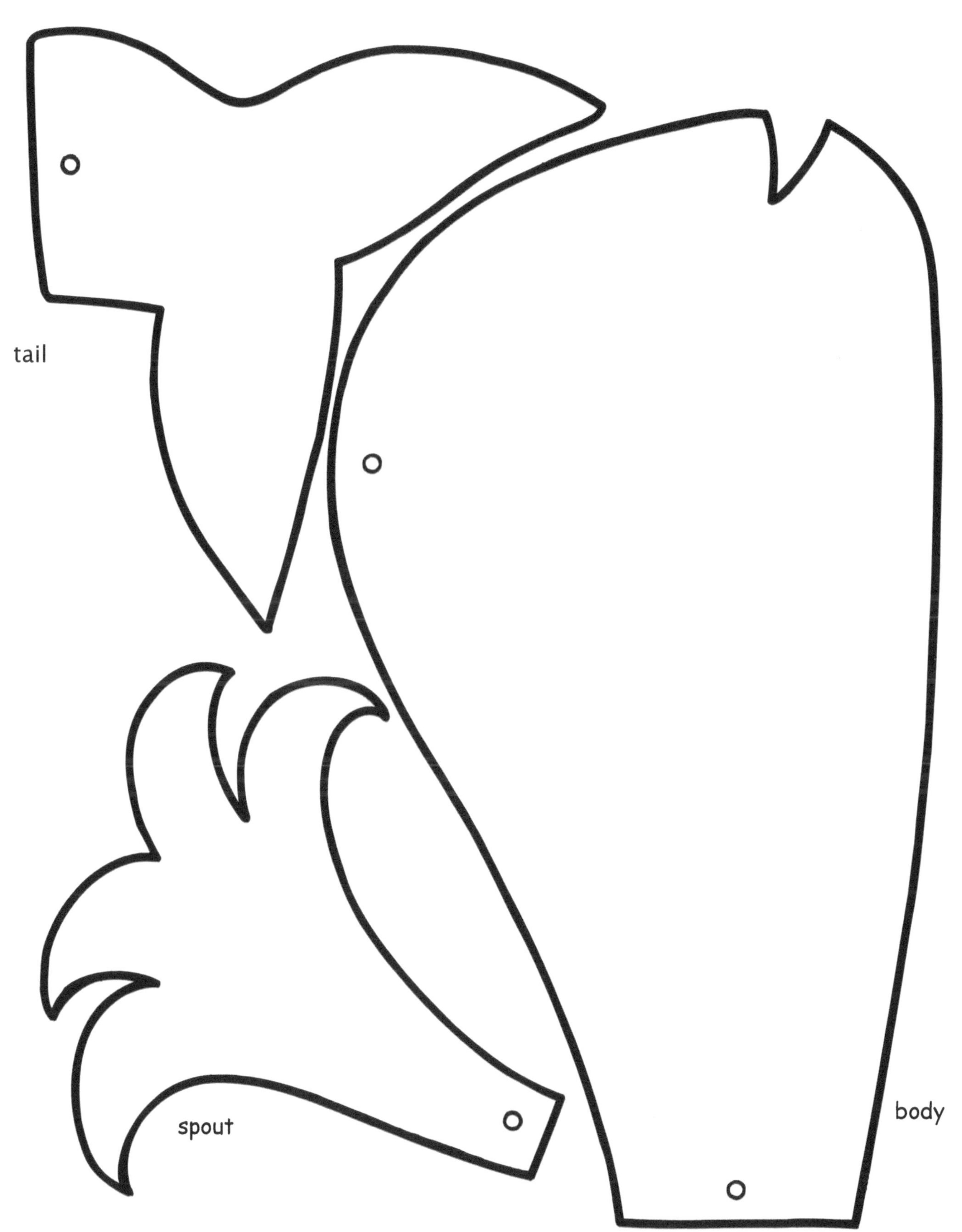
tail
spout
body

Star Chain Decoration

Materials

- star pattern and small pictures (p. 73)
- yellow card stock
- silver wrapping paper and gold wrapping paper
- scissors
- ruler
- markers
- glue sticks
- tape
- birth of Jesus and star stickers *(optional)*
- December calendar for the current year

Before Class

Copy the star pattern and pictures onto yellow card stock. Cut out the stars and pictures, one set for each child. Cut 1" x 5" strips of silver and gold wrapping paper, approximately 12 strips of each color for each child.

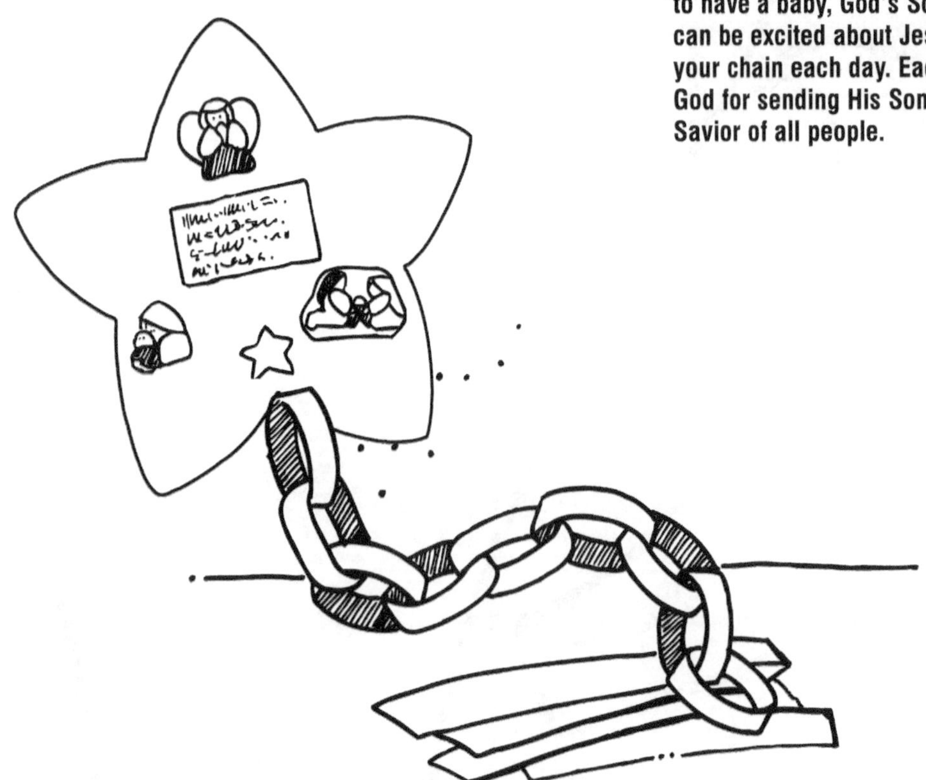

Instructions for Children

- Look at a calendar. Count to see how many days there are until Christmas Day (December 25). That's the day we celebrate Jesus' birthday.

- Use silver and gold strips to make a paper chain. Use tape to secure the ends of each link on the chain. Make one link for each day until Christmas Day.

- Color the small star, angel, and baby pictures. Glue the pictures onto the large star. Add other stickers, if desired.

- Tape one end of the paper chain to the bottom of the star.

Talk About

Have you ever seen a newborn baby? How did you feel? Allow children to share. **When Mary learned she was going to have a baby, God's Son, she must have been excited. We can be excited about Jesus' birth too. Remove one link from your chain each day. Each time you remove a link, thank God for sending His Son, Jesus, to earth to become the Savior of all people.**

Little star, shining bright,
How many days till the special night?
Jesus' birthday will soon be here.
Thank You, God, for Your Son so dear.

Paper-Plate Angel

Materials

- white paper plates
- yarn
- ruler
- scissors
- curly doll hair (or crinkled paper shred)
- fine-tip marker
- crayons
- stapler and staples
- tape
- glue
- hole punch
- star stickers
- glitter *(optional)*

Before Class

Cut an angel from a paper plate as shown in sketch a. With the plate facing up, draw a face on the angel's head. Prepare an angel for each child. Cut yarn into 12" lengths. Cut doll hair into short lengths.

Instructions for Children

- Color the portion of the plate below the angel's head to look like a robe. Then turn the plate over and color the bottom portion of the back side of the paper plate.
- With a teacher's help, bend the robe portion of the plate to overlap in the front and staple the ends in place (sketch b).
- Carefully bend the wings down behind the robe portion and tape or staple the wings to the back of the robe.
- With a teacher's help, punch a hole in the top of the head. Thread yarn through the hole and tie the ends together.
- Glue a small amount of curly doll hair to the head.
- Add star stickers to decorate the robe.
- Hang the angel and let it fly in the breeze!

Enrichment Idea

Older children may enjoy adding glitter to the wings. They can spread glue on the wings, sprinkle with glitter, and then shake off any excess.

Talk About

Have you ever received a special card or package? Who delivered it to you? Allow children to share. **Angels are God's special messengers. What did the angel tell Mary?** (Jesus would be born.) **What did angels tell the shepherds?** (Jesus was born.) **We can be messengers for God too. We can tell others that Jesus is God's Son!**

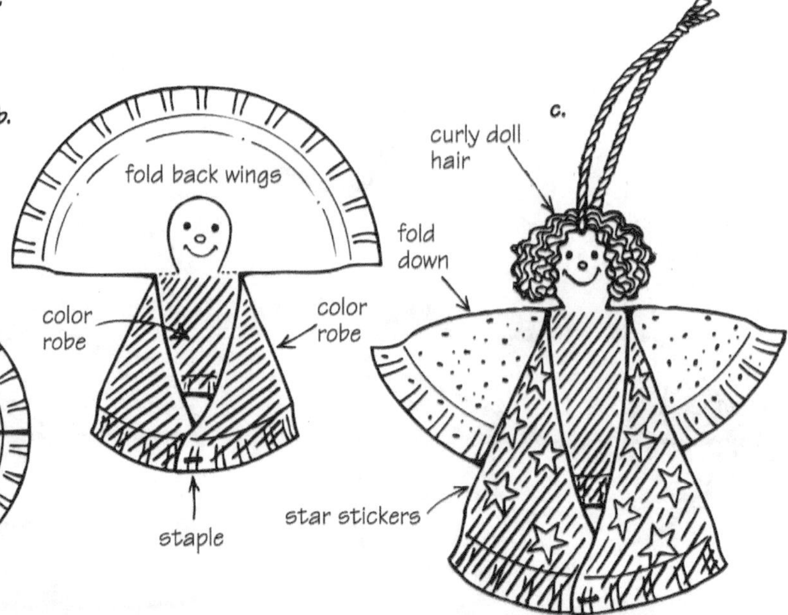

Baby Jesus Doll

Materials

- fabric
- ruler
- scissors
- jumbo craft sticks
- yarn
- small cardboard jewelry boxes (type used for earrings)
- straw (or dried grass)
- glue
- fine-tip markers

Before Class

Cut fabric into 2" squares. Cut jumbo craft sticks to fit inside a small jewelry box. Cut yarn into small pieces.

Simplification Idea

Draw facial features on the craft sticks before class.

Instructions for Children

- Spread a little glue on one side of the rounded edge of a craft stick (sketch a).
- Press a few yarn pieces onto the glue to make hair (sketch b).
- Glue straw to the inside of a small jewelry box.
- Use a fine-tip marker to draw facial features on the craft-stick doll (sketch b).
- Place the doll in the straw and cover the doll with a piece of fabric (sketch c).

Talk About

What is the name of God's Son? (Jesus) **Where was Jesus born?** (in Bethlehem) **Jesus' mother laid baby Jesus in a manger, a box used to hold food for animals. Jesus came to earth as a baby, and then He grew to be a man. Jesus came to tell people about God's love for them.**

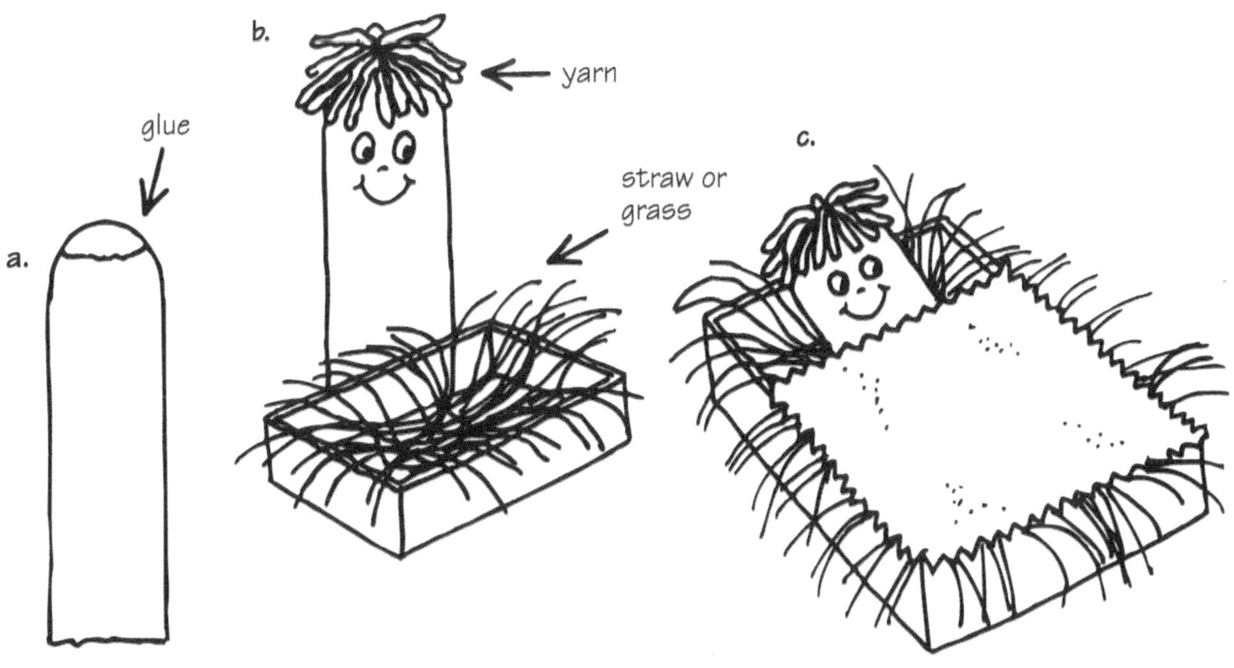

Mary and Joseph Manger Scene

Materials

- manger scene patterns (p. 77)
- craft foam (or colored paper) in light blue, dark blue, tan, and brown
- fabric scraps
- yellow tissue paper
- pen
- scissors
- ruler
- jumbo craft sticks (4 per child)
- 8½" x 11" sheets of purple card stock (1 per child)
- brown crayons (or washable markers)
- glue

Before Class

Copy the patterns and cut them out. Trace the head pattern onto tan craft foam and cut out, two for each child. Trace the body pattern onto dark- and light-blue craft foam and cut out, one of each color for each child. Trace the manger pattern onto brown craft foam and cut out, one per child. Trace the head covering pattern onto fabric scraps and cut out, two per child. Cut tissue paper into 5" squares, one per child.

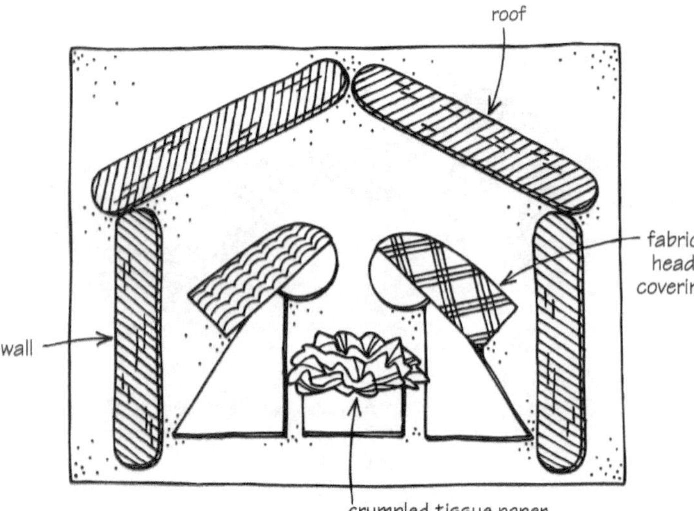

Simplification Idea

Glue four craft sticks to a sheet of purple paper to form the manger scene (see sketch). Prepare one for each child and allow the glue to dry before class.

Instructions for Children

- Color four craft sticks, using brown crayons.
- Lay a sheet of purple card stock on the table, horizontally. Glue two craft sticks near the top edge to make the stable's roof (see sketch). Glue two craft sticks onto the card stock to make the stable's walls.
- Glue a brown foam manger in the center bottom of the stable.
- Crumple a square of tissue paper and glue it to the top of the manger for hay.
- Glue one triangle body piece on each side of the manger to make the Mary and Joseph figures (see sketch).
- Glue the head circles on top of the triangle bodies.
- Glue fabric pieces onto the heads to make head coverings.
- Allow the glue to dry.

Talk About

Have you ever helped to take care of a baby? What did you have to do for the baby? Allow children to share. **Jesus was God's Son. Joseph and Mary were glad that God had chosen them to take care of baby Jesus.**

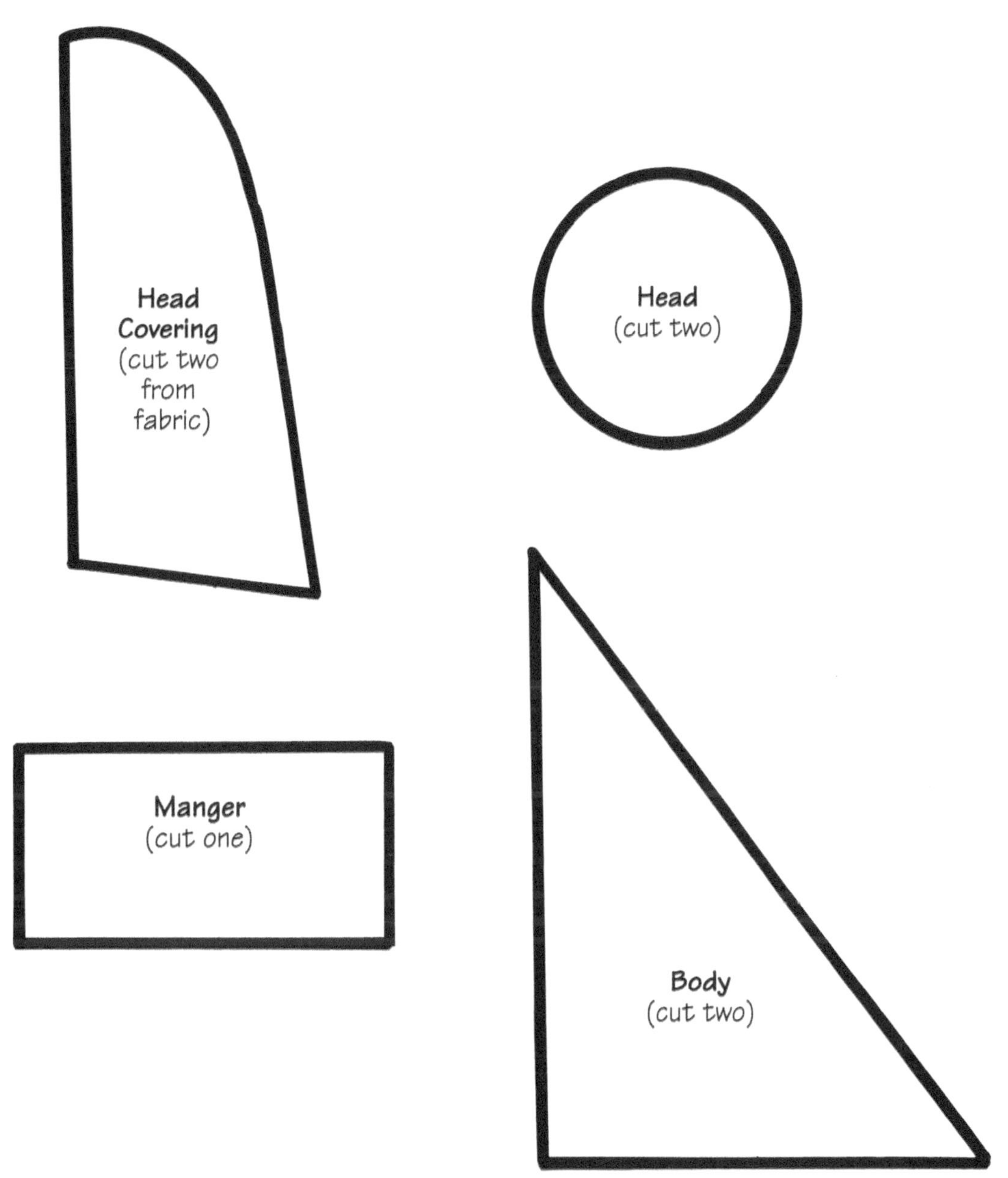
Head
Covering
(cut two
from
fabric)
Head
(cut two)
Manger
(cut one)
Body
(cut two)

"Jesus Is Born" Stained-Glass Picture

Materials

- "Jesus Is Born" picture (p. 79)
- white copy paper
- crayons
- old magazines (1 per child)
- baby oil
- cotton balls

Before Class

Copy the "Jesus Is Born" picture onto white paper, one for each child.

Instructions for Children

- Color the picture, using crayons.
- Lay the picture on top of a magazine.
- With a teacher's help, apply baby oil to a cotton ball.
- Rub the cotton ball over the picture to spread the oil (sketch a). The oil will make the picture translucent. Allow the oil to dry.

Talk About

Has a bright light or sudden noise ever frightened you? What happened? Allow children to share. **The shepherds were afraid when an angel suddenly appeared to them. What news did the angel tell the shepherds?** (Jesus had been born.) **Where were the shepherds to find the baby?** (lying in a manger in the town of Bethlehem) **Jesus is God's Son. He came to show God's love to everyone.** Encourage children to tape their pictures in windows at home to see the light shining through the pictures (sketch b).

a.

b.

"Today a Savior has been born to you" (from Luke 2:11).

Star Viewer

Materials

- toilet paper tubes (1 per child)
- construction paper
- 4" squares of blue cellophane paper
- scissors
- crayons
- glitter markers
- tape
- star stickers
- rubber bands

Before Class

Cut 4" x 5" pieces of construction paper, one for each child. Cut 4" squares of blue cellophane paper, one for each child.

Instructions for Children

- Using crayons and glitter markers, draw designs to decorate a precut piece of construction paper.
- With a teacher's help, cover a toilet paper tube with the construction paper. Fasten it in place using tape.
- Put a few star stickers in the center of a square of cellophane paper.
- Place the cellophane paper over one end of the tube and hold it in place with a rubber band.

Talk About

Have the children hold their star viewers toward a light to make the stars shine. When you look at the sky at nighttime, what do you see? (the moon, stars, clouds) **Wise men followed a bright star to find Jesus. How did the wise men worship Jesus?** (bowed down, gave gifts to Him) **How can we worship Jesus?** (pray and thank God for Jesus, sing and take part in worship times at church)

Crown

Materials

- 12" x 18" sheets of construction paper
- scissors
- decorative supplies (crayons, glitter glue or glitter markers, stickers, self-adhesive jewels, etc.)
- tape

Before Class

Cut simple crown shapes from construction paper (see sketch).

Instructions for Children

- Color and decorate a crown, using the supplies provided.

- With a teacher's help, tape the ends of the crown so it fits and can be worn.

Talk About

The wise men who came to see Jesus were probably wealthy. They may have been kings or rulers in their countries. Have the children put the crowns on their heads and pretend to be wise men. **What would you say to Jesus? What do you own that you could give to Jesus?**

"Grow Like Jesus" Growth Chart

Materials

- ruler strips (p. 83)
- card stock
- scissors
- copy paper
- tape
- decorative stickers of children (or happy faces)
- marker

Before Class

Cut a sheet of card stock in half. On each half-sheet, draw a happy face and print "I Grow Like Jesus Grew" (see sketch). Copy the ruler strips onto copy paper and cut them out. (Note: When making copies of the ruler strips, be sure to set the copier to print the page at 100%.) Make a set of six strips for each child.

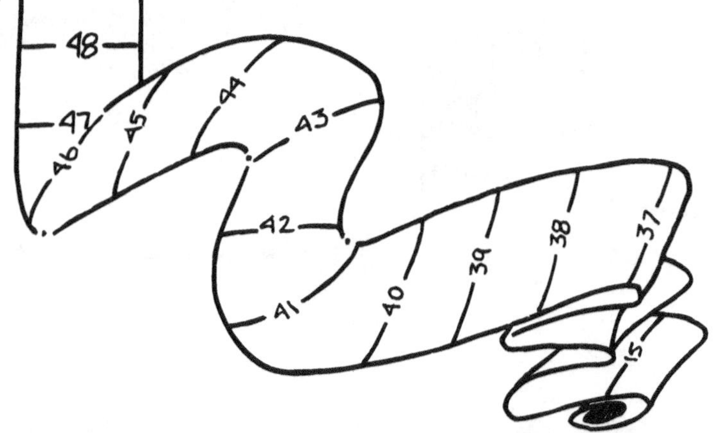

Simplification Idea

Attach and number the six strips before class.

Instructions for Children

- Tape six strips together to make a 48" strip.
- Starting at the bottom and working up, print numerals 1 to 48 on the strip.
- Tape the top of the long strip to a prepared header piece.
- Add decorative stickers of children along the strip.

Talk About

What did you do when you were a baby? What can you do now that you are bigger? Encourage the children to share. **As Jesus grew up, He grew wiser and taller. He grew in pleasing both God and people. You can grow just like Jesus did. How can you please God? What can you do to please people?** Hold each child's growth chart next to a wall with the bottom end of the strip touching the floor. Have the child stand in front of the strip, and mark the child's height on the strip.

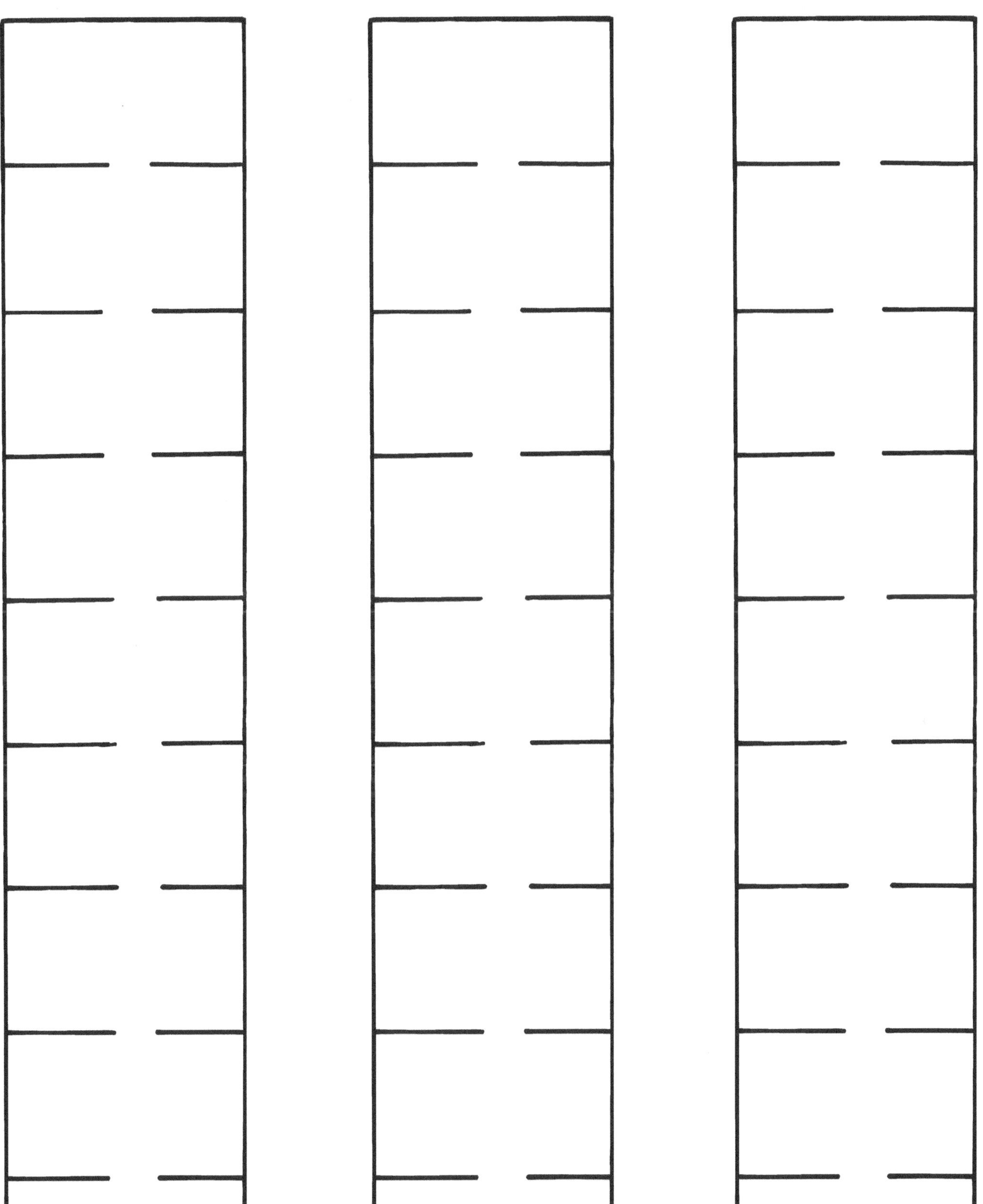

Surprise Me! Picture

Materials

- white paper plates
- construction paper in a various skin tones
- ruler
- scissors
- compass
- variety of stickers
- paper fasteners (1 per child)
- markers
- glue sticks
- hole punch
- rubber stamps, washable ink pads *(optional)*

Before Class

Cut the paper plates in half, one for each child (sketch a). Print "God loves" on the back side of the top half of each plate. Print a child's name on the back side of the bottom half of each plate. Using the compass, draw 5" circles onto construction paper and cut out. (Cut circles from a variety of skin-tone colors so children can choose the color they want to use.)

Instructions for Children

- Choose a construction paper circle. With a marker, draw your face on the circle (sketch b).
- Rub glue on the front lower edge of the face and attach it to the bottom plate half so the face is peeking out above where your name is (sketch c).
- Decorate the plate halves with stickers.
- With the printed sides up, overlap the top "God loves" plate half over the bottom plate half (sketch c).
- With a teacher's help, punch a hole in the left edge of each plate half, then fasten the plates halves together with a paper fastener (sketch c).

Enrichment Idea

- Older children can print their own names on their bottom paper plate halves. They can print the names in bubble lettering or add their own designs.
- Instead of stickers, provide rubber stamps and washable ink pads.

Talk About

Have the children take turns opening their plate halves to reveal the faces they drew of themselves. **Look! God loves _____** (child's name)**! John 3:16 tells us that because God loves us so much, He sent His only Son, Jesus, to the world. If we believe in Jesus, we can live with Him forever. I'm glad God loves each one of us!**

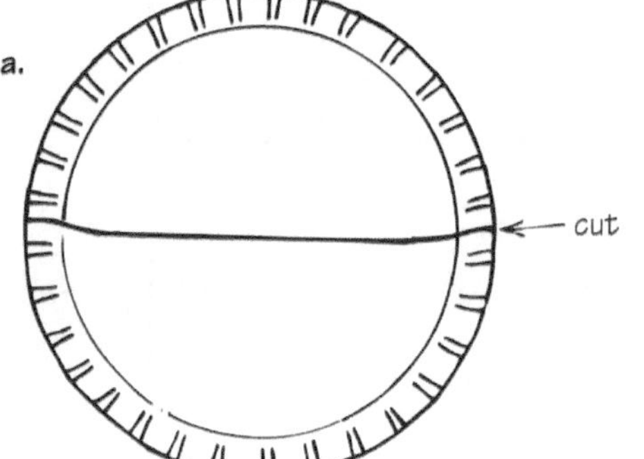

Fishing Boat

Materials

- 1"-thick household sponges (1 per child)
- craft foam in various colors
- scissors
- ruler
- drinking straws (1 per child)
- markers
- variety of foam stickers
- hole punch
- hot-glue gun and hot-glue sticks
- large containers of shallow water *(optional)*

Before Class

Cut the corners off one end of each sponge (sketch a); prepare one for each child. In the center of each sponge, use the tip of a pair of scissors to poke a hole large enough for a straw to fit into (sketch a). Cut the craft foam into 4" x 6" rectangles, one for every two children. Then cut the rectangles in half diagonally to make two sails (sketch b). Just before the project begins, plug in a glue gun out of the reach of the children.

Instructions for Children

- Use markers and foam stickers to decorate the sail.
- With a teacher's help, punch a hole at the top and bottom of the sail (sketch c).
- Insert a straw through the two holes for the mast.
- Pull the sail near the top of the straw (sketch d).
- Have a teacher use a hot-glue gun to glue the bottom end of the straw into the sponge hole (sketch d).

Enrichment Idea

Provide large containers of shallow water in which children sail their boats.

Talk About

When Jesus was walking beside a sea, He saw two brothers. Do you know what they were doing? (fishing) **Yes, Peter and Andrew were casting their nets to catch fish. Jesus said, "Come, follow me." And they did! What can we do to follow Jesus today?** (love God, love others)

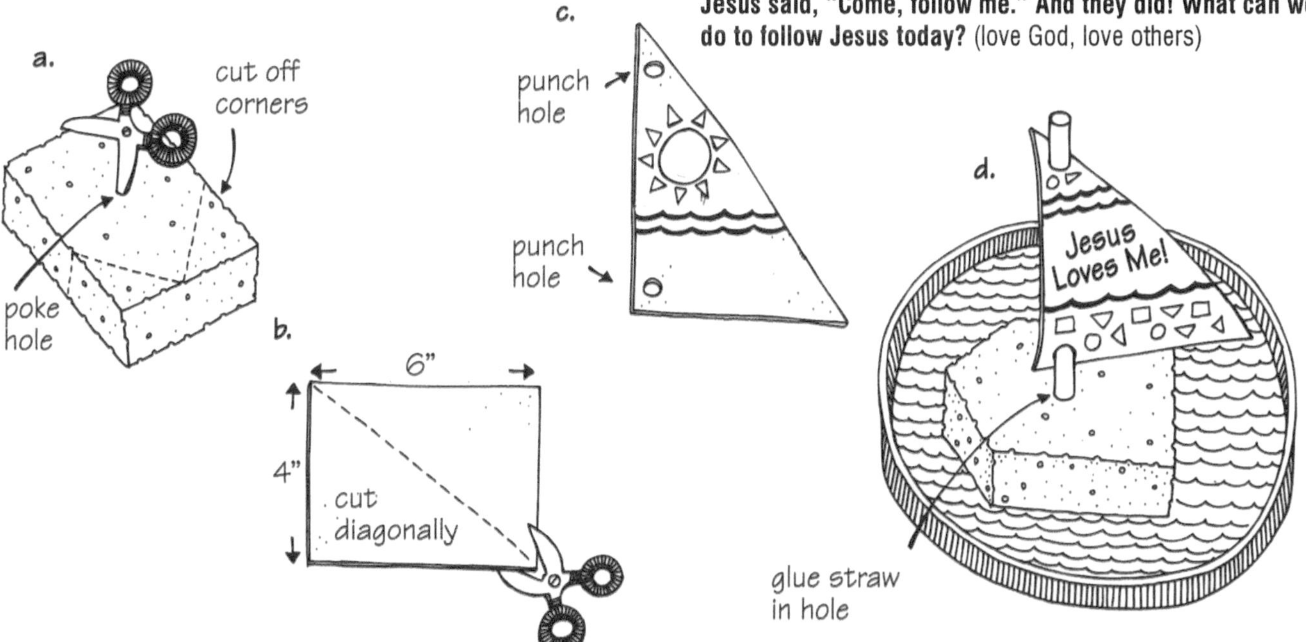

Paper-Bag Fish

Materials

- yarn
- ruler
- scissors
- paper lunch bags (1 per child)
- tempera paint in various colors
- shallow containers
- paintbrushes
- paint shirts
- newspapers
- large wiggle eyes (2 per child)
- craft glue
- a fishnet, available at craft or party supply stores, crayons or markers *(optional)*

Before Class

Cut yarn into 6" pieces, one for each child. Cover the work area with newspaper. Pour paint into shallow containers.

Simplification Idea

Color the fish with crayons or markers, if there is not time for painting.

Instructions for Children

- Crumple pieces of newspaper and stuff them into a paper bag until the bag is half full.
- Gather the top unstuffed portion of the bag to make the fish's tail. Hold the tail together while a teacher ties yarn around it (sketch a). Trim the yarn ends.
- Paint the entire bag to look like a fish. Decorate it with various colors. Paint the fish's mouth on the end (bottom) of the bag (sketch b). Allow the paint to dry.
- Glue a wiggle eye on each side of the fish (sketch b).

Enrichment Idea

When they are dry, put all the fish together in a fishnet and reenact the story of Jesus calling the fishermen to be His disciples.

Talk About

What did Jesus say to the fishermen when He passed by them? ("Come, follow me.") **Jesus wanted these men to become His friends and help Him tell people about God. The fishermen left their fishing boats and nets to go with Jesus. They knew that Jesus was special. Jesus is God's Son.**

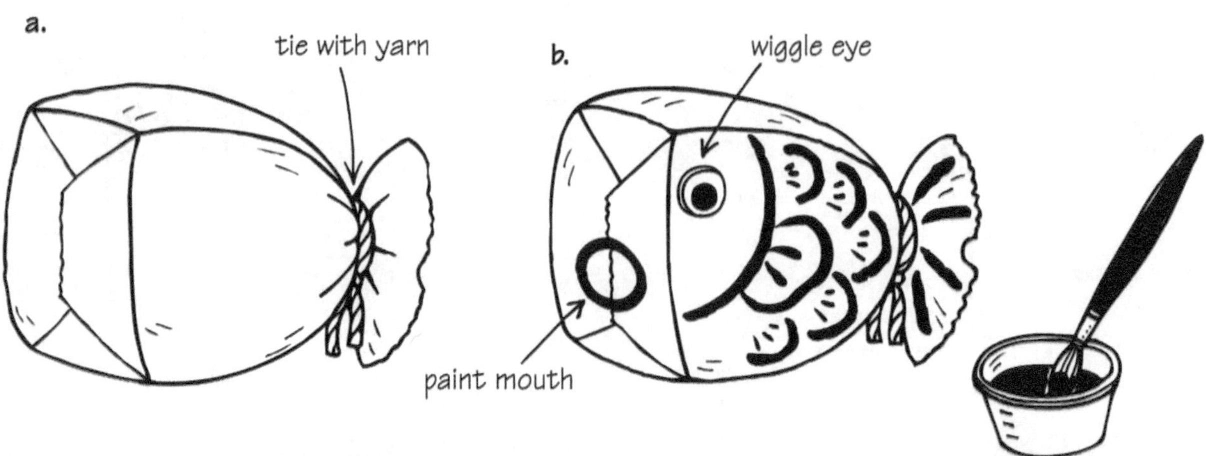

Helper Bee Note Holder

Materials

- bee pattern
- yellow poster board (or card stock)
- black chenille wires
- scissors
- pencil
- ruler
- black markers
- black crayons
- 7 mm wiggle eyes (2 per child)
- spring clothespins (1 per child)
- craft glue (or tape)
- ½"-wide adhesive-backed magnet tape
- tape *(optional)*

Before Class

Copy and cut out the bee pattern. (Note: Copy the page at 100%.) Trace the pattern onto yellow poster board and cut out, one for each child. Cut magnet tape into 1½" lengths, one for each child. Cut black chenille wires into six ¾" lengths and two 1½" lengths, one set for each child.

Instructions for Children

- With a black marker, draw a smile on the bee's face.
- Color black stripes on the bee's body.
- Glue wiggle eyes on the bee's face.
- Glue (or tape) onto the bee's body six small black chenille wires for legs (sketch a).
- Bend the ends of the two longer black chenille wires to make antennae. Glue (or tape) them to the bee's head.
- Glue the bee to a spring clothespin (see sketch b). Allow the glue to dry.
- Attach a magnet to the back of the clothespin (sketch b).

Talk About

Have you ever helped a friend? What did you do? Encourage children to share. **One day some men brought to Jesus a man who could not walk. Jesus said to the man, "Get up and go home." And the man did! Jesus wants us to be helpers too. Your Helper Bee can keep papers clipped together in one place. It can remind you to help others.**

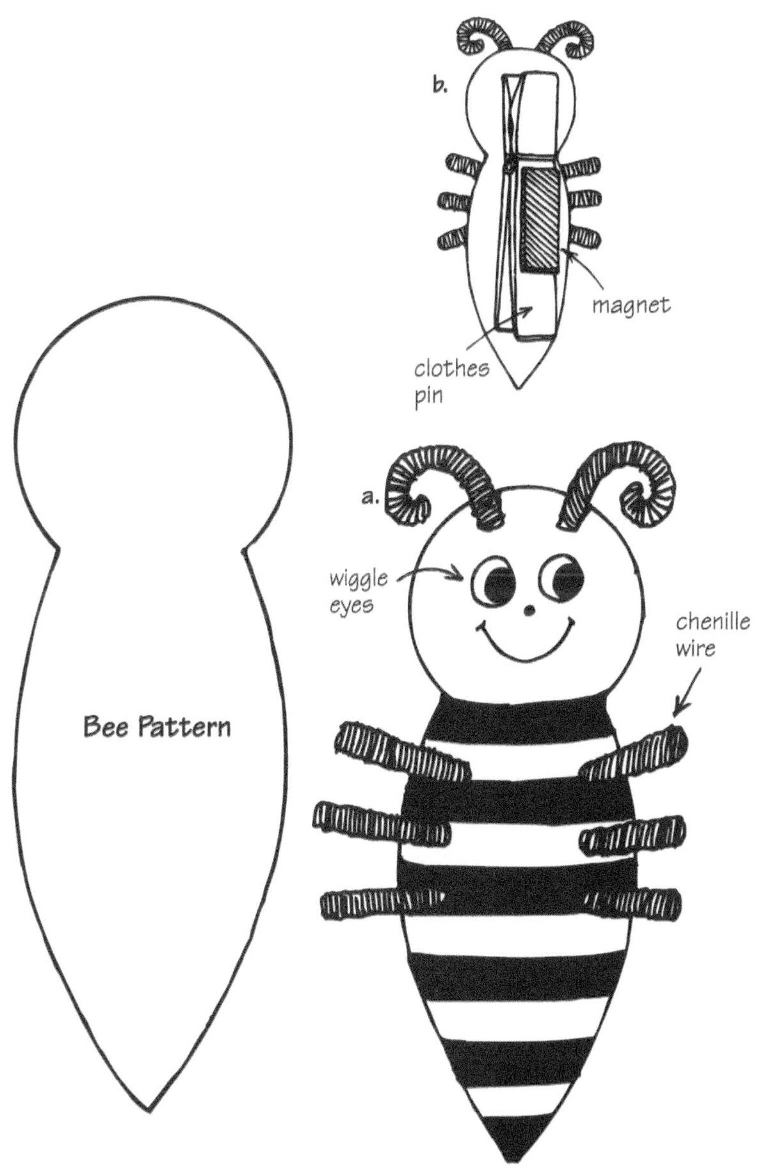

Prayer Place Mat

Materials

- magazines and retail store flyers with a variety of pictures (animals, foods, people, nature, etc.)
- poster board in various colors
- ruler
- scissors
- marker
- glue sticks
- clear adhesive covering

Before Class

Cut the poster board into 9" x 12" mats, one for each child. On each mat, print at the top, "Dear God, thank You for …" and at the bottom print "Amen." Cut clear adhesive covering into 10" x 13" rectangles, two for each child. Look through magazines and flyers and tear out appropriate pages. (Note: If you do not have magazines or store flyers, find and print appropriate images from the Internet.)

Simplification Idea

For younger children, cut out individual pictures in appropriate sizes for the children to choose from and add to their place mats.

Instructions for Children

- Look through magazine pages and store ads and cut out pictures of people or things you are thankful God has made or given to you. Glue the cutouts onto a poster board mat.

- With a teacher's help, peel the paper backing from a piece of clear adhesive covering. Place the clear covering over the front of the place mat, smoothing out any wrinkles. Then peel the backing from a second piece of clear covering and repeat the process on the back of the place mat.

- With a teacher's help, trim the edges of the adhesive covering as close as possible to the edges of the place mat.

Talk About

If your family prays together at mealtimes, what do you pray about? What do you thank God for? Allow children to share. **Jesus taught people to ask God for the food they need each day. You can use your place mat when you eat a meal or a snack. The words and pictures can help you remember to thank God for all the good things He gives you.**

"Do Not Worry" Bird Puppet

Materials

- paper lunch bags (1 per child)
- bird patterns (pp. 90–91)
- yellow and white card stock
- crayons
- glue
- scissors
- colored feathers *(optional)*

Enrichment Ideas

- Glue feathers onto the head, wings, body, and tail, as desired.
- Have the children use their puppets to name things kids might worry about (grades, friends, health, where they will live, what they will eat, etc.). Make up simple puppet plays in which the birds tell the kids not to worry—and why.

Before Class

Copy the head, claws, tail, and wing patterns onto white card stock. Copy the beak pattern pieces onto yellow card stock. You will need a complete set (body, two beak pieces, two claws, two wings, tail) for each child.

Talk About

What kinds of birds live in your yard? Allow children to share. **Jesus taught that God provides food for the birds. Instead of worrying, we should seek God. We should follow and love God. God cares for us and knows what we need. Use your puppet to say, "I won't worry. God cares for me!"**

Simplification Idea

Cut out all the puppet pieces before class.

Instructions for Children

- Use crayons to color the bird's head, claws, wings, and tail. Cut out all the pieces, including the beak pieces.
- Glue the head to bottom flap of a paper bag.
- With a teacher's help, bend the top beak piece into a cone shape. Fold under the tabs and glue this piece onto the bird's head. Then fold up the bottom beak piece and glue the tab to the head, inside and under the top beak piece (sketch a).
- Glue the claws to the bottom edge of the bag. Then glue the wings to the inside folds of the bag sides (sketch b).
- Fold the tab on the tail and glue it to the back of the paper bag.

Glue beak here.
bottom beak piece
top beak piece
claws

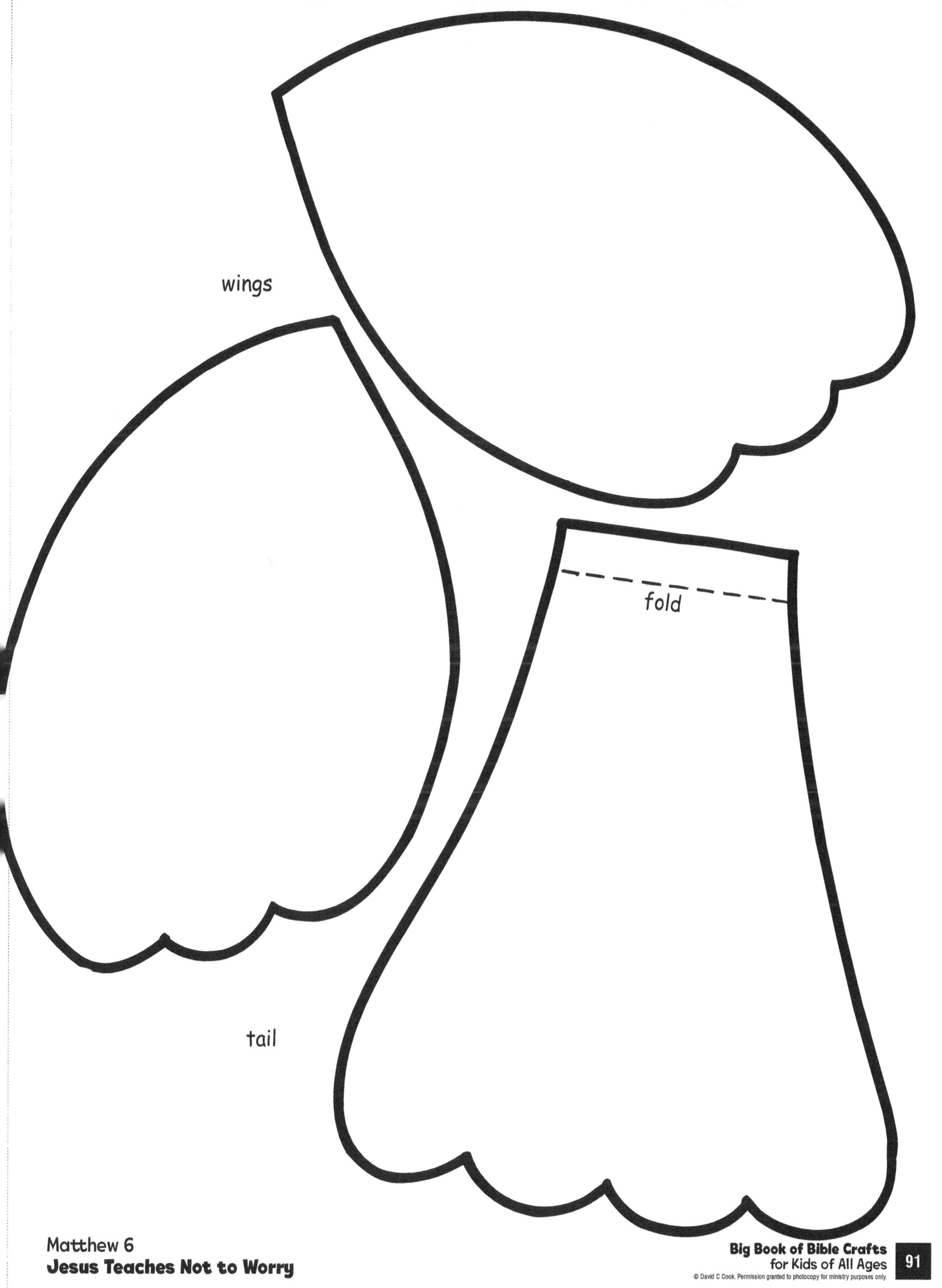
wings
fold
tail

Stormy and Calm Sea Picture

Materials

- 11" x 17" sheets of construction paper (1 per child)
- black felt
- small pieces of construction paper in various colors
- scissors
- crayons (or washable markers)
- glue
- fish-shape crackers (or fish stickers)

Before Class

Prepare one sheet of construction paper for each child. Divide the paper in half by drawing a line down the center. Print "Stormy" at the top of the left half; print "Calm" at the top of the right half. Cut clouds out of black felt, one for each child.

Instructions for Children

- On the "Stormy" side, use crayons to draw a sea that is stormy.
- Glue on a black felt cloud in the sky.

- From construction paper, cut a triangle for a sail and a rectangle for a boat. Glue the sail and boat onto the stormy waves.
- Glue on a few fish that are struggling to swim in the stormy water.
- On the "Calm" side, use crayons to draw a sea that is calm.
- From construction paper, cut out a circle to represent a warm sun; glue the sun in the sky.
- Cut a triangle for a sail and a rectangle for a boat. Glue the sail and boat onto the calm sea.
- Glue on a few fish that are happily swimming in the water.

Talk About

Have you ever been in a boat on the water? What did you do while you were in the boat? Allow children to share. **The Bible tells about a time when Jesus was in a boat with some of His disciples. Jesus lay down and went to sleep. A big storm came and Jesus' friends were afraid. But Jesus spoke to the wind and the waves. He told them, "Quiet! Be still!" And they were! How does Jesus help you when you are afraid?**

Get-Well Card

Materials

- card stock
- black permanent marker
- old greeting cards (or seed catalogs and magazines that have pictures of flowers and nature items)
- scissors
- glue sticks
- washable markers

Before Class

Fold sheets of card stock in half to create cards, one for each child. Inside each card, print "Get well soon. I will pray for you." Cut pictures from old greeting cards to use on the cards that children will create.

Instructions for Children

- Choose a picture to glue to the front of a card. Use markers to add drawings and designs.

- Draw (or glue on) other pictures inside the card.

- Print (Sign) your name on the inside of the card.

- A teacher will collect the cards to give to someone who is sick. Or you can ask an adult to help you deliver your card to someone you know who is sick.

Talk About

Have you ever received a get-well card? If you did, how did the card make you feel? Allow children to share. **The Bible tells about a time when a young girl was very sick. The girl's father asked Jesus to heal the girl. And Jesus did! Jesus helped the girl and her family. How does Jesus help your family? How can you help someone who is sick?**

Food Basket

Materials

- basket, loaf, and fish patterns (p. 95)
- white card stock
- scissors
- glue sticks
- crayons (or markers)
- whiteboard and dry-erase marker

Before Class

Copy the patterns onto card stock and cut out a basket, two fish, and five loaves of bread for each child. Each child will also need one full sheet of card stock. Print on the whiteboard, "Jesus has power!"

Simplification Idea

For younger children, print on full sheets of card stock: "Jesus has power!"

Instructions for Children

- Print at the top of a sheet of paper: "Jesus has power!"
- Color a basket, two fish, and five loaves of bread.
- With a teacher's help, put glue on the outside edges only (sides and bottom) of the basket. Glue the basket to your paper. Make sure the top of the basket is open so the fish and bread can be put inside.

Talk About

What do you like to eat for lunch? Allow children to share. Jesus once used a boy's small lunch to feed over 5,000 hungry people. Help the children count together as they put two fish and five loaves of bread into their baskets. Jesus has power to give us what we need. How can we thank Jesus for what He gives to us? (Possible answers: Obey God. Pray and thank Jesus. Tell others about Jesus.)

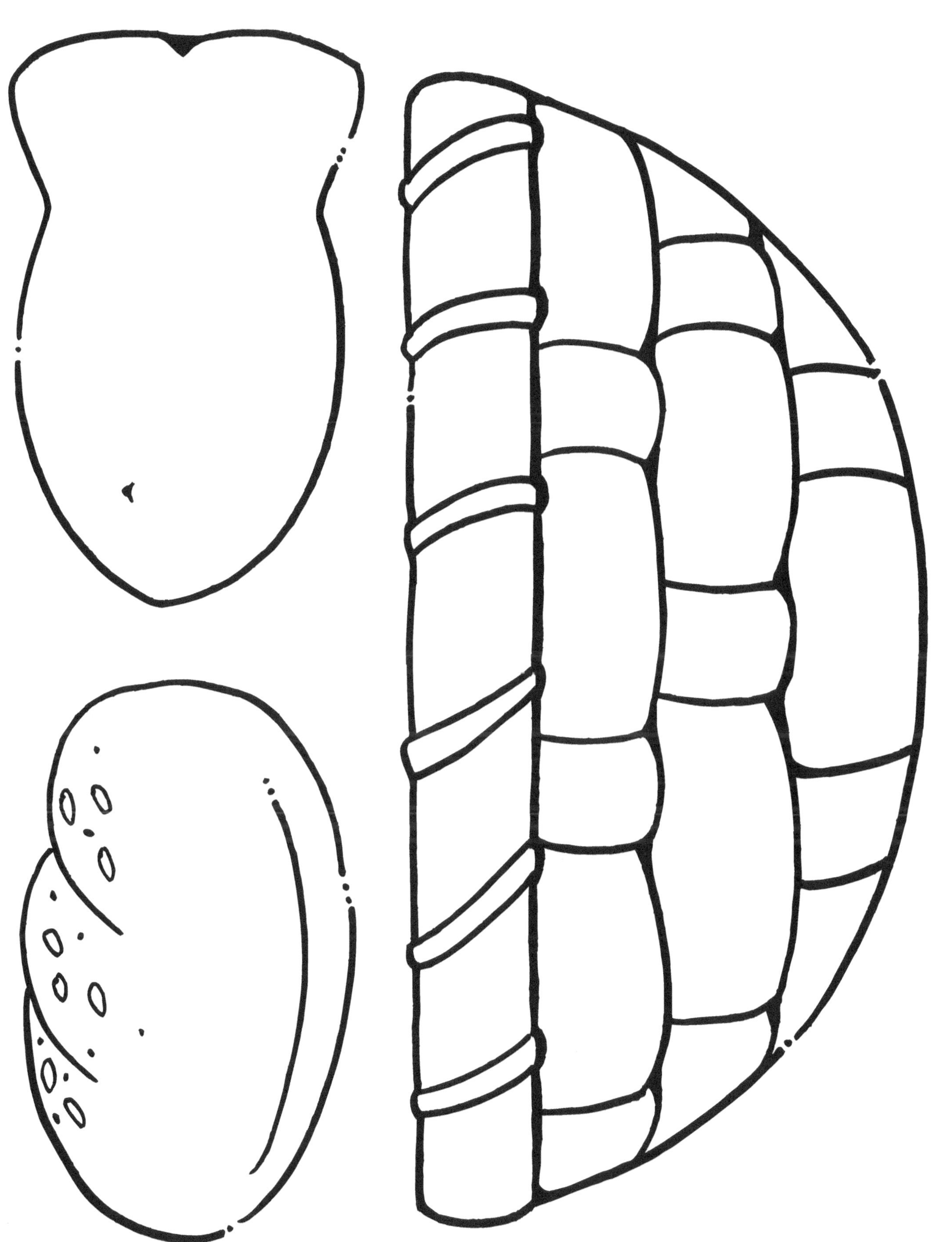

"Miracle" Picture

Materials

- powdered drink mixes in various colors
- several empty salt shakers with lids
- plastic tub (or bucket)
- white paper (1 sheet per child)
- newspaper (or plastic tablecloth)
- water
- roll of art paper *(optional)*

Before Class

Remove the lids from the salt shakers. Pour one color of powdered drink mix into each shaker and replace the lid. Fill a plastic tub with water. Cover the work area with a thick layer of newspaper.

Instructions for Children

- Carefully dip a sheet of white paper into the water to get it wet (sketch a).

- Lay the paper flat on the newspaper.

- Gently sprinkle drink mix from a shaker onto the paper (sketch b). Observe how color suddenly appears on the paper.

- Shake on several colors, as desired.

- Keep the paper flat to dry.

Enrichment Idea

Allow children to make several pictures, or use a large piece of art paper and have the children work together to create a mural.

Talk About

We can make colors appear on sheets of white paper. Is that a miracle? (no) **People can do a lot of amazing things, but only God and Jesus can do real miracles. Jesus performed many miracles to help people. He made sick people well. He fed thousands of people with just a boy's lunch. Jesus even walked on water! We can praise Jesus because He has power to help us!**

Flip-Flop Face

Materials

- craft foam (or construction paper) in various colors
- yarn (yellow, black, brown, red)
- small paper plates (2 per child)
- jumbo craft sticks (1 per child)
- scissors
- ruler
- craft glue
- paintbrushes
- small shallow containers
- tape
- stapler and staples
- markers *(optional)*

Before Class

From the craft foam, cut out shapes for eyebrows, eyes, noses, and mouths (see sketches a and b). Cut 6" and 7" lengths of yarn for hair. Pour craft glue into small containers.

Simplification Idea

Instead of gluing on shapes, have the children use markers to draw faces on the paper plates.

Instructions for Children

- Using paintbrushes and craft glue, glue happy-face features to the back side of one paper plate. Glue on pieces of yarn for hair (sketch a).
- Glue angry-face features to the back side of a second paper plate. Glue on pieces of yarn for hair (sketch b).
- Allow the glue to dry. Then tape a craft stick to the front bottom edge of one plate (sketch c).
- With a teacher's help, staple the front rims of the plates together.

Talk About

Ask the kids to use their flip-flop faces to tell about attitudes or actions that make people angry. Then have them tell about attitudes or actions that make people happy. **Jesus said we should forgive others "seventy-seven times"—or as many times as is needed. When you feel angry, you can ask God to help you forgive and show love instead of hurting others.**

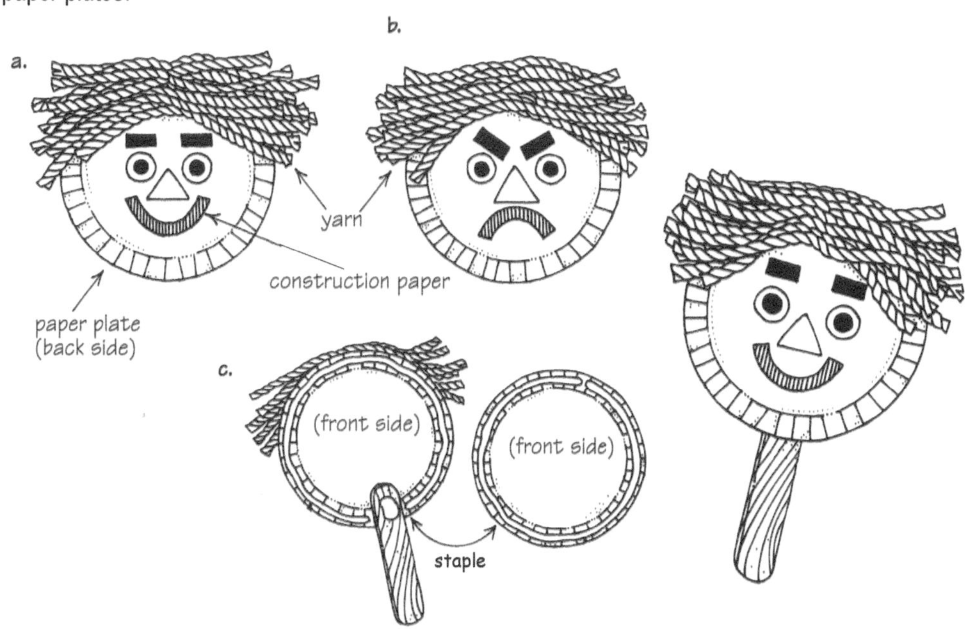

Love Medallion

Materials

- elbow macaroni
- gold spray paint
- newspaper
- small-size margarine lid
- pencil
- poster board
- scissors
- markers
- hole punch
- yarn
- ruler
- scissors
- glue

Before Class

Trace around a margarine lid to make circles on poster board, one circle for each child. Cut out the circles. With a marker, outline the letters "Love" on each circle. Punch a hole at the top of each circle. Cut a 24" length of yarn for each child. Place uncooked macaroni on a newspaper in a well-ventilated area; spray the pieces with gold paint.

Instructions for Children

- Use markers to color the letters or add designs to the poster board medallion.
- Glue macaroni around the edge of the medallion (see sketch).
- With a teacher's help, push one end of a piece of yarn through the hole on the medallion. Tie the two yarn ends together to make a necklace.

Enrichment Idea

Older children may print "Love" on the medallions by themselves.

Talk About

Jesus told a story about a man who stopped to help a person who was hurt. Two other men had seen the hurt man, but they didn't stop to help. God wants us to show love to one another. How do people show love to you? What are some ways you can show love to others?

Praying Hands Design

Materials

- colored card stock (2 sheets per child)
- pencil
- scissors
- yarn
- ruler
- hole punch
- tape
- colored chalk
- markers
- stickers
- unscented aerosol hairspray *(optional)*

Before Class

To create a handprint stencil pattern: Place one hand palm down, with fingers together, on a sheet of card stock. (A child's hand will work best.) Trace around the hand, and then cut out the handprint shape. Lay the pattern you have created on another sheet of card stock and trace around it, leaving at least a ½" margin at the top, bottom, and right edge. Then cut out and discard the handprint you have just traced (sketch a). Prepare a handprint stencil for each child. (Or prepare one stencil for every three or four children to share.) Cut 14" lengths of yarn, one for each child.

Instructions for Children

- Tape a handprint stencil over another sheet of card stock (sketch b).
- Color the inside of the stencil area with colored chalk.
- If desired, have a teacher lightly spray the colored area with hairspray to set the chalk. Then remove the stencil.
- With a teacher's help, print a simple prayer or sentence about prayer next to the handprint (sketch c).
- Decorate the edges of the card stock with stickers.
- Punch holes in the top corners. With a teacher's help, thread yarn through the holes and tie the ends to make a hanger.

Talk About

Jesus told His disciples that they should ask God for the things they needed. When we pray, we are talking to God. When are times that you pray? What would you like to talk to God about right now? Allow children to name things they want to pray about. Then lead in a time of prayer.

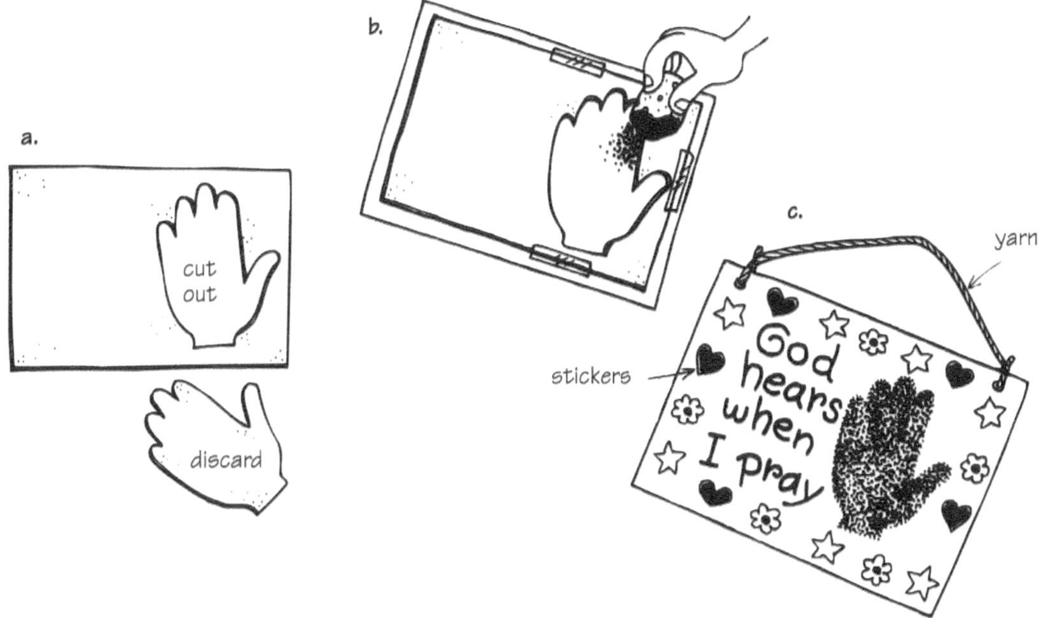

Sunshine Mobile

Materials

- large yellow paper plates (1 for every 2 children)
- scissors
- yarn (various colors)
- ruler
- yellow construction paper
- lids from small plastic butter tubs (or potato chip canisters, 4 per child)
- hole punch
- magazines (or store ad flyers) with various pictures
- markers
- glue

Before Class

Cut the paper plates in half, one half for each child. Cut the yarn into 12" lengths, five for each child. Cut construction paper into 2" squares, then cut the squares in half to make triangles. Punch a hole in each plastic lid and tie a length of yarn to the lid. Prepare four lids for each child. Look through magazines and tear out pages with small pictures of items that a child might be thankful for. With a marker, print "Thank You, God, for ..." on the bottom of each paper plate (see sketch).

Simplification Idea

For younger children, cut out a variety of small pictures and punch the holes in the plates before class.

Instructions for Children

- With a teacher's help, punch four evenly spaced holes along the bottom edge and one at the top of a half paper plate (see sketch).
- To make the sun rays, glue paper triangles around the curved edge of the paper plate.
- Look through the magazine pages and cut out pictures of people, animals, or things you are thankful for. Glue the pictures onto both sides of four plastic lids.
- With a teacher's help, tie the lids to the plate (see sketch). Trim the yarn ends as needed.
- To make a hanger for the mobile, thread a piece of yarn through the hole at the top of the plate and tie the ends together.

Talk About

What are you thankful for? Encourage the children to show their mobiles and name other people or things they are thankful for. **Jesus once healed ten men, but only one of the men remembered to thank Jesus. God takes care of us. He helps us have what we need to be safe and healthy and strong. We should remember to thank God for taking care of us.**

Heart Magnet

Materials

- heart pattern
- red (or pink) poster board (or card stock)
- pencil
- scissors
- adhesive-backed magnet tape
- ruler
- ½" pom-poms in various colors
- small pictures (or stickers) of Jesus (1 per child)
- markers
- glue

Before Class

Trace the heart pattern onto poster board, one for each child. Cut out the heart shapes. Cut magnet tape into 1" pieces, one for each child.

Instructions for Children

- Color and glue a picture of Jesus in the center of a poster board heart.
- Turn the heart over, and attach a piece of magnet tape to the back of the heart shape (sketch a).
- Turn the heart faceup again. Squeeze a thin line of glue around the outside edge of the heart.
- Glue some pom-poms around the edge of the heart (sketch b).

Talk About

People brought young children to Jesus, and Jesus took time for them. Jesus loves all people. When you look at your heart magnet, you can remember how much Jesus loves you. What is one thing Jesus did to show how much He loves us? (He died so our sins could be forgiven.)

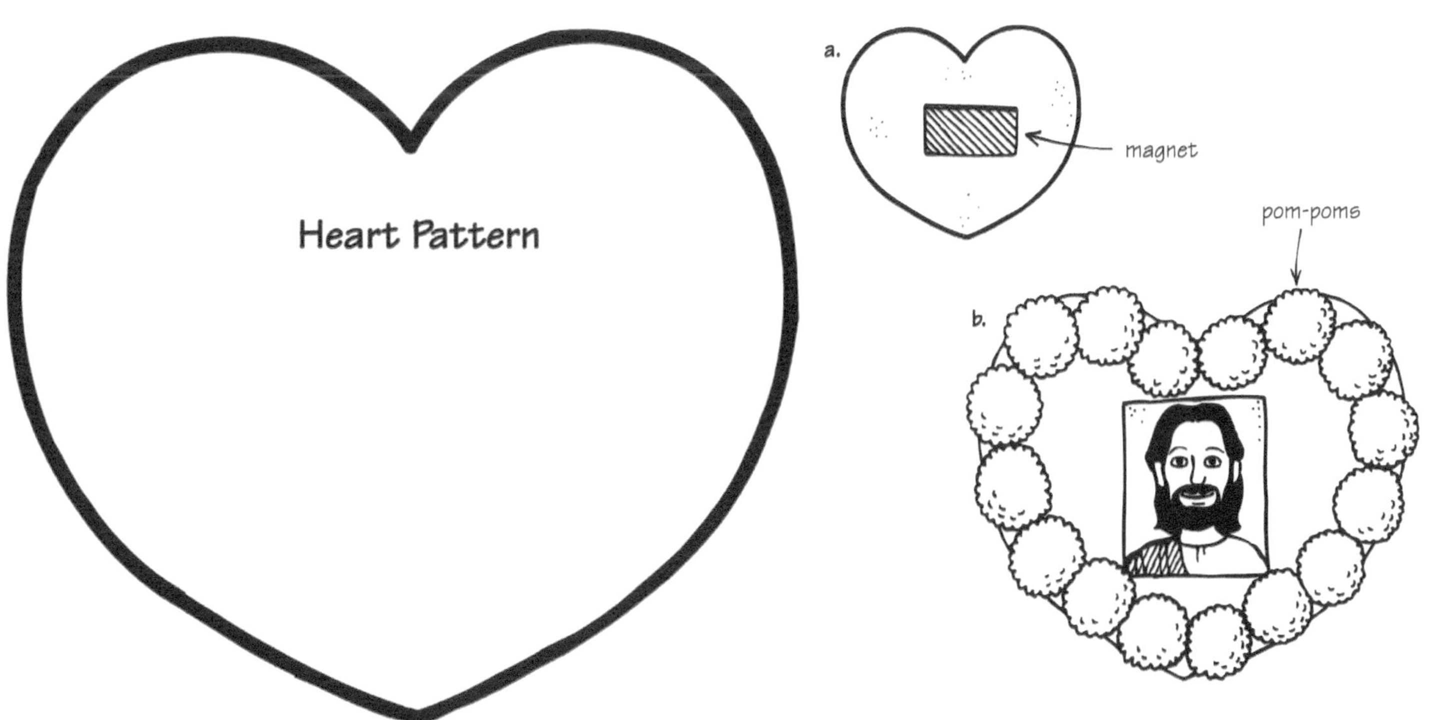

Stand-Up Sycamore Tree

Materials

- tree pattern (p. 103)
- white card stock
- scissors
- ruler
- green and yellow tissue paper
- brown crayons
- paintbrushes
- glue
- shallow containers
- water
- newspapers
- green crayons *(optional)*

Before Class

Copy the tree pattern onto card stock. Cut out two tree pieces for each child. On one tree piece, cut slit 1 from the top to the middle. On the other tree piece, cut slit 2 from the bottom to middle. Cut or tear tissue paper into 2" squares. Pour glue into shallow containers and dilute it with a little water. Cover the work area with newspaper for easier cleanup.

Simplification Idea

Younger children may color the treetops green and then crumple and glue just a few pieces of tissue onto their tree pieces.

Instructions for Children

- Use brown crayons to color both sides of two tree trunks.
- Brush a thin layer of glue on the treetop of one piece (sketch a). Lay several pieces of tissue onto the glue. Make sure the slits in the trees are not covered with tissue.
- Repeat this process until both sides of the treetops on both trees are covered with tissue (sketch b). Allow the glue to dry.
- With a teacher's help, slide one tree piece into the slit of the other tree piece (sketch c) and stand the tree up (sketch d).

Talk About

Have you ever tried to climb a tree? What might you see if you were sitting on a tree branch? Allow the children to share. **Zacchaeus climbed a tree so he could see Jesus coming into town. Zacchaeus wanted to see who Jesus was. How can we learn about Jesus?** (listen to or read stories from the Bible, watch Bible story videos, etc.) **What would you like to know about Jesus?**

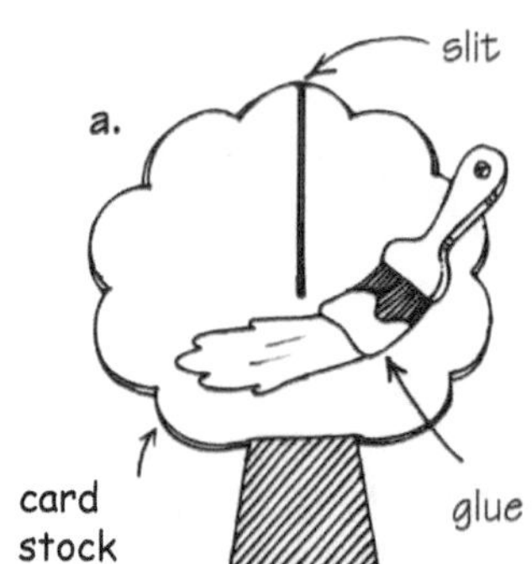

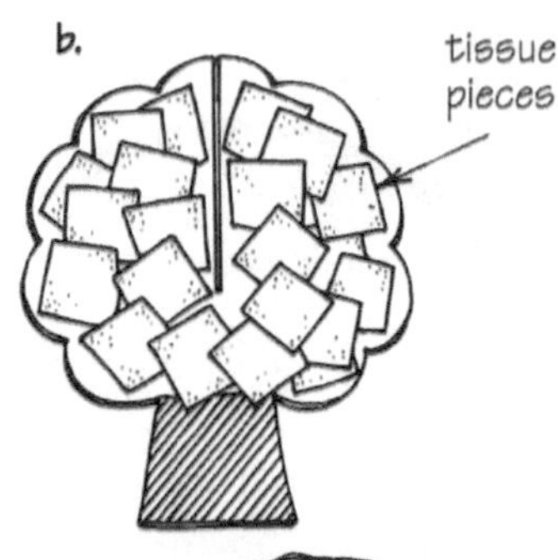

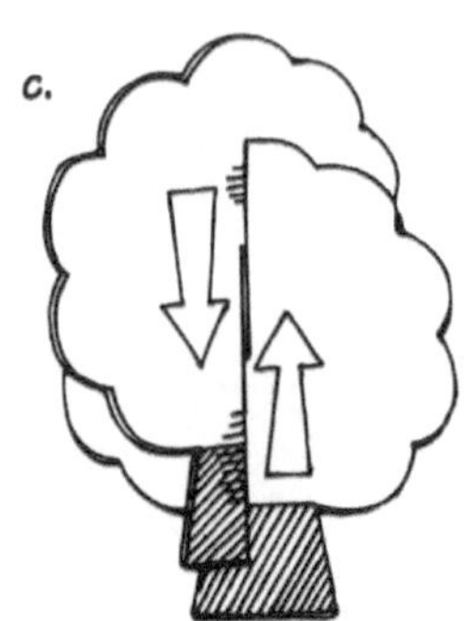

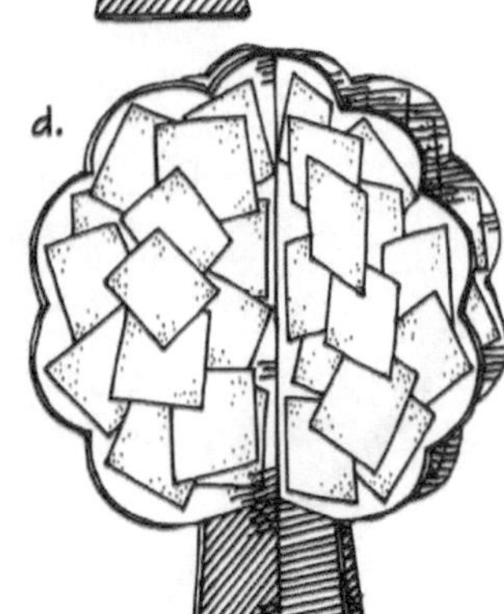

slit 1
slit 2

Zacchaeus Puppet Theater

Materials

- Jesus and Zacchaeus puppet patterns (p. 105)
- sheets of green poster board (1 for every 2 children)
- white card stock
- brown paper lunch bags (or brown construction paper)
- scissors
- ruler
- jumbo craft sticks (2 per child)
- crayons
- glue
- tape
- markers
- nature stickers, resealable plastic sandwich bags *(optional)*

Before Class

Cut a sheet of green poster board in half widthwise, one half for each child. Cut the top of each half to look like treetops (sketch a). Fold each side of the poster board to meet in the middle. Cut out a 2" circle in the center section. Copy the Jesus and Zacchaeus puppets onto card stock, one set for each child. Cut simple tree trunk shapes from brown paper bags, three for each child.

Simplification Idea

You may want to cut out the Jesus and Zacchaeus puppets for younger children.

Instructions for Children

- Glue three tree trunk shapes along the bottom edge of a poster-board puppet theater (sketch a).
- Draw (or use nature stickers) to add birds, animals, and flowers to the theater scene.
- Color and cut out a Jesus puppet and a Zacchaeus puppet. Tape craft sticks to the back sides of the Jesus and Zacchaeus puppets (sketch b).
- If desired, tape the sides of a plastic bag to back of the poster board theater (sketch c). The puppets can be kept in the bag, so they won't get lost.

Enrichment Idea

Children may draw people in a crowd near the bottom of the poster board scene.

Talk About

Have you ever had an unexpected guest come to your house? What happened? Allow children to share. **When Jesus saw Zacchaeus in the tree, Jesus said, "Come down immediately. I must stay at your house today." Zacchaeus was glad to have Jesus come to his house. How can we show Jesus that we are glad He is our friend too?** (Possible answers: pray to Jesus, read about Jesus in the Bible, show love to others)

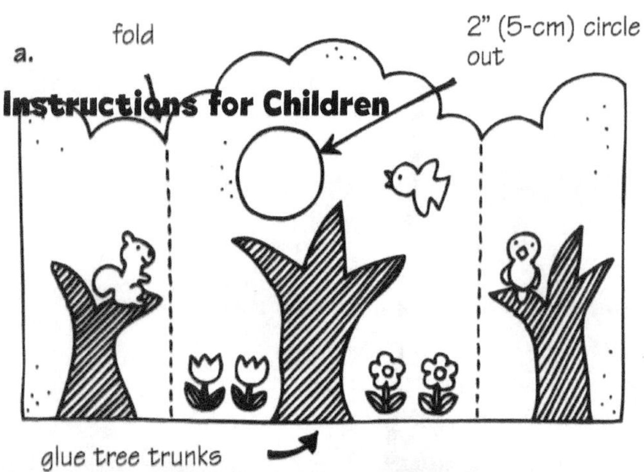

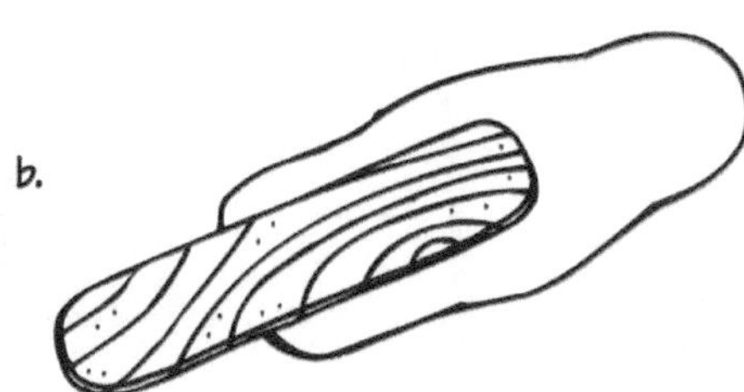

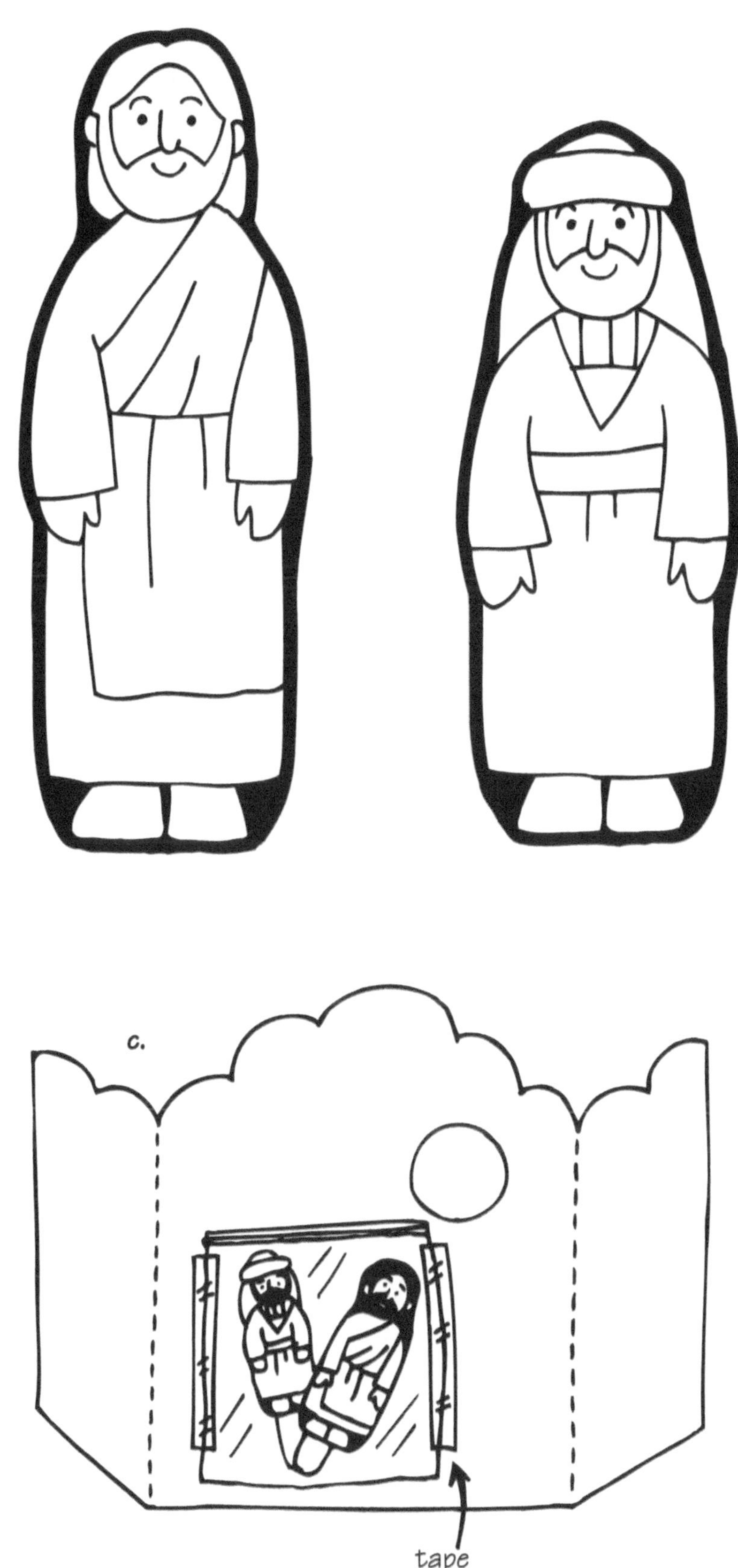
c.
tape

"Hosanna!" Streamers

Materials

- crepe-paper streamers in various bright colors
- yarn
- scissors
- ruler
- large plastic thread spools (1 per child)
- tape
- assorted stickers
- toilet paper tubes *(optional)*

Before Class

Remove the labels on the ends of the spools. Cut crepe-paper streamers into 3' lengths, three different colors for each child. Cut yarn into 18" lengths, one for each child.

Simplification Idea

If you don't have spools available, cut toilet paper tubes in half, one half for each child.

Instructions for Children

- Fold one end of a streamer into a point (sketch a). Repeat for the other two streamers.
- Tape the points of the streamers onto a spool (sketch b).
- Decorate the streamers with stickers.
- Thread a length of yarn through the center of the spool. With a teacher's help, tie the ends of the yarn together to make a loop (sketch b).

Talk About

When Jesus came into town, the people were happy to see Him. What did they shout? ("Hosanna to the Son of David!" and "Hosanna in the highest heavens!") **The people were glad Jesus had come. We are glad Jesus came too. Jesus came to earth because He loves each of us. What are some things we can say to praise Jesus?** Allow children to suggest a few praise phrases. Then have the children hold on to the loops and wave their streamers in the air as they say the praise phrases and shout, "Hosanna!"

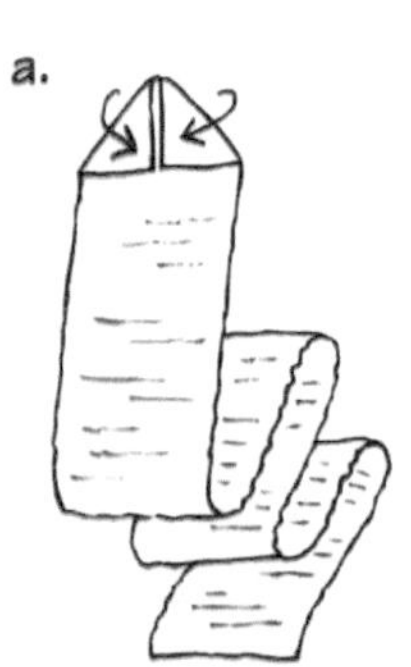

Clay Coins

Materials

- air-drying clay
- wax paper
- permanent marker
- coins (pennies, nickels, quarters)
- embossed buttons
- gold and silver tempera paint, paintbrushes, paint shirts *(optional)*

Before Class

Tear squares of wax paper for children to work on, one for each child. Using a permanent marker, print each child's name on a waxed paper square. Give each child a lump of clay.

Instructions for Children

- Divide a lump of clay into several small balls.
- Flatten each ball with your thumb (sketch a).
- Press a coin or button onto the top of each clay circle to make a design (sketch b).
- Let the clay coins dry on waxed paper overnight until hard.

Enrichment Idea

After the clay has dried, allow the children to paint their coins.

Talk About

Jesus told a story about a master who asked his servants to help take care of his money (bags of gold) while he was gone. Two of the servants used the money to make even more money for their master. The master was very happy with them and gave them a reward. But the third servant didn't help his master at all. This servant just buried his master's money in the ground. The master was very unhappy with the lazy servant. Jesus wants us to be good workers and use the abilities that God has given us. What are some things you can do to help others and please God? Discuss individual abilities the children have and suggest ways those abilities can be used to help others.

a.

b.

Rollaway Stone

Materials

- tomb and stone patterns (p. 109)
- white copy paper
- card stock
- scissors
- crayons
- paper fasteners (1 per child)
- glitter markers *(optional)*

Before Class

Copy the tomb and stone patterns onto white paper, a set for each child.

Simplification Idea

For younger children, cut out the tombs and stones before class.

Instructions for Children

- Color the tomb and the stone. Cut out the two pieces.
- Glue the tomb onto a sheet of card stock.
- Draw flowers, clouds, and grass around the tomb.
- With a teacher's help, use a paper fastener to attach the stone at the top of the tomb.
- Practice lifting (or moving to one side) the stone so the message inside the tomb can be read.

Enrichment Idea

Provide glitter markers that children can use to color the burst around the words "Jesus Lives!"

Talk About

After Jesus was put to death on a cross, His body was put inside a tomb. A large stone was rolled over the entrance to the tomb. What did the women find when they went to the tomb on the first day of the week? (The stone had been rolled away from the tomb's entrance. The tomb was empty. Jesus had come back to life!) **Who can you tell that Jesus is alive?**

Jesus
Lives!

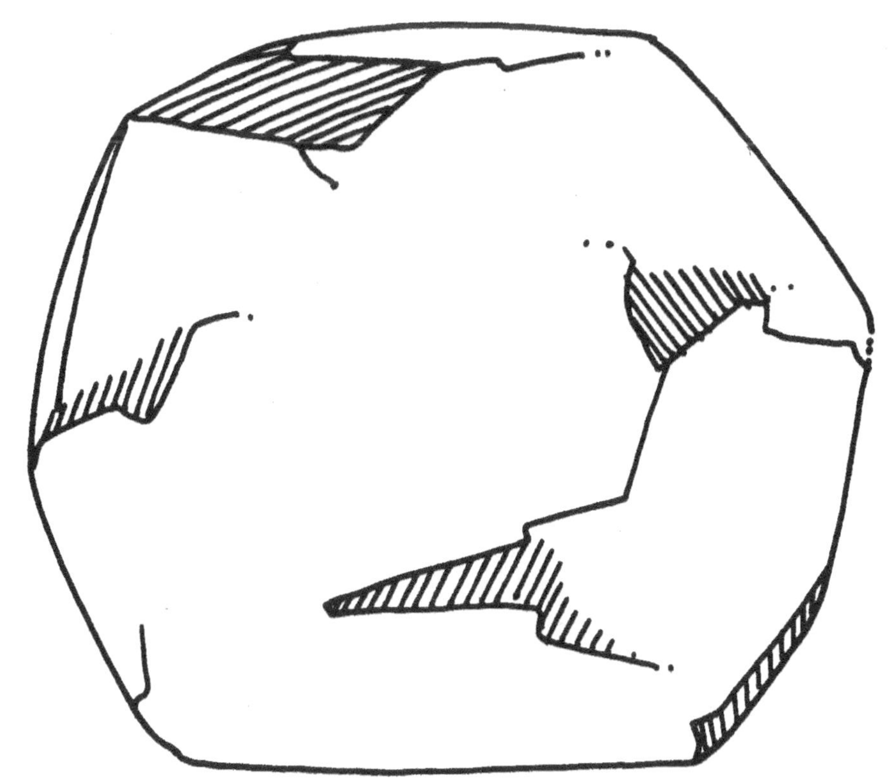

"He Is Risen" Message Plate

Materials

- angel picture (p. 111)
- large paper plates (1 per child)
- brown and green tempera paint
- paintbrushes
- fine-grit sandpaper (or brown construction paper)
- scissors
- compass
- ruler
- yarn
- copy paper
- glue
- crayons
- hole punch
- pencil
- shallow containers
- newspaper
- paper fasteners (1 per child)
- green crinkle paper *(optional)*

Before Class

Make copies of the angel picture, one for each child. Draw a line across each paper plate, two-thirds down. Using a compass, draw and cut 5" circles from sheets of sandpaper, one for each child. With a hole punch, punch one hole close to the edge of each sandpaper circle. Cut yarn into 6" lengths, one length for each child. Cover the work area with newspaper. Pour brown and green paint into shallow containers.

Simplification Idea

Children can color the cave brown and the grass green, rather than using paint.

Instructions for Children

- With a paper plate faceup, paint the top two-thirds brown for a cave. Paint the bottom third green for grass (sketch a). Allow the paint to dry.
- Use crayons to color an angel picture. Cut out the picture and glue it to the front center of the painted plate.
- With brown and gray crayons, add color to a sandpaper "stone."
- With a teacher's help, punch two holes in the paper plate as shown on sketch b.
- With a paper fastener, attach the stone to the paper plate near the angel picture (sketch c).
- Thread a piece of yarn through the hole at the top of the plate and tie the ends together for a hanger.

Enrichment Idea

Children can glue green crinkle paper onto the grass portion of the paper plate.

Talk About

Have you ever told good news to someone? What was the news? Allow children to share. **When some women came and found the empty tomb, an angel told the women the best news ever! The angel said, "He is not here; he has risen, just as he said." Then the women got to share that news with Jesus' disciples. We can share this good news too.** Have the children cover the opening of their caves with the stone, and then "roll away" the stone to see the angel. **We can tell others that Jesus is alive!**

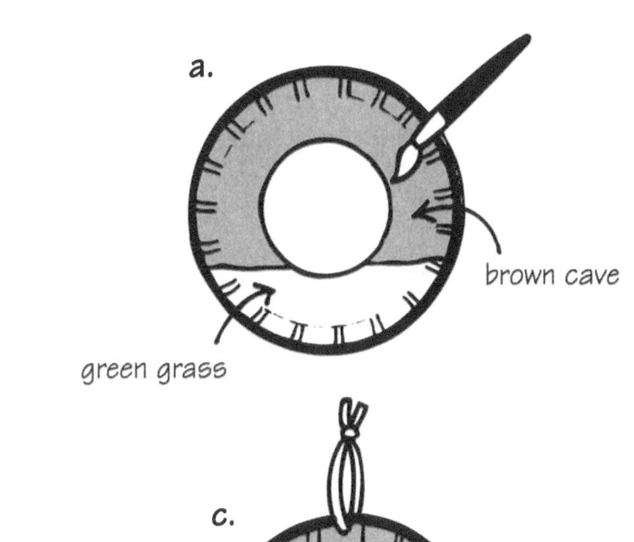
a.
brown cave
green grass

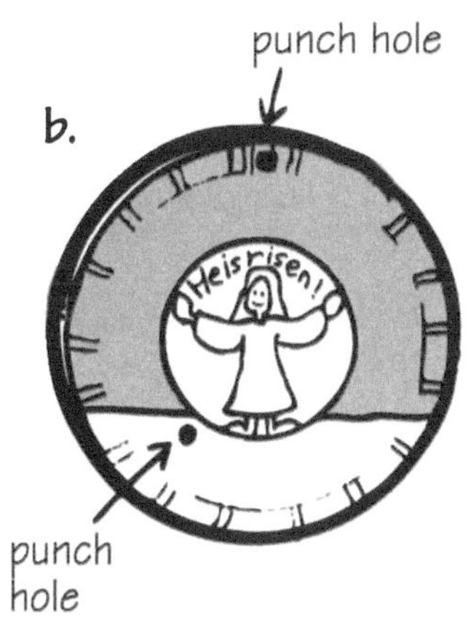
punch hole
b.
He is risen!
punch
hole

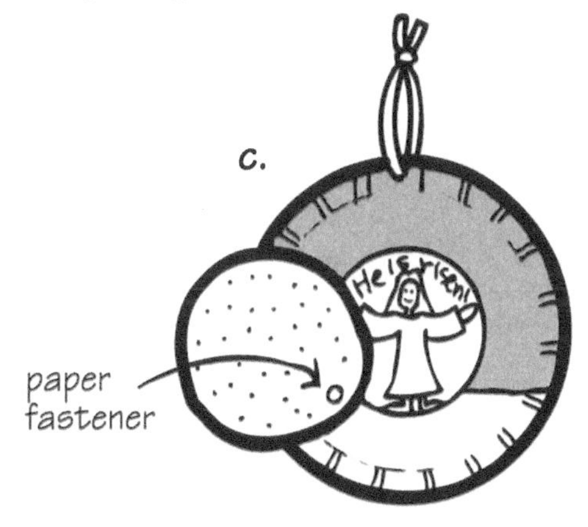
c.
He is risen!
paper
fastener

He is risen!

Beanbag Fish

Materials

- fish and eye patterns (p. 113)
- plain or small-print fabric
- white felt
- narrow ribbon
- pinking shears
- thread
- sewing machine
- pencil
- fabric scissors
- ruler
- dried beans
- plastic spoons
- small containers
- craft glue
- small wiggle eyes (2 per child)
- liquid fabric adhesive *(optional)*

Before Class

Trace the fish pattern onto double-layered fabric (wrong sides of the fabric together). Use pinking shears to cut out two fish pieces. With a sewing machine, sew the two pieces together around the long outer edges. Leave the straight end open (sketch a). Prepare a fabric fish for each child. Cut ribbon into 8" lengths, one for each child. Trace the eye pattern onto white felt and cut out, two for each child.

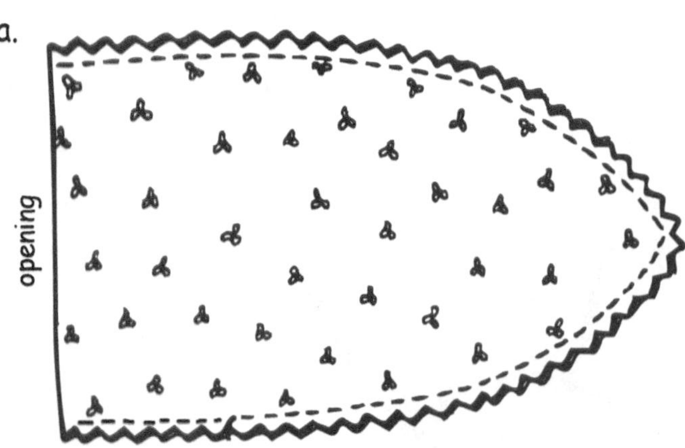

Simplification Idea

If you do not have a sewing machine, you can use liquid fabric adhesive to glue the fabric pieces together along the long outer edges of the fish.

Instructions for Children

- Spoon dried beans into the opening at the end of a fabric fish until the fish is about two-thirds full.
- With a teacher's help, gather the fabric and securely knot a ribbon near the back end of the fish to form a tail (sketch b). (Note: You may want to seal the open end of the fish with fabric adhesive.)
- Glue a felt circle on each side of the fish for eyes. Glue a wiggle eye in the center of each felt circle.

Talk About

How would you feel if you went fishing but you didn't catch any fish? Allow children to respond. **After Jesus died and came back to life, some of His followers decided to go fishing. They fished all night, but they didn't catch any fish. When Jesus came, He called to them from the beach shore and told them to throw their nets on the right side of the boat. Suddenly their nets were full of fish! Jesus is the Son of God. He has power to help us.**

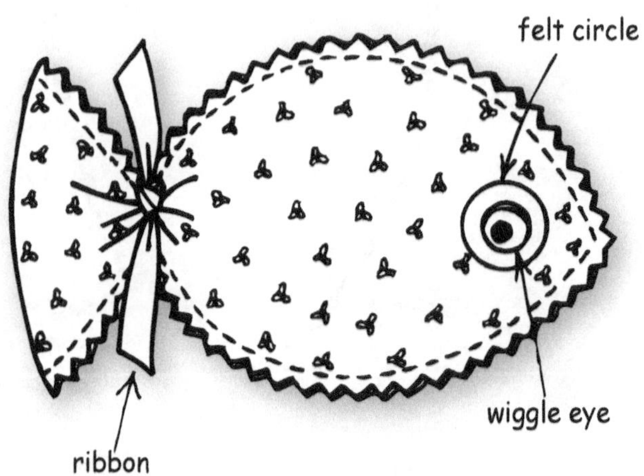

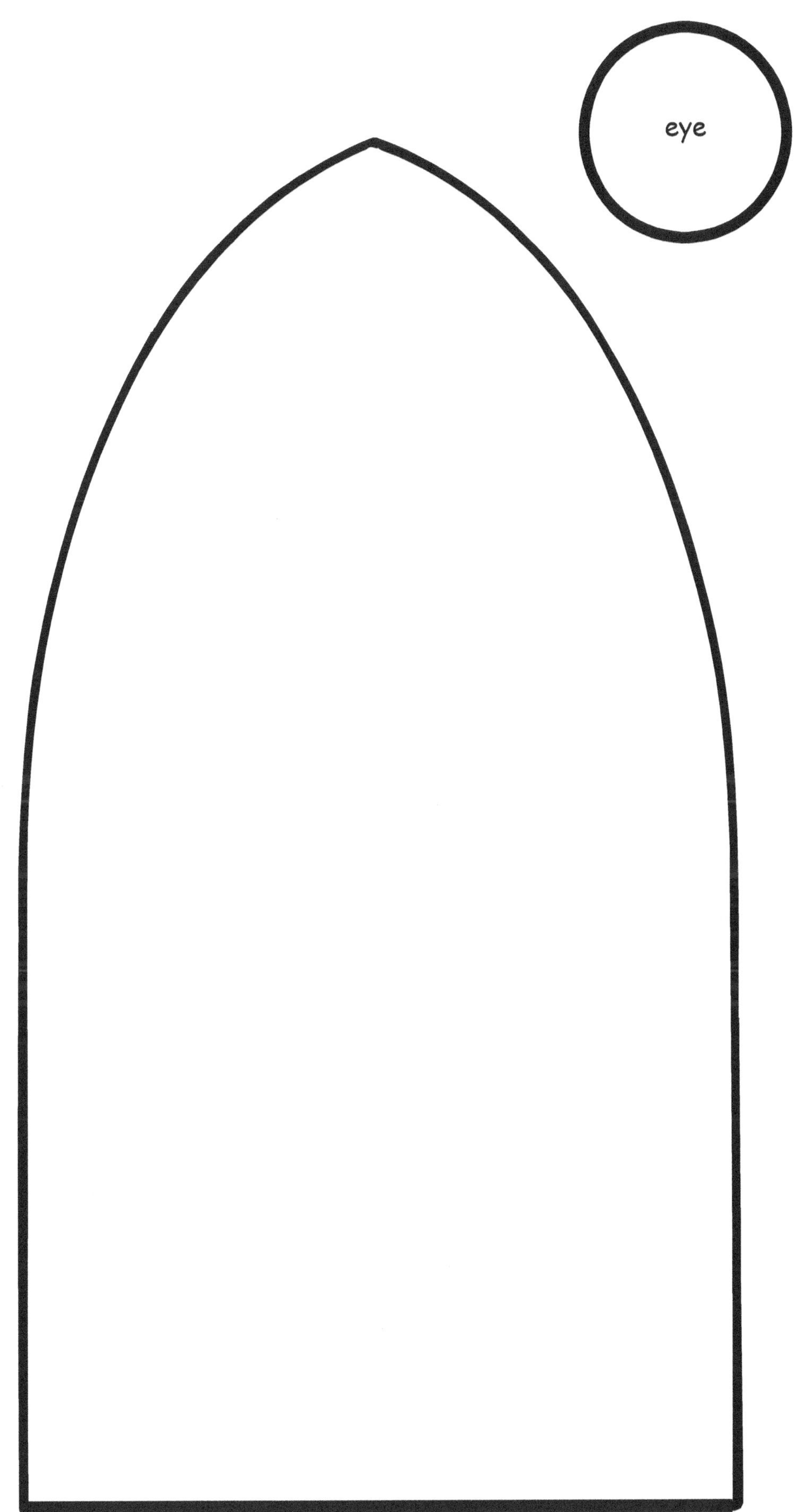
eye

New Life Butterfly

Materials

- butterfly wings pattern (p. 115)
- craft foam (or felt) in various colors
- scissors
- ruler
- black chenille wires
- fine-tip permanent marker
- plastic spoons (1 per child)
- pen
- craft glue
- acrylic jewels
- sequins
- tape
- double-sided mounting tape or a hot-glue gun and hot-glue sticks *(optional)*

Before Class

With a marker, trace the butterfly wings pattern onto craft foam and cut out, one for each child. With a permanent marker, draw a face on the bowl of a spoon and print "Jesus Is Alive!" on the spoon handle. Prepare a spoon for each child. Cut chenille wires in half, one half for each child. Cut craft foam scraps into 1"-size triangles, circles, and squares (see sketch).

Simplification Idea

Using double-sided mounting tape or a hot-glue gun (out of the reach of children) to attach the spoon to the wings can make this project go faster and eliminate some of the drying time.

Instructions for Children

- Bend a piece of chenille wire in half and curl each end to make antennae. Glue (or tape) the antennae to the back of a spoon.
- Glue craft foam wings to the back of a prepared spoon (see sketch). Then glue some jewels, sequins, and craft foam shapes onto the wings.
- Allow the glue to dry.

Talk About

What happens when a caterpillar spins a cocoon? (No one sees it for a long time. When it finally comes out of the cocoon, it has become a butterfly.) **Because Jesus died, came back to life, and returned to heaven, we can have new life too and live with Him in heaven someday. Your butterfly will help you remember that Jesus is alive!** Have the children hold their butterflies by the spoon handles and wave the spoons back and forth to make the butterflies "fly."

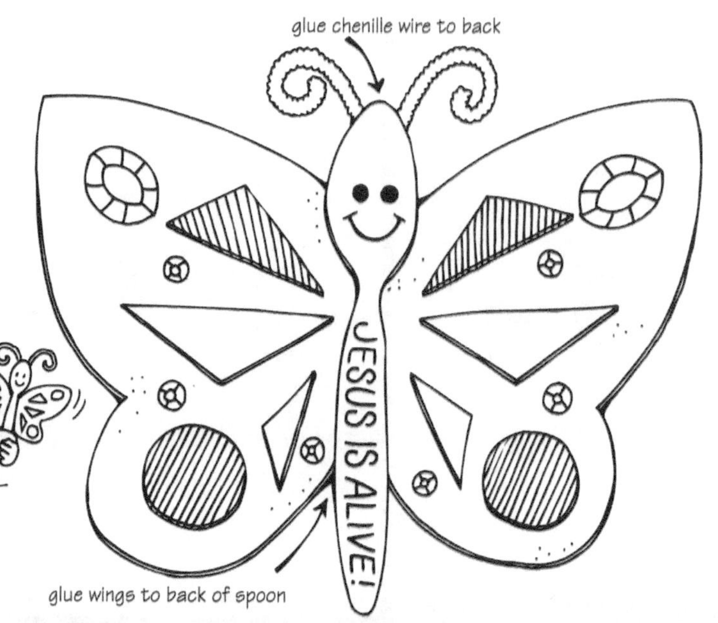

Framed Silhouette

Materials

- black, white, and colorful sheets of 12" x 18" construction paper
- scissors
- black permanent marker
- bright lamp (or flashlight)
- reusable adhesive
- white pencil
- glitter markers
- craft foam stickers
- glue

Before Class

Cut large oval picture frames from colorful construction paper, one for each child. Make the frame border 1½" wide. Print "Jesus' Follower" at the bottom of each frame.

Instructions for Children

- Have a child sit on a chair that is close to a blank wall. Shine a bright light on the wall. Using reusable adhesive, attach a sheet of black construction paper where the child's shadow falls. Move the light around until you get a clear silhouette. Trace around the image with a white pencil on the black construction paper. Cut out the silhouette.
- As they are waiting for their turn, children can decorate their frames with markers and foam stickers.
- Help the children glue their silhouettes onto white paper. Place a decorated frame over the child's silhouette, centering the image inside the frame. Glue the frame in place. Trim around the edges as needed.

Talk About

Have you or your family ever planned to go somewhere but then something happened that changed your plans? What happened? Allow the children to share. **Saul's plans changed when he was traveling on a road. A bright light from heaven flashed around Saul, and Jesus spoke to him. Saul obeyed what Jesus told him to do, and he became a follower of Jesus. What can we do to follow Jesus?**

"Serve One Another" Helper Jewels

Materials

- Bible
- dry pasta suitable for beading (elbow macaroni, rigatoni, penne, ziti, rotelle, etc.)
- gold (or silver) metallic spray paint
- gold (or silver) cord
- ruler
- scissors
- tape
- gold or silver chenille wires
- clear jewel-colored pony beads
- shallow containers
- newspaper

Before Class

Cover a work area with newspaper. Lay pieces of various kinds of pasta on newspaper and lightly spray-paint one side of the pasta. When the paint is dry, turn the pasta over and spray-paint the other side. Cut the cord into 3' lengths, one for each child. Wrap one end of each cord with tape. Tie the other end of each cord to a pony bead so that beads won't slide off while the children are beading (sketch a). Place pasta in shallow containers.

Instructions for Children

- To make a necklace, string two or three pasta beads onto a cord. Then add a pony bead "jewel" (sketch b).
- Continue threading pasta and pony beads in the same manner until the necklace is finished.
- With a teacher's help, tie the ends of the cord together and cut off the bead tied to the cord end (sketch c).
- To make a bracelet, thread a few pasta and pony beads onto a chenille wire.
- With a teacher's help, twist the ends of the wire together to finish the bracelet (sketch d). Make the bracelet large enough to slip over your hand. A teacher can trim the wire ends with scissors, if necessary.

Talk About

In what ways do people help you every day? Who helps you? Allow time for discussion. Remind the children of people who help them at home, at school, at church, and in the community. Open a Bible to Galatians 5:13. **Galatians 5:13 says, "Serve one another humbly in love." What should your attitude be when someone asks you for help?** (cheerful, loving, kind) **When we help and serve others in love, we are serving God too. We are serving in God's royal kingdom.** Have the children wear their jewelry as they pray and ask God to help them serve others in love.

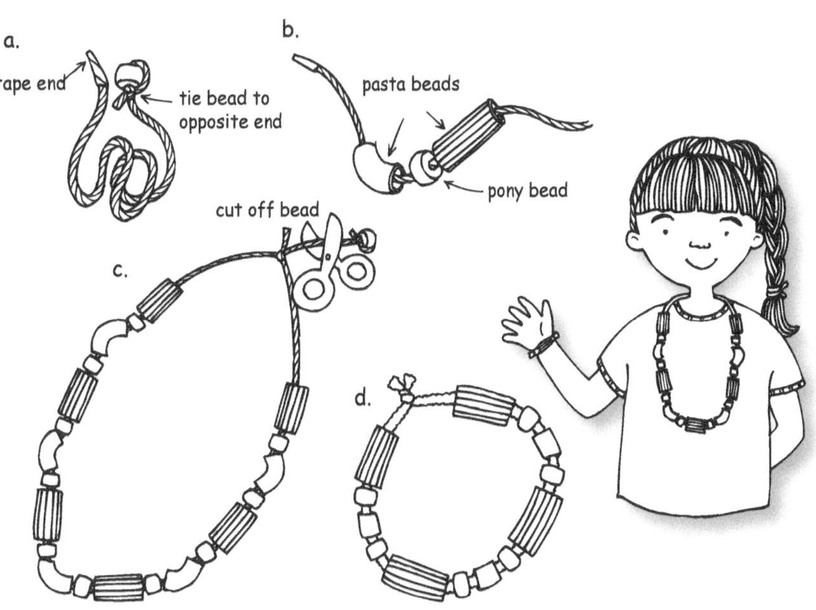

"Be Kind" Heart Hanging

Materials

- Bible
- heart patterns (p. 119)
- brightly colored poster board
- colored copy paper
- fine-grit sandpaper
- scissors
- ribbon
- markers
- glue
- hole punch
- whiteboard and dry-erase marker

Before Class

Make a copy of the heart patterns. To make a template for cutting out large hearts, trace the large half heart onto poster board. Then flip the pattern and trace around it to make a complete heart. Cut out the template. Trace the shape onto poster board and cut out a large heart for each child. Copy the different-size smaller hearts onto colorful copy paper. Cut some smaller hearts out of sandpaper. Print "Be Kind" on a whiteboard. Cut 8" lengths of ribbon, one for each child.

Simplification Idea

For younger children, you may want to print "Be Kind" on some of the smaller hearts.

Instructions for Children

- Cut out a few colorful paper hearts. Color a few sandpaper hearts.
- Print "Be Kind" on each heart.
- Glue paper hearts and sandpaper hearts onto a large poster board heart.
- With a teacher's help, punch a hole in the top of the poster board heart. Thread a ribbon through the hole and tie the ends together for a hanger.

Talk About

Did you ever have a hard time being kind to someone? What made you want to be unkind to that person? Allow children to share. Be ready to share your own story. Open a Bible to Ephesian 4:32. **Ephesians 4:32 says we are to be kind to others. We are to forgive others. It's not always easy to be kind and forgive others. What are ways we can be kind at home? At school? When we are with friends?**

fold

Section Two

Grades 1–6

Crafts for Elementary Kids

Most kids in the first few years of elementary school delight in completing craft projects. They have a handle on most of the basic skills needed and are eager to participate. They enjoy the challenge presented by a new craft and generally like the things they make.

Trying to plan craft projects for older elementary students can be more of a challenge. Today's 9- to 11-year-olds generally favor social activities that engage both their hands and their minds. A project that challenges their abilities may be scorned because it somehow doesn't appeal to these young sophisticates. Yet another project that seems too juvenile to an adult may click with the kids. Being flexible and keeping your sense of humor can certainly help!

Remember these guiding principles as you work on any craft with older students:

- The process kids go through is more important than the finished product.
- Kids should have the freedom to make the craft the way they want it to look, as long as it achieves the purpose of linking the Bible teaching to their lives.
- Each student should leave your room with a unique item that will spark his memory of what was learned and talked about.

Cutting with Scissors

- If your craft involves cutting fabric, felt, or ribbon, have several extra pairs of fabric scissors.
- Have available two or three pairs of left-handed scissors for students who need these.

Using Paints

- Provide smocks or old shirts for the kids to wear, as some paints may stain clothes.
- To make paint go further, dilute thicker paint (such as acrylic) with a small amount of water.
- Have paper towels and shallow containers filled with soapy water on hand. Encourage kids to clean their paintbrushes both before switching colors and immediately after finishing a project.

God Rocks!

Materials

- water
- 2-cup glass measuring cup
- small glass jars with lids (1 per student)
- powdered alum
- small rocks (or pebbles or seashells)
- spoons
- pot holder (or oven mitt)
- electric boiling pot (or another way to heat water)

Before Class

Prepare a sample crystal garden several weeks before class so the crystals have time to grow. Then for your students, gather an assortment of small rocks, enough to fill the bottom half of a glass jar for each student. Wash the rocks. For safety reasons, plan to pour the hot water for the students. Alum can be found in the spice section of most grocery stores. While it's not specifically toxic, discourage kids from drinking the crystal garden solution.

Instructions for Kids

- Gently place clean rocks inside a glass jar, filling the jar half full.
- To make a crystal garden solution, place 2½ tablespoons alum into the measuring cup and add 1½ cups boiling water. (Note: A teacher should pour the boiling water.) Stir until the alum is completely dissolved, or until no more will dissolve. Let any remaining solids settle to the bottom of the measuring cup.
- Pour the crystal garden solution into the jar until the rocks are covered. Do not pour any leftover solids into the jar. Set the jar aside to cool.
- Attach the lid securely onto the jar for the trip home. Avoid shaking the jar and disturbing the crystals that may be forming.
- Remove the lid at home so the water can evaporate, leaving crystals on the rocks.

Enrichment Idea

If possible, let the students collect and wash their own rocks before placing them into jars.

Talk About

Show your sample to the class so they see what their crystals should look like in a few days or weeks. **Growing a miniature garden of crystals can bring to mind the creative force God used in designing the earth. What words come to mind when you think about how God made everything?** (Possible answers: amazing, incredible, weird, etc.) **What part of creation is the most interesting or special to you, and why?** Accept all genuine responses. Encourage kids to come back to the next class with descriptions of what developed in their crystal gardens.

"God Made the World" Nature Dome

Materials

- poster board
- felt
- ruler
- scissors
- small nature items (shells, dried flowers, small pinecones, pebbles, etc.)
- 9-oz. clear plastic cups (or clear glass custard cups, 1 per kid)
- paper
- fine-tip markers
- craft glue
- whiteboard and dry-erase marker

Before Class

Cut the poster board and felt into 5" squares, one for each student. Cut small strips of paper, approximately ¾" x 2½", one for each student. Print "God made the world" on the whiteboard.

Instructions for Kids

- Turn a plastic cup upside down on a poster board square and trace around the rim of the cup, using a marker. Cut out the circle.
- Repeat the above process with a square of felt (sketch a).
- Glue the felt circle to the poster board circle.
- With a marker, print "God made the world" on a strip of paper. Then glue the strip onto the felt circle (sketch b).
- Choose some nature items, and glue them onto the felt circle.
- Squeeze a line of glue around the outer edge of the felt circle, and press an inverted cup onto the glue.
- Set the project aside to dry.

Talk About

What are some things you might see if you were hiking in the woods? Walking on the beach? Camping in the desert? Allow kids to share. **We can be thankful that God has made so many wonderful things for us to enjoy. How can you let God know how you feel about the amazing world He made?** (Possible answers: write a poem, talk to Him while doing a project outdoors, take care of the environment, create a piece of art, etc.)

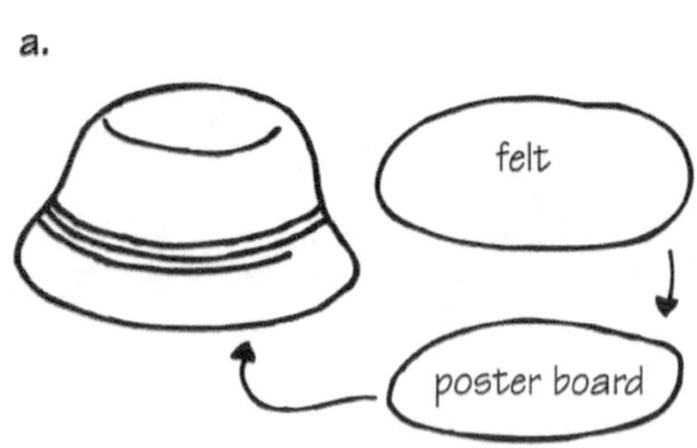

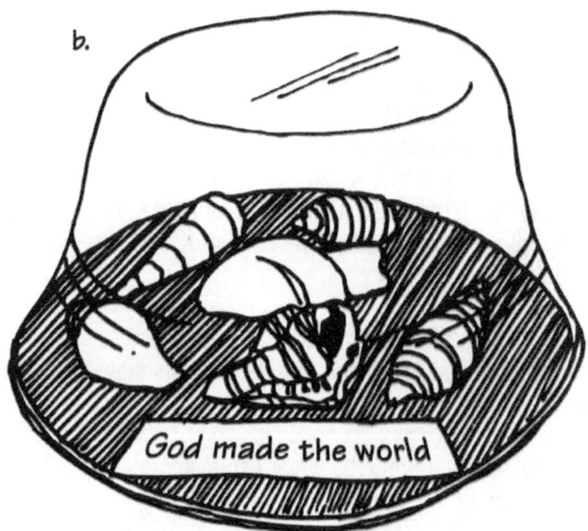

"God Made All Things" Bookmark

Materials

- Bible
- colored card stock
- clear adhesive covering
- scissors
- ruler
- small dried flowers and leaves
- fine-tip washable markers
- glue
- hole punch
- yarn
- whiteboard and dry-erase marker

Before Class

Cut the card stock into 2" x 6" strips and clear adhesive covering into 2½" x 6½" strips, one each for each kid. Cut the yarn into 8" lengths, one for each kid. Print "God made all things" on the whiteboard.

Instructions for Kids

- Print "God made all things" on a card stock strip.
- Decorate the bookmark by gluing on dried flowers and leaves (sketch a). Use a very small amount of glue and allow the glue to dry for a few minutes.
- Peel the backing off the clear adhesive covering strip and carefully cover the bookmark (sketch b). Trim off the excess.
- Use a hole punch to make a hole near the bottom edge of the bookmark.
- Thread a length of yarn through the hole, tie it in a knot, and then tie a bow. Trim the yarn ends to make them even.

Talk About

The Bible tells us about God's creation of the world. God made all things, including people. God made you. That's why God loves you so much. Open a Bible and read aloud Genesis 1:26–31. Encourage the kids to place their bookmarks in Bibles at home and remember that God made all things.

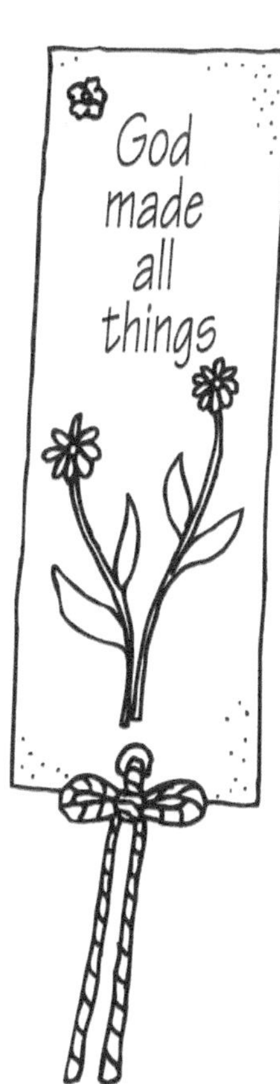

One-of-a-Kind Butterfly

Materials

- butterfly wings pattern (p. 125)
- white copy paper
- black chenille wires
- scissors
- tempera paints in squeeze bottles
- drinking straws
- jumbo craft sticks (1 per kid)
- black wide-tip markers
- spring clothespins (1 per kid)
- glue
- newspapers

Before Class

Copy the butterfly wings pattern onto the copy paper, one for each kid. Cut the chenille wires in half, one half for each kid. Cover the work area with newspaper.

Instructions for Kids

- Cut out the butterfly wings.
- Fold the wings on the center fold line; then fold back on the outer fold lines (sketch a). Lay the wings with the center fold pointing down.
- Squeeze small drops of paint onto one butterfly wing. With a straw, gently blow the paint drops to create abstract designs.
- Press the wings together to print a mirror image of the painted wing design on the unpainted wing. Open the wings and allow the paint to dry.
- Color both sides of a craft stick with a black marker.
- Fold a precut length of chenille wire around one end of the jumbo craft stick. Twist the wire ends together a couple of times to secure the wire to the stick. Spread the ends apart and bend the tips to make antennae (sketch b).
- Spread glue inside the fold of the wings; then place the craft stick inside.
- Clip a clothespin to the underside of the butterfly (see sketch b).

Talk About

God created butterflies with many different colors and patterns. He created people with different colors of eyes, hair, and skin tones. Genesis 1:31 says, "God saw all that he had made, and it was very good." God made you, and He loves each of you. What are some ways God made you unique? What abilities did He give you? As kids share, they can hold their butterflies by the clip clothespins and move their hands up and down to make the butterflies flutter.

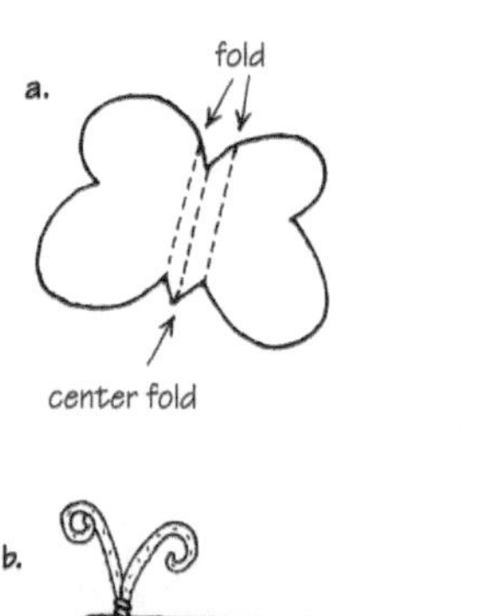

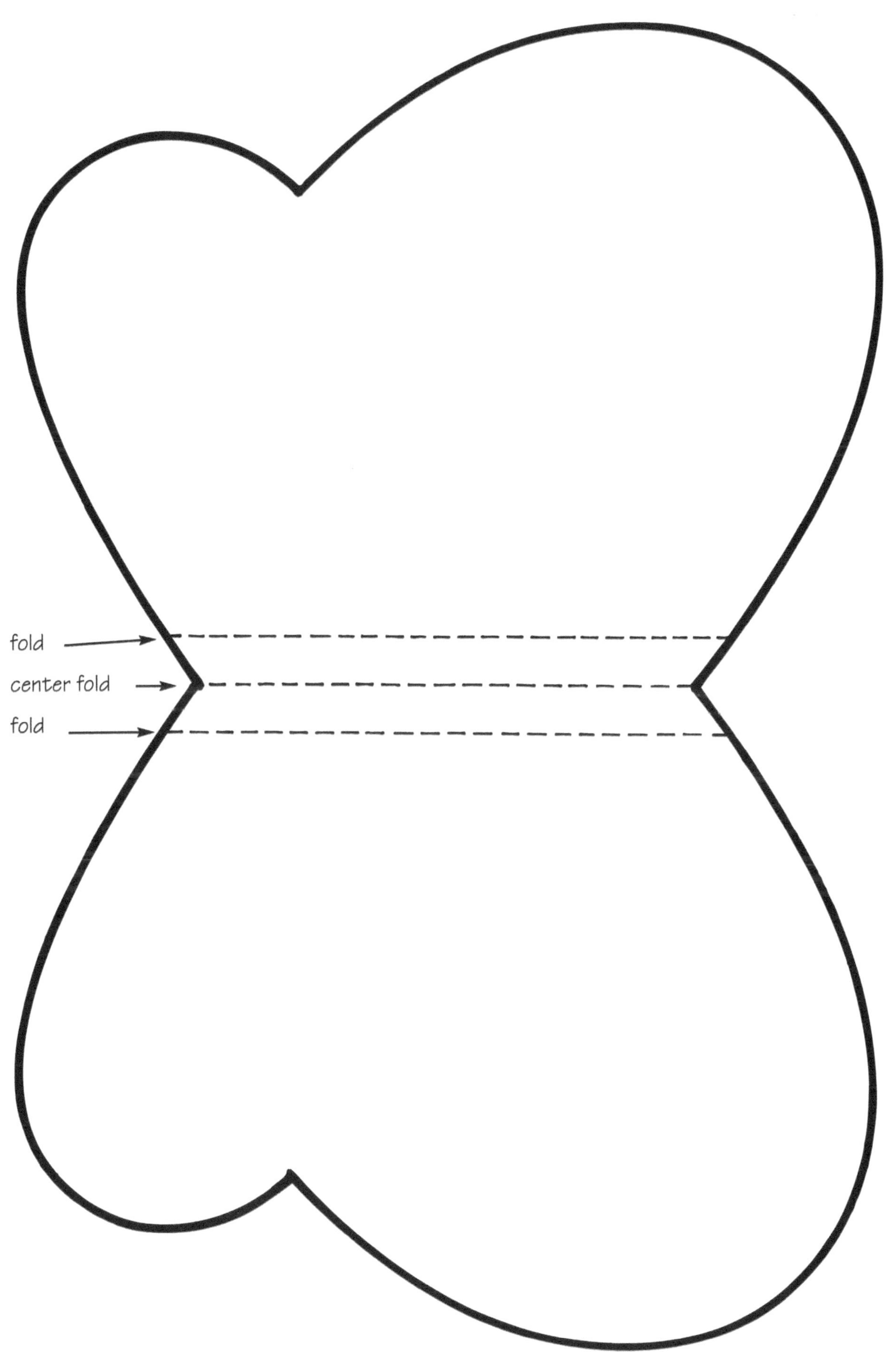
fold
center fold
fold

Wired for Purpose

Materials

- bare and color-coated wire
- wire cutters
- needle-nose pliers
- tools for curling, bending, and shaping wire (pencils, nails, spoons, etc.)
- wiggle eyes (2 per kid)
- craft glue
- colorful chenille wires
- scissors

Before Class

From a hardware store or craft store, obtain wire that's easy to sculpt by hand. Cut the wire to various lengths, ranging from 8" to 12". Cut several pieces of wire for each student. Try your hand at wire sculpting to gain experience and for giving creative pointers to students.

Instructions for Kids

- Select a piece of bare or color-coated wire to bend and shape to resemble the basic outline of an animal or person God created. Be careful to not poke yourself or others with the ends of the wires.

- By hand or with pliers and other tools, twist, wrap, and shape additional wires that add form, shape, and detailed features to the sculpture.

- Twist on colorful chenille wires, and glue on wiggle eyes for additional features or accents.

Talk About

Unlike some of our sculptures, when God designed people and animals, each one came out just as He planned! Ask several students to name a creature and share something about it that shows God's purpose in creation. **One reason God made people was to care for His creation. How can you care for God's creation?**

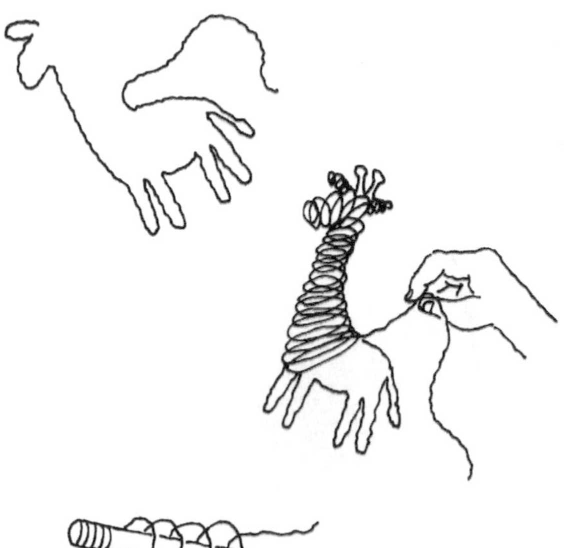

Adam's Animal Magnets

Materials

- Bible
- adhesive-backed magnet tape
- scissors
- ruler
- animal crackers
- acrylic paint in various colors
- clear nail polish (or clear acrylic coating)
- paintbrushes
- small shallow containers
- newspapers
- clear acrylic coating, poster board, small jewelry pin backs *(optional)*

Before Class

Cut the magnet tape into ¾" lengths, two for each student. Cover the work area with newspaper. Pour the paint into shallow containers. Have extra crackers available, as they break easily (and some will get eaten!).

Simplification Idea

Omit the painting and just use clear nail polish to coat and preserve the animal crackers. Or spray the crackers with clear acrylic coating.

Instructions for Kids

- Choose two unbroken crackers.
- Paint the fronts of the crackers. Allow the paint to dry.
- In a well-ventilated area, brush clear nail polish on the fronts and backs of the crackers. Let the nail polish dry.
- Attach a piece of magnet tape onto the back of each cracker (sketch a).

Enrichment Idea

Make a jewelry pin by gluing a piece of poster board onto the back of a painted cracker. Glue a pin back onto the poster board (sketch b).

Talk About

God gave Adam the important task of naming each animal God had created. Open a Bible and read aloud Genesis 2:19–20. **What would you name some of the animals if you could name (or rename) them?** Encourage the kids' creativity as they make suggestions.

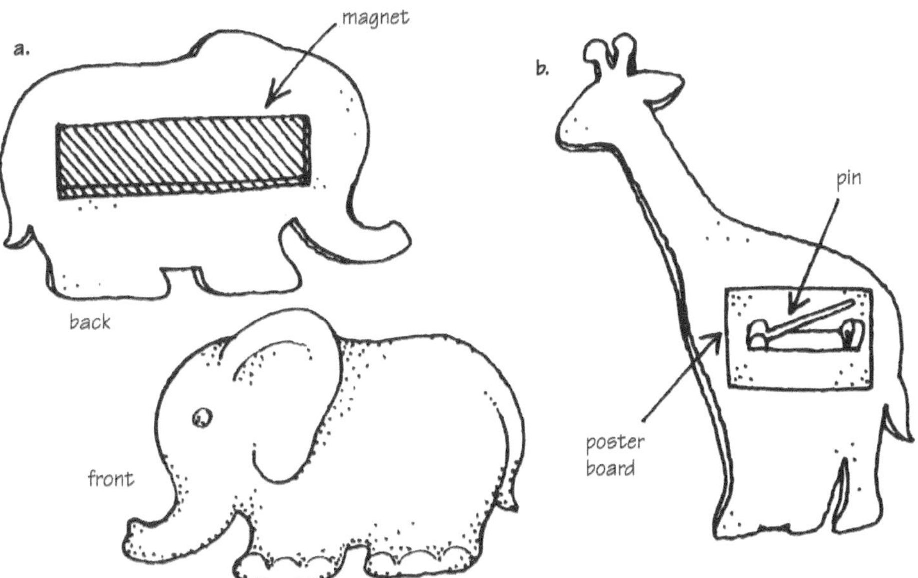

"Make Good Choices" Apple

Materials

- apple and leaf patterns (p. 129)
- lightweight cardboard
- red and green felt
- fine-tip markers
- pencils
- scissors
- ruler
- medium-size beads
- white paper
- craft glue
- whiteboard and dry-erase marker

Before Class

Trace the apple pattern onto lightweight cardboard and cut out the apple shape. You will need a cardboard apple for each kid. Trace the leaf pattern onto cardboard and cut it out, one for every two or three kids. Cut 1" x 6" cardboard strips, one for each kid. Cut the paper into 3" squares, one for each kid. Print "God says" and "Make good choices" on the whiteboard.

Simplification Idea

Precut the apples and leaves from felt.

Instructions for Kids

- Using the cardboard apple, trace the outline of an apple onto red felt, then cut it out. Using the cardboard leaf, trace the outline of a leaf onto green felt, then cut it out.
- Cut a door in the middle of the felt apple, using the pattern as a guide. Be sure to cut out only the top, bottom, and right edge (sketch a).
- Using a marker, print "God says" on the door flap.
- To make a knob, glue a bead onto the right edge of the door.
- Print "Make good choices" on a 3" square of paper.
- Glue the paper square onto the center of the cardboard apple so it will be directly under the felt door (sketch b). Then glue the felt apple on top of the cardboard apple. (Do *not* put glue on the back of the door. The door should open to reveal the message behind it.)
- Glue the leaf behind the stem of the apple.
- Fold down the ends of the cardboard strip and then fold the cardboard strip in half to create a stand. Glue the stand to the back of the cardboard apple (sketch c).

Talk About

Adam and Eve chose to eat fruit from the tree that God had told them not to eat from. Did they make a good choice? (no) **They disobeyed God, but He still loved them. God loves you too. He wants you to choose to obey Him. In what ways can you obey God? What good choices can you make?**

a.
God says
bead
cut
felt
b.
paper
Make good choices
cardboard
c.
glue stand to back of apple
cut door here

Noah Plant Stick

Materials

- Noah patterns (p. 131)
- white card stock
- crayons (or washable markers)
- scissors
- jumbo craft sticks (2 per kid)
- cotton balls
- small wiggle eyes (3 per kid)
- craft glue
- 6" bamboo skewers
- tape *(optional)*

Before Class

Copy the Noah patterns onto white card stock. Use scissors to cut the skewers in half, one half for each student.

Simplification Idea

Tape can be used to assemble some pieces, reducing the time needed for glue to dry.

Instructions for Kids

- Color and cut out the Noah pieces.
- Glue two wiggle eyes onto Noah's face. Glue one wiggle eye onto the giraffe's head.
- Glue Noah's head to the top of one craft stick. Glue the coat below the head and the boots below the coat.
- Pull three small pieces of cotton from a cotton ball and glue them on top and on either side of the head for hair. Glue some cotton to the face for a beard. (See sketch a.)
- Glue the hands behind the coat sleeves (with thumbs up). Glue the giraffe head behind Noah's shoulder. Glue the dove to the front of the opposite shoulder.
- Overlapping two inches, glue a second craft stick to the back of the first craft stick (sketch b).
- Glue the bamboo skewer to the back of the umbrella piece, with the point above umbrella top. Glue the bottom of the skewer to one of Noah's hands. Lay the puppet stick flat until the glue is dry.

Enrichment Idea

The students may want to use their Noah projects as stick puppets to tell the story of Noah and the flood.

Talk About

If you had to take care of all the animals in the ark, which would be your favorite and why? What would be the hardest part of living in an ark for over a year? Encourage the kids to share. **Place your Noah project in a favorite potted plant to decorate a room. Remember that God protected Noah and his family inside the ark. God can protect you too!**

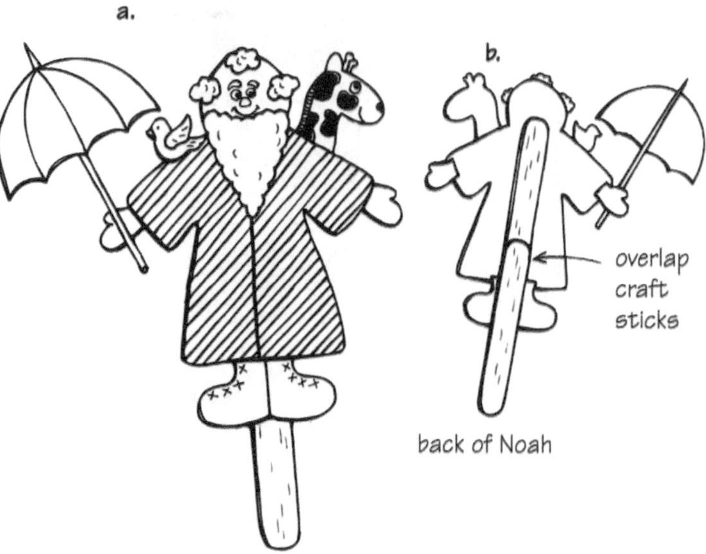

Boots
Umbrella
Hand
Dove
Giraffe
Coat
Head

"Trust in God's Wisdom" Rainbow Reminder

Materials

- rainbow pattern (p. 133)
- white card stock (1 sheet per kid)
- colored card stock
- scissors
- ruler
- yarn
- tissue paper (blue, green, yellow, and red)
- liquid starch
- paintbrushes
- shallow containers
- newspapers
- whiteboard and dry-erase marker
- markers
- hole punches
- glue, water *(optional)*

Before Class

Copy the rainbow pattern onto the white card stock, one for each student. Cut colored card stock into 2" x 3" rectangles, four for each student. Cut yarn into 6" lengths, four for each student. Cut 20" lengths of yarn, one for each student. Cut tissue paper into 1" squares. Cover the work area with newspaper. Pour small amounts of liquid starch into shallow containers. Print "Trust in God's Wisdom" on the whiteboard.

Simplification Idea

Precut the rainbows from card stock and punch the holes. Use glue, diluted with a little water, instead of using liquid starch.

Instructions for Kids

- Cut out a rainbow. Use a hole punch to punch holes in the rainbow where indicated on the pattern.
- Use a paintbrush to paint liquid starch onto the top row of the rainbow. Place squares of blue tissue paper onto the top row, fitting within the lines on the pattern (or overlapping slightly for a blended effect; see sketch).
- Brush starch onto the next row and add green tissue-paper squares in the same manner. Continue, adding rows of yellow tissue and red tissue. Allow starch to dry.
- If necessary, trim the tissue paper edges even with the rainbow edges.
- On the card stock rectangles, print "Trust in God's Wisdom," one word on each rectangle.
- Punch a hole at the top of each rectangle. Thread a 6" length of yarn through the hole in each rectangle and tie the yarn with a knot.
- Keeping the words in sentence order, thread the free end of each length of yarn through a hole at the bottom of the rainbow. Secure each end with a knot.
- Tie each end of the 20" length of yarn in the holes at the top of the rainbow to form a hanger.

Talk About

Even when flood waters covered the earth, God had a plan. Noah, his family, and every kind of animal were kept safe on the ark. What are some ways God keeps you safe? Lead kids in a discussion about God's care for them. **Every time you see a rainbow, remember that you can trust God's wisdom to take care of you.**

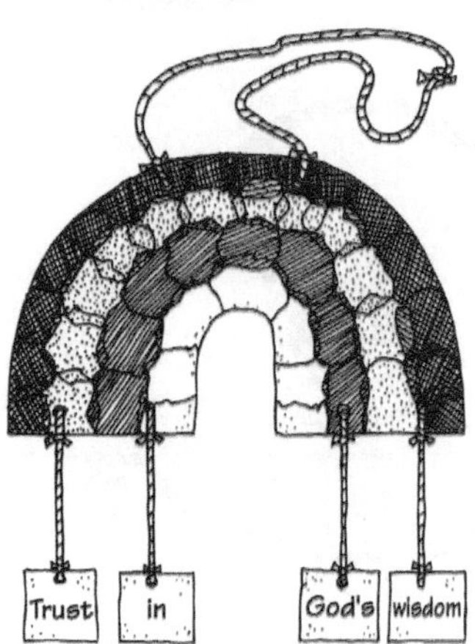

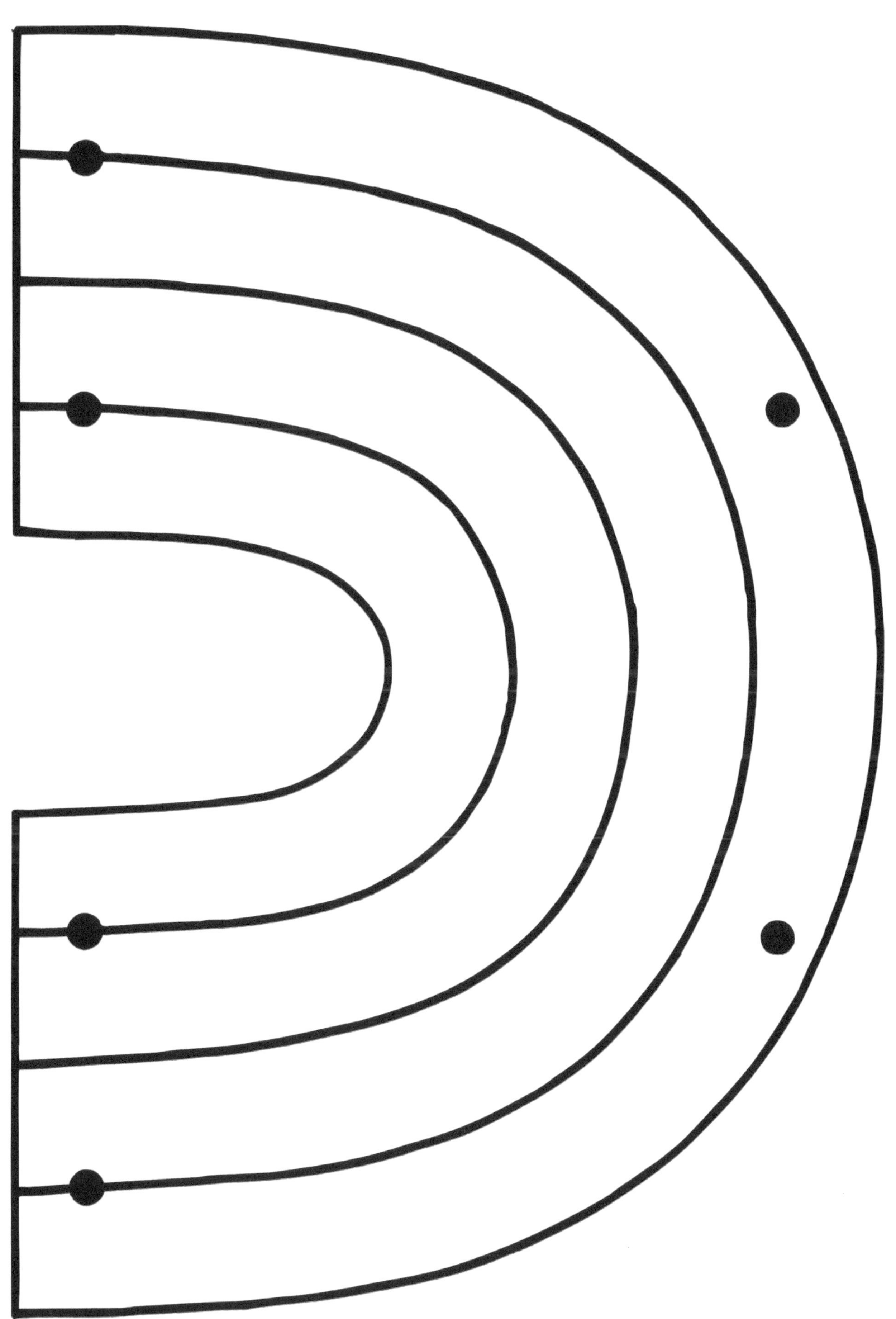

Point the Way Compass

Materials

- 3" diameter clear plastic cups (2 per kid)
- small corks (1 per kid)
- large tapestry needles with blunt-tip ends (1 per kid)
- thread
- pliers
- scissors
- ruler
- magnet
- fine-tip permanent markers
- tape

Before Class

Thread the needle with a 6" length of thread. Push and pull the needle (use pliers as needed) through the center of a cork from top to bottom to pull about 2" of thread through the cork (sketch a). Knot the end of the thread to keep it from pulling completely through the cork. Remove the needle. Prepare a cork for each student.

Instructions for Kids

- Magnetize a needle by holding just the tip of the eye end and stroking a magnet over the needle from the eye to the sharp end of the needle about 100 times. Stroke in one direction only (sketch b).

- Push the magnetized needle through the middle of the cork from side to side. Do not push it completely through—most of the needle should poke out of the cork in one direction (sketch c).

- Tape the loose end of the thread to the inside center of a plastic cup so the cork and needle dangle freely without touching the sides when the cup is turned upside down. Get as near the center of the bottom of the cup as possible (sketch d).

- Lay a ruler over the closed end of a second cup and hold it in place. Draw a line with a permanent marker across the bottom center of the cup (sketch e). Move the ruler and draw another line, perpendicular to the first line, so there is a "+" on the bottom of the second cup.

- On the bottom inside of the cup, write an N at the end of one of the lines (it doesn't matter which one). Then, moving clockwise, write an E at the end of the next line, an S on the line opposite the N, and a W on the line opposite the E to complete a compass rose.

- Stack the two cups rim-to-rim with the compass rose on the bottom and the cup with the taped thread on top. The cork and needle should dangle freely in the center. If the needle touches the cup, adjust the length of thread hanging from the cup.

- Hold the cups steady. Wait for the needle to settle, pointing north. This may take a minute. Rotate the bottom cup until the N orients to the needle.

- Tape the two cups together (sketch f).

Enrichment Idea

Have the kids compare their compasses with a real compass to see whether their compasses point in the correct direction.

Talk About

Abraham listened to and followed God's directions, and God led Abraham to the promised land. Just like following a good compass, we can trust God to lead us in the right direction for living lives that are pleasing to Him. In what areas of your life do you feel like you could use some direction from God? What are some ways we learn God's direction for our lives? (find Scripture verses that help us with a decision, listen to advice from wise adults)

cork

a.

magnet

b.

needle
thread
cork
thread

c.

tape to bottom of cup
in center

d.

e.

N
E
S
W

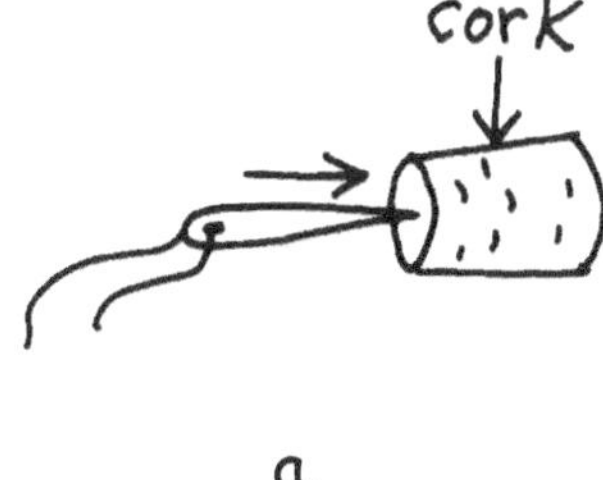

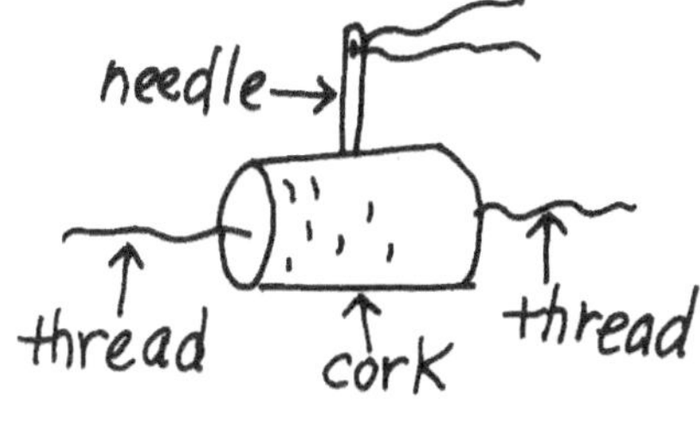

f.

Indestructible Lunch Bag

Materials

- duct tape in a variety of colors
- paper lunch bags (1 per kid)
- craft scissors
- stickers
- permanent markers

Before Class

Prepare a sample bag. Gather craft scissors that will make cutting the duct tape easier.

Instructions for Kids

- Lay a paper bag facedown, with the bottom flap folded and against the table.
- Cut (or tear) strips of duct tape to go across the width of the bag. Lay the strips down one at a time, overlapping the tape a bit and extending it over the edges of the bag (sketch a).
- After this surface is completely covered, use scissors to trim the edges close to the bag (or fold the edges over the side folds of the bag).
- Turn the bag over and fold the bottom flap under again. Repeat the above process, covering this side of the bag with strips of duct tape and trimming the edges.
- Open the bag and stand it up. Cut strips of duct tape, one at a time, to cover both sides of the bag going up and down, the long way.
- Place your hand inside the bag to support the bag as you attach each strip (sketch b). Cut off (or fold over) any tape that extends beyond the bag edges.
- Cover the outside bottom of the bag, placing your hand inside the bag for support. Cut off extra tape that extends beyond the edges.
- Refold the bag, using the original fold lines, and then press down to create new fold lines in the tape.
- Decorate the outside of the bag with other colors of tape, stickers, or permanent markers.

Enrichment Idea

Have the kids work with partners to cut the strips and hold the bag while the other person is applying the tape. Emphasize the importance of cooperation and helping one another.

Talk About

Jacob tricked Esau twice, and both times food was part of the plot. But food can be used in better ways—especially to treat others the way we like to be treated. What are some ways you like others to treat you? What can you do to treat others in these same ways? How can you use your lunch bag to treat others well? Encourage kids to share honestly and think creatively.

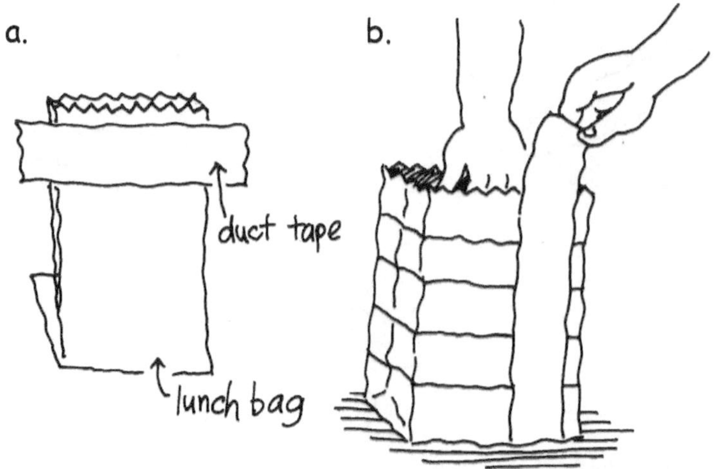

Time Capsule Keeper

Materials

- small gift boxes (or tins or jars with lids, 1 per kid)
- variety of papers (wrapping paper, comic and magazine pages, colorful tissue paper)
- stickers
- decoupage medium (or diluted glue)
- ½"- to 1"-wide paintbrushes
- newspapers
- shallow containers
- scissors
- plastic cups

Before Class

Cover the work area with newspaper. Pour decoupage medium into shallow containers.

Instructions for Kids

- Select a gift box to make into a time capsule.

- Tear or cut small pieces of paper, and select stickers to cover the box.

- Position a piece of paper or sticker on the box and paint a thin layer of decoupage medium over it. Apply one paper or sticker at a time, slightly overlapping pieces until the entire box has been covered (see sketches).

- When finished with the decoupage process, prop the box on a plastic cup so that the least amount of wet surface touches the table during the drying process. The box lid should be left off and dried separately to avoid sealing the container shut.

- When dry, fill the time capsule with items to be left for people in a future time. Close the box and hide the time capsule.

Talk About

What do you think is the hardest part of making peace with someone? (talking to the person while you are still angry, getting over hurt feelings, apologizing, taking the blame) **When Isaac moved to Gerar, the Philistines became hostile, filling Isaac's wells with dirt and telling him to leave. But Isaac remained faithful to God and demonstrated how we can live peacefully with others and reflect God's way in challenging situations. What are some rewards that come from making peace?** (friendships are fixed, God is honored, other people don't get hurt) **One thing that all time capsules have in common is that they get buried or put away. Conflicts should also be buried and put away.**

Joseph's Coat Pencil Holder

Materials

- Joseph patterns (p. 139)
- 12-oz. frozen juice cans (1 per kid)
- 12" chenille wires in various colors
- white card stock
- crayons in various colors (including flesh tone)
- craft glue
- sponge brushes
- scissors
- shallow containers
- colorful copy paper, ruler, tape *(optional)*

Before Class

Copy the Joseph patterns onto card stock—a head and pair of hands for each student. Cut chenille wires in half, up to 20 per student. Pour the glue into shallow containers.

Simplification Idea

Cut 4¾" x 9" pieces of colorful copy paper, and wrap a piece around each juice can. Seal the open edge of the paper with tape. Providing a solid color covering will reduce the number of chenille wires needed for each can.

Instructions for Kids

- Brush glue on the outside of a can, one section at a time. Lay a chenille wire onto the glue with one end of wire even with the bottom of the can. Bend the top end of the wire to the inside of the can and glue it in place (sketch a).

- To make Joseph's colorful coat, continue gluing on different colors of chenille wires until the entire outside of the can is covered.

- Color Joseph's face, neck, headdress, and hands. Cut out the pieces.

- Cut and glue short pieces of chenille wire to the base of each hand for cuffs. Cut and glue a piece of chenille wire to the middle of the headdress for a band. Bend the ends of the wires to the backs of the card stock (sketches b and c).

- Glue the neck to the upper inside front of the can. (See finished sketch.)

- Make a shepherd's crook by bending one end of a chenille wire over one of your fingers. Glue the crook to the front of the body. Then glue the wrist of each hand to Joseph's coat, with one hand over the crook.

Talk About

Have you ever been jealous of someone because the person was given something special that you didn't get? What happened? Encourage honest discussion. **Joseph's brothers were jealous because their father gave Joseph a special coat. Joseph was kind to his brothers even though they were mean to him. How do you show kindness to others?**

a.
b.
hand
c.
wire
pieces
Head
Hands

Kickin' Jealousy Footbag

Materials

- 5" round balloons (3 per kid)
- dried grain (split peas, lentils, popcorn, rice)
- measuring cup
- small paper cups
- funnels
- chopsticks
- scissors
- permanent markers

Before Class

Measure grain into small paper cups, ½ cup for each student.

Instructions for Kids

- Blow up a balloon and release the air just to stretch it.
- Stretch the opening of the balloon over the end of a funnel.
- Slowly pour in approximately ½ cup of grain, filling the balloon to the bottom of the balloon neck (sketch a). As needed, push the grain through the balloon neck with a chopstick, being careful not to puncture the balloon.
- Knot the balloon as close to the bottom of the neck as possible. Cut off the extra part of the neck.
- Blow up a second balloon to stretch it. Cut off the neck, then stretch the round part around the filled balloon (sketch b).
- Repeat with the third balloon.
- Decorate the outer balloon with permanent markers.

Enrichment Idea

Provide additional supplies if students want to make three juggling balls rather than a footbag.

Talk About

Making a footbag (or hacky sack) is easy; learning to play is harder. (Note: Generally accepted footbag rules are to keep the footbag in the air or volley it between friends, using only your feet and legs.) **It's hard to get rid of jealousy too. Joseph's entire family suffered for years because of his brothers' jealousy. Jealousy creeps in when we compare ourselves to others. How can you keep from comparing your looks, possessions, or talents with those of other people?** (Think about and be thankful for what you have, not what you don't have or wish you had.) **Each time you play with your footbag, think of how you can kick jealousy out of your thoughts.**

Knot One, Forgive Two

Materials

- smooth cord
- ruler
- pencil or dowel
- scissors
- split key-chain rings, beads *(optional)*

Before Class

Select cord that is smooth, flexible, and at least ¼" but no more than ½" in diameter. Cut the cord into 2' lengths, one to three lengths for each student. Practice tying the following three types of knots so you can demonstrate each one (or invite an experienced guest to join your class and teach the students how to make the knots).

Instructions for Kids

- Follow the step-by-step instructions to learn how to tie the following three kinds of knots.
- Choose and learn how to tie one type of knot. Practice tying the knot a few times before moving to the next type of knot.

Talk About

Joseph forgave his brothers for the way they had treated him. Forgiving others is like learning to tie knots—you get better at it the more you do it. What are some of the things people do to us that we should forgive? Accept all genuine responses. **How can you show others that you have truly forgiven them?** (don't keep on talking about the incident or event; continue to be a friend, treat the person well)

Figure 8 Knot

This is a large knot that is easy to undo. Sailors use this knot to prevent ropes from slipping.

1. Lay a 2' length of cord vertical on a table. Bring the top end down on the right and then over to the left, going under the vertical rope to make a loop. Keep a loop while pulling with a 6" tail extending to the right of your vertical rope.
2. Pass the end of the 6" tail over the vertical rope toward the left.
3. Continue taking the end under the left side of the loop you made in step 1 (this completes the figure 8).
4. Bring the end up through the loop so an inch or two extends above and beyond the top loop.
5. Pull both ends of your rope tight into a knot.

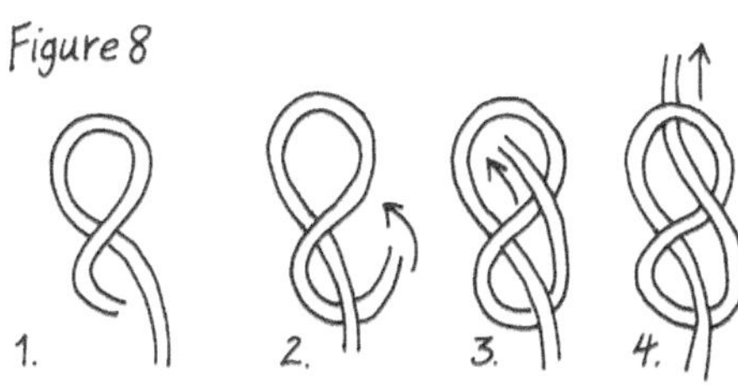

Square Knot

This is a handy knot for tying off the ends of one rope for packaging, first aid, and sewing because it doesn't let go. It is also good for joining two ropes so they won't slip apart.

1. Hold the rope horizontally with one end in each hand. Cross the ends so the end coming from the right goes over the one coming from the left. Leave a loop hanging below.

2. Wrap the end that is now on your left over the top of the loop to the back side and then up through the loop.

3. Gently pull both ends to draw the loop smaller and gain some length on each end of rope to finish the knot.

4. Cross the ends again, but this time the one coming from the left goes over the end coming from the right. Leave a second and smaller loop just below.

5. Wrap the end that is now on your right over the top of the second loop to the back side and then up through the loop.

6. Pull both ends tight to complete the square knot.

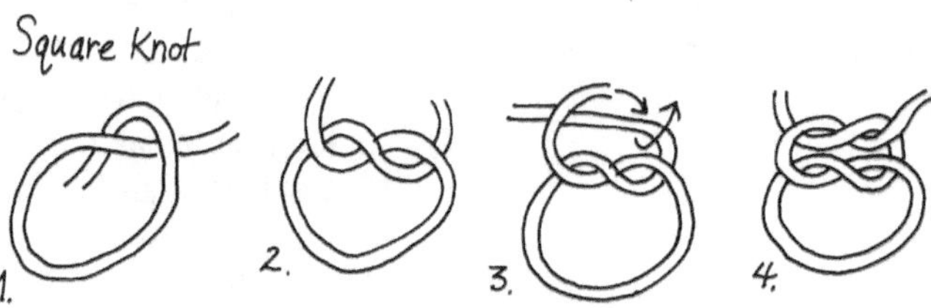

Half Hitch

A half hitch ties the end of a rope to a tree or post to secure any number of things, such as a horse, a pet, or a tent. To learn how to tie this knot, secure your rope with a half-hitch onto a chair leg.

1. Hold the longer end as you pass the shorter end around the back side of a chair leg.

2. Working with the shorter end of the rope, and a few inches from the chair leg, take the shorter end under the longer rope and then up, back over, and down through the space between the ropes and the chair leg.

3. Pull the ends in opposite directions to draw the half-hitch tight around the leg. To secure a strong horse, repeat steps 2 and 3 to create two half hitches (or a double hitch).

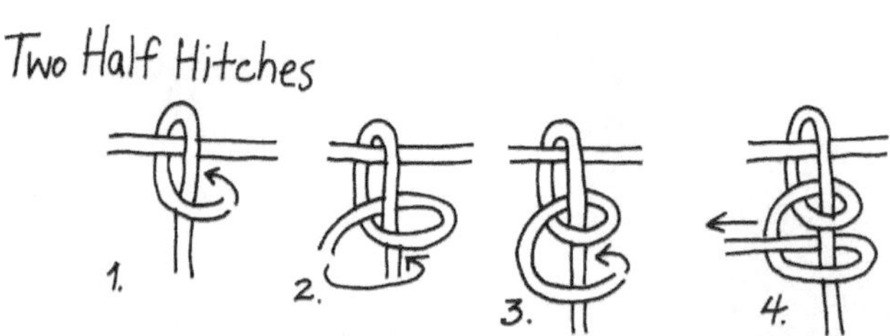

Stone Magnets

Materials

- Bibles
- paint pens in gold and white
- damp paper towels (or wet wipes)
- craft glue
- smooth stones (several per kid)
- ½" round heavy-duty magnets (or magnet strip cut into ½" pieces)
- whiteboard and dry-erase marker

Instructions for Kids

- Use damp paper towels to clean off the surface of several stones.
- Glue a magnet to the back of each stone (sketch a). Allow the glue to dry.
- Find Exodus 20 in a Bible. With a teacher or the rest of the class, read the commands God gave to Moses. Try to summarize each command in two or three words. (Examples: Obey parents. Speak truth.) Write the summaries on a whiteboard.
- Choose a few commandments to remember. Using a white paint pen, print on each stone a summary of one of the commandments.
- Use a gold paint pen to decorate the stones. Allow the paint to dry.

Talk About

What rules do you have at home? At school? Why is it important to obey those rules? Point out that rules often protect us. **God gave Moses and the people of Israel some commandments, or rules. And God gave the people a way to remember His rules—He wrote them on stone tablets! Why is it important for us to remember God's commands?** (Knowing God's commands can help us grow in our relationships with God and others.) **Put your magnets where you will see them often. Remember to love and obey God and to show His love to others.**

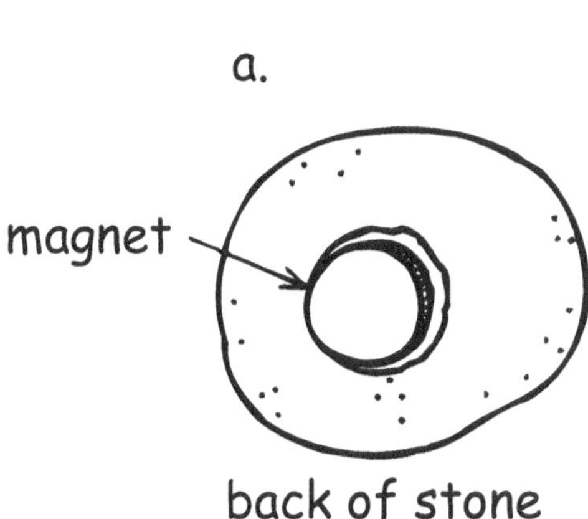

Travel Trunk

Materials

- Bible
- 1/8"-wide black elastic
- ruler
- awl
- scissors
- craft foam
- plastic wet wipes boxes with flip-up lids (1 per kid)
- masking tape
- brown shoe polish paste
- soft cloths
- paper towels
- large 2-hole buttons (or pony beads, 1 per kid)
- index cards, pencils *(optional)*

Before Class

Cut the elastic into 3½" lengths—two for each student. Cut craft foam into 2" squares, one for each student. Use the point of a pair of scissors to cut two vertical slits in the front edge of each box lid, near the center (sketch a). Use the awl to poke two small holes in the box front, near the center (sketch a).

Instructions for Kids

- Tear (or cut) short pieces of masking tape. Cover the top and all four sides of a plastic box with the tape. Overlap and crisscross the pieces if desired (sketch b).
- Use a soft cloth and brown shoe polish paste to stain the masking tape. Use a paper towel to wipe off any extra paste.
- Cut a craft foam square into a decorative shape. Then punch two small holes near the middle of the shape.
- Thread the two ends of one elastic piece through the two slits in the top of the box. Tie the ends together inside the box, leaving a loop in front.
- Thread the two ends of a second elastic piece through the two holes in the large button. Then thread the ends through the holes in the foam shape and, finally, through the holes in the box front (sketch b). Tightly tie together the ends of this piece of elastic inside the box.
- Close the lid by stretching the elastic loop over the button.

Enrichment Idea

Have the kids write Deuteronomy 31:8 on index cards and place the cards inside their travel trunks.

Talk About

Your boxes look like moving trunks. Have you ever moved? How did you feel about the move? Allow the kids to share. **Joshua was going to be moving into a new land—the land God had promised to His people.** Read Deuteronomy 31:8 aloud. **Moses told Joshua, "The Lord himself goes before you and will be with you." God will go with you wherever you go too!**

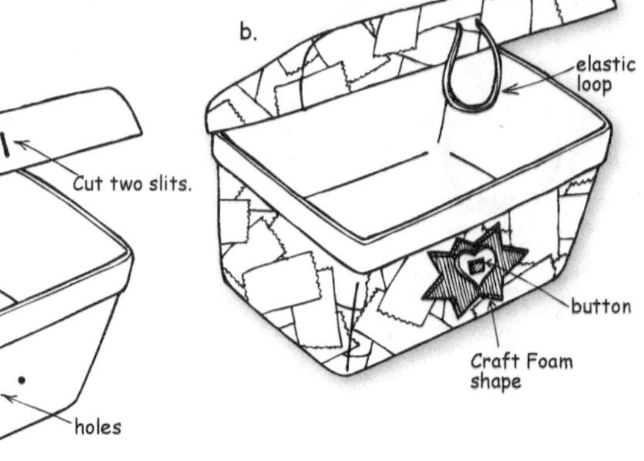

Adventure Kit

Materials

- old maps
- boxes with lids (shoeboxes, gift boxes, photo boxes; 1 per kid)
- scissors
- yarn
- hole punch (or awl)
- glue
- water
- paintbrushes
- shallow containers
- markers
- index cards
- Bibles
- thick yarn or cording *(optional)*

Before Class

With a hole punch, make holes in opposite sides of the boxes just below where the lid will lie (sketch a). Cut the yarn into lengths suitable for a box handle, three equal lengths for each box. Pour glue into shallow containers and dilute the glue with a small amount of water.

Instructions for Kids

- Tear a map into various-size strips and pieces, no smaller than 2" x 2". Brush glue over one side of a box and place the map pieces over the glue, overlapping the pieces. Brush glue over the edges of the pieces to smooth them down (sketch b).

- Continue in this manner, covering each side of the box and smoothing the map pieces around the corners and edges.

- Brush glue onto the top and sides of the lid. Cover the lid with map pieces, just as you did on the box.

- Find the holes on the box sides, and use a hole punch to poke through the map pieces that are now covering the holes.

- To form a handle, push three lengths of yarn through one hole, and knot the pieces together inside the box (sketch c).

- Braid the lengths of yarn. Then push the free ends of the yarn through the opposite hole in the box, and knot the yarn ends together inside the box. (Or use thick yarn or cording for the handle.)

- Print your name and "Adventure Kit" on an index card. Glue the card to the box front or onto the top of the lid.

- After the glue is completely dry, put the lid on the box.

Enrichment Idea

Print Joshua 1:9 and other Bible verses on index cards. Place the cards inside the kit.

Talk About

If you could travel anywhere in the world, where would you like to go? Allow students to share their ideas. **The Bible says God will be with us wherever we go.** Read Joshua 1:9 aloud. **Your Adventure Kit can hold items you would like to take on your next adventure. Be sure to include a Bible or some Bible verse cards in the kit!**

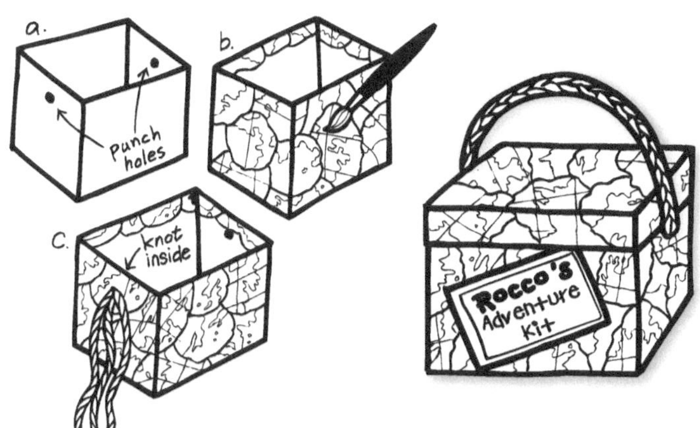

Bible People Puppets

Materials

- Bible people puppet patterns (p. 147)
- ¼"-wide ribbon
- markers
- 7 mm wiggle eyes
- jumbo craft sticks
- white card stock
- glue
- scissors

Before Class

Copy the Bible people puppet patterns onto the card stock. Make enough copies for kids to choose one or more sets of puppet patterns to use.

Simplification Idea

Use markers to draw eyes on the puppets, rather than gluing on wiggle eyes

Instructions for Kids

- Choose the patterns you want to use to create one or more Bible people puppets. Use markers to color the pattern pieces and add details to the faces, hair, and clothing (such as curly or wavy lines). Cut out the pieces you have colored.
- Glue a face piece onto one end of a craft stick. Then glue either a front hair piece or a beard and/or a headdress onto the face piece (sketch a).
- Glue a back hair piece or a back headdress piece onto the back of the craft stick and face piece (sketch b). Be sure to glue together the uncolored sides of the pieces.
- Cut a short piece of ribbon and glue it across the forehead for a headband, if desired (sketch c).
- Glue two wiggle eyes onto the face.
- Use a black marker to write the name of your Bible character on the bottom end of the craft stick.

Enrichment Idea

Have kids work with partners (or in small groups) to create a complete set of puppets for retelling the story of Ruth. Each person can make one or more of the Bible characters: Naomi, Orpah, Ruth, Boaz, Boaz's servants, townspeople. When finished, the partners can put on a puppet show.

Talk About

What are some ways we can show kindness to others? Encourage the kids to be creative in their thinking. **In the Bible book of Ruth, we learn that Ruth showed kindness to Naomi. Boaz showed kindness to Ruth. All of this was part of God's plan for His nation. We can be part of God's plan too. We can show kindness, acceptance, and God's love to others.**

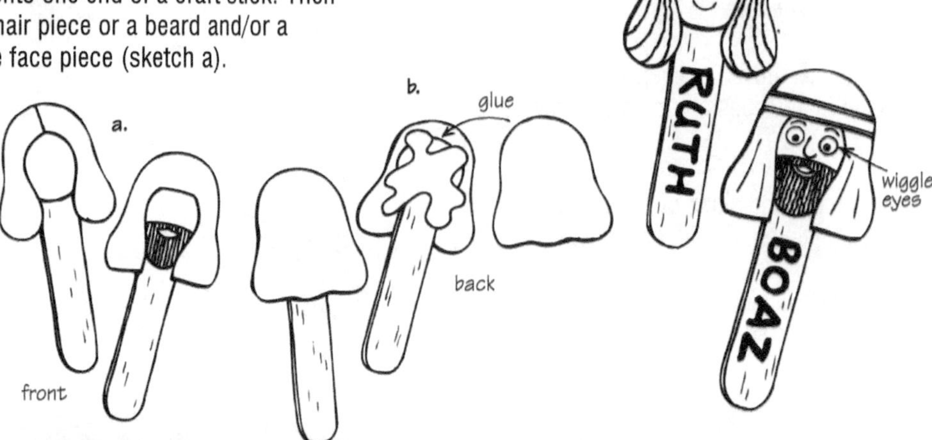

Face
Long Hair
Front
Medium Hair
Front
Short Hair
Front
Long Hair
and
Headdress
Back
Medium Hair and
Headdress Back
Short Hair and
Headdress Back
Beard
Medium
Headdress
Front
Long
Headdress
Front

David's Sheep

Materials

- small saw
- white cotton balls
- black felt
- black markers
- flat wood clothespins
- craft sticks
- glue
- scissors
- ruler

Before Class

Using the patterns provided, cut ears and tails out of black felt, two ears and one tail for each student (sketch a). Use a saw to cut the prongs off each clothespin (sketch b). Discard the prongs. Use a saw to cut craft sticks into three even pieces (sketch c). Discard the middle piece of the craft sticks.

Instructions for Kids

- To create a sheep's head, use a black marker to color the round head of a wood clothespin.
- Color the rounded ends of four craft stick pieces to make feet.
- Tear two cotton balls in half. Gently stretch each half into a 2" strip. Glue a cotton strip around each leg piece, just above the colored feet (sketch d).
- Glue the legs onto the clothespin body (sketch e). Make sure the legs are even by standing the sheep on a flat surface. Lay the sheep on its side to dry.
- Tear several cotton balls in half. Glue cotton pieces to the clothespin until the entire body of the sheep is covered (sketch f).
- Glue one felt ear to each side of the head. Glue a tail onto the rear of the sheep's body (sketch f).

Enrichment Idea

If time allows, have each student make a flock of sheep.

Talk About

What do you know about taking care of farm animals, such as sheep? Allow the kids to share. Discuss feeding and taking animals to pasture, shearing sheep, etc. **When David was young, he spent many hours watching and caring for his father's sheep. God used what David did as a shepherd to prepare him for the jobs he would do later in life. How does God help us prepare for the work we do—or will do?**

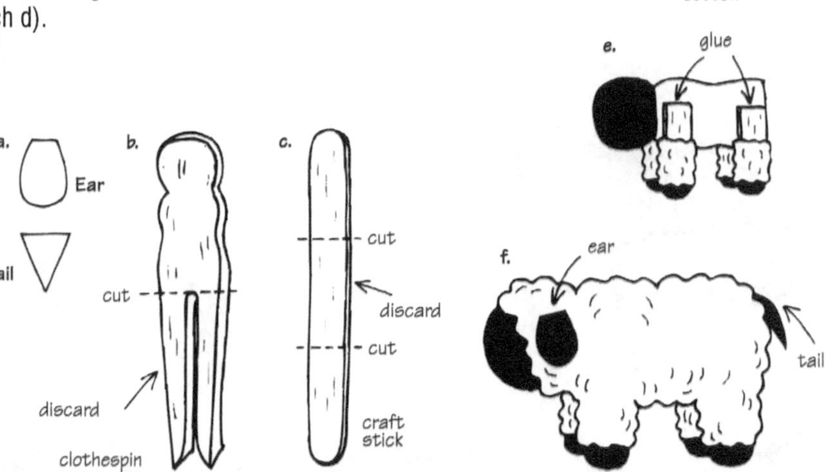

"My Times" Sand Glass

Materials

- Bible
- individual-size clear plastic water bottles (2 per kid)
- rubbing alcohol
- paper towels
- pencils
- lightweight cardboard
- scissors
- hole punch
- fine sand (or salt)
- measuring cups
- funnels
- small bowls
- craft glue
- timer
- electrical tape
- decorative ribbon
- permanent markers in metallic colors
- newspapers

Before Class

Remove the labels from the plastic bottles. Apply rubbing alcohol with paper towels to remove any remaining adhesive. Cover the work area with newspaper.

Instructions for Kids

- Trace around the opening of a bottle onto lightweight cardboard. Cut out the circle (sketch a). Punch a hole in the middle of the cardboard circle.
- Use a funnel to fill the bottle with two cups of sand.
- Set a bowl next to you. Place the cardboard circle on top of the opening of the bottle. A teacher will time two minutes. When the teacher signals to start, turn the bottle upside down over the bowl, holding the cardboard circle firmly against the bottle opening (sketch b). Allow the sand to flow through the hole in the cardboard circle into the bowl for exactly two minutes.
- When the teacher signals that time is up, quickly turn the bottle right side up. Discard any sand that is left in the bottle. Then use a funnel to pour the sand from the bowl back into the bottle.
- Glue the cardboard circle to the bottle opening. Then turn a second bottle upside down and glue the opening of that bottle on top of the cardboard circle on the first bottle (sketch c). Be careful not to get glue inside the hole on the cardboard circle.
- Wrap electrical tape securely around the bottle necks to fasten them together.
- Decorate the bottle necks, wrapping ribbon over the electrical tape.
- Use metallic markers to decorate the outside of the bottles. Write the words of Psalm 31:15 on the bottles.

Talk About

Let kids practice using their sand glasses to time something that requires two minutes. (Examples: a simple chore, a time of silence) **Why is it important for people to know what time it is?** Allow kids to make suggestions. Read Psalm 31:15 aloud. **King David said all our times are in God's hands. When we're hurried or worried, that's a good truth to remember.**

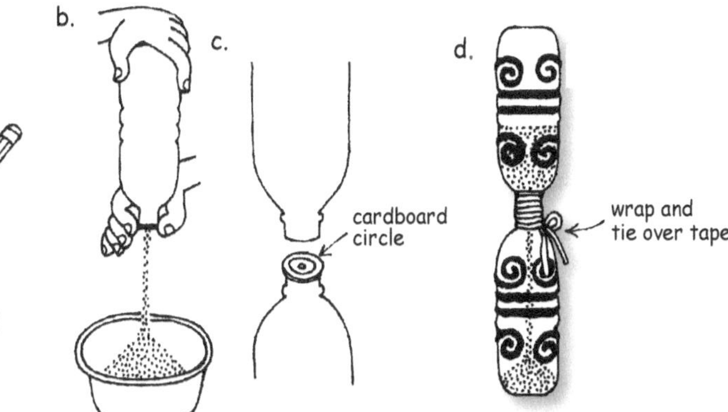

Mighty God Wind Tube

Materials

- Bible
- half-gallon round ice cream containers without lids (1 per kid)
- utility knife
- blue construction paper
- white crepe-paper streamers
- string
- scissors
- ruler
- tape
- hole punches
- gold and silver star stickers
- markers *(optional)*

Before Class

Use a utility knife to cut the bottom off the ice cream containers, one for each student. Cut blue construction paper the height and circumference of the containers, one for each student. Cut crepe-paper streamers into 2' lengths, five for each student. Cut the string into 2' lengths, four for each student.

Instructions for Kids

- Glue a piece of blue construction paper around an ice cream container (sketch a). Tape the overlapping edges to secure the paper.

- Tape one end of four strips of streamer paper around the bottom edge of the blue paper (sketch b). Then glue one strip of streamer around the bottom edge, covering the taped ends of the four streamers (sketch c).

- Add star stickers randomly onto the blue paper to decorate the wind tube.

- Punch four evenly spaced holes around the top of the wind tube, directly under the top rim of the container. Then tie one length of string through each hole (sketch d).

- Gather the loose ends of the strings and tie the ends together in a knot. Tie a second knot halfway down the length of the strings (sketch e).

Enrichment Idea

Older students can measure and cut their own paper, streamers, and string. Provide markers and have the kids write "No Limit" on the blue construction paper, before gluing the paper to the container.

Talk About

Have you ever tried to count the stars in the night sky? How high did you count? Let the students share. **Even with telescopes, scientists have never been able to count the total number of stars in our galaxy. The Bible says God determines the number of stars in the sky.** Read aloud Psalm 147:4–5. **God is mighty. His power has no limit. Tie your wind tube to a pole or a porch railing. When the wind blows, the wind tube will float in the air and remind you of God's mighty power.** Encourage students to memorize Psalm 147:4–5.

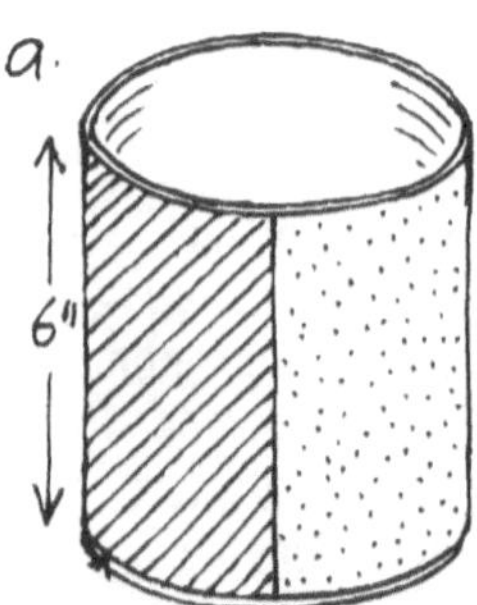

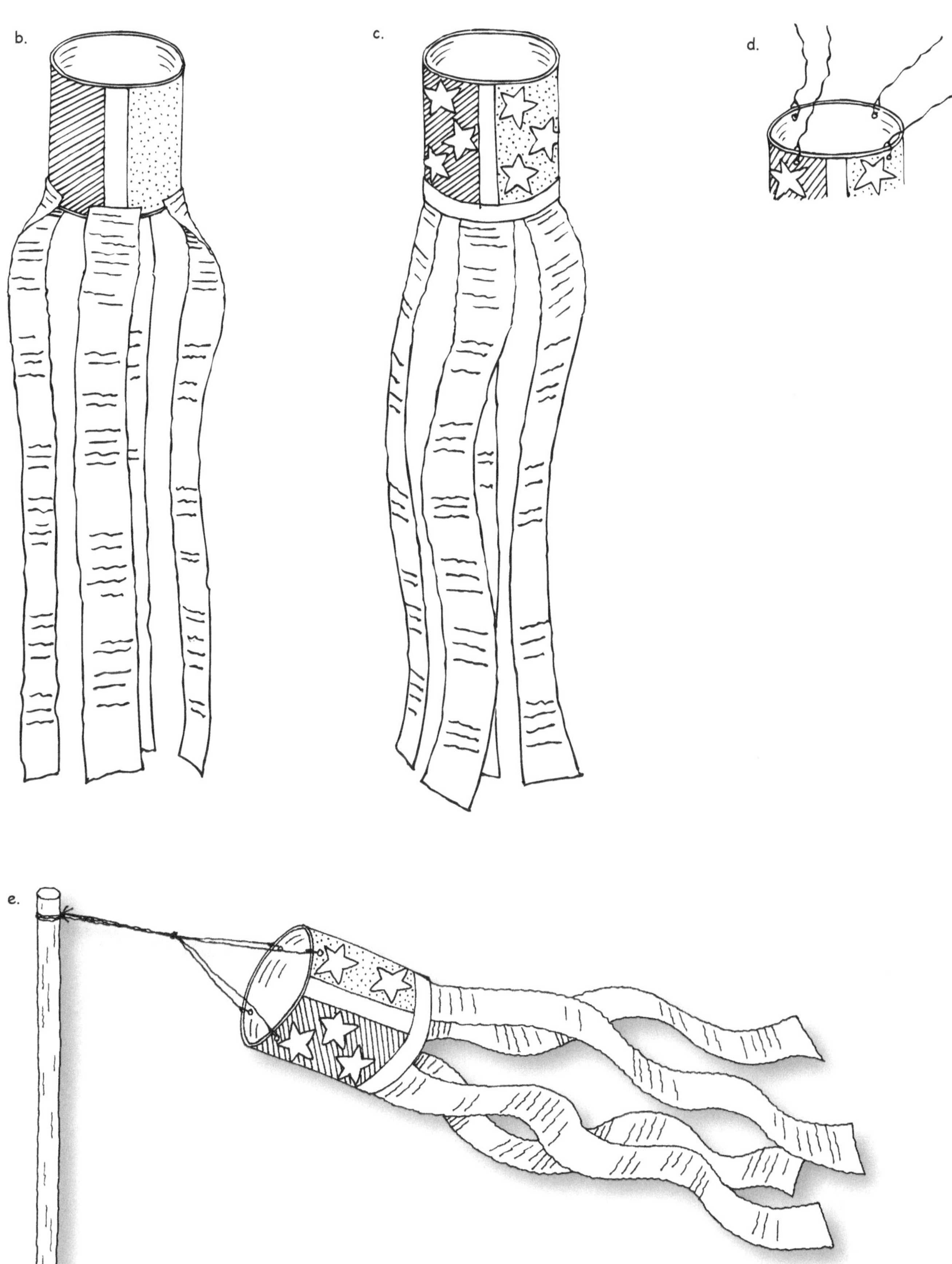
b.
c.
d.
e.

Shadrach, Meshach, and Abednego Pop-Up

Materials

- ½-gallon cardboard juice (or milk) cartons (1 per kid)
- scissors
- ruler
- jumbo craft sticks (1 per kid)
- wood craft spoons (available at craft supply stores, 4 per kid)
- small wiggle eyes (6 per kid)
- construction paper (yellow, red, and orange)
- black fine-tip markers
- craft glue
- small colorful rubber bands
- fabric scraps
- hot-glue gun and hot-glue sticks, Bible, index cards *(optional)*

Before Class

Cut juice cartons to stand 4" high, one per student (sketch a). Cut a 1" slit in the bottom center of each carton (sketch a). Cut construction paper into 5" x 12" rectangles, one of each color for each student. Cut fabric scraps into 2" x 3" rectangles, three for each student.

Simplification Idea

Out of the reach of students, use a hot-glue gun to glue together the wood spoons and craft stick.

Instructions for Kids

- Wrap and glue fabric scraps onto three wood craft spoons for headdresses. Secure the fabric with small rubber bands as headbands (sketch b).
- Glue two wiggle eyes onto each of the three wood spoons. Use markers to draw a nose and a mouth on each spoon.
- Using a fourth wood spoon, glue a jumbo craft stick and the decorated wood spoons together (sketch c). Let the glue dry.
- Cut construction-paper rectangles into 5"-high flames, each approximately 1" wide (sketch d). Fold up the flat edge of some flames (sketch e) and glue these flames around the top inside of the juice carton (sketch f). Then glue more flames around all four sides on the outside of the carton (sketch g).
- Push the jumbo craft stick down through the slot in the bottom of the carton and pull Shadrach, Meshach, and Abednego inside the fiery furnace. Push the craft stick up out of the pop-up to show that the men come out of the fire unharmed!

Enrichment Idea

Read Daniel 3:16–18 aloud. On index cards, have the kids print, "The God we serve is able to deliver us." Then have the kids glue the cards to the front of their fiery furnaces.

Talk About

Shadrach, Meshach, and Abednego knew they should worship only the one true God. They loved God and wanted to obey Him, even if they faced danger! It's not always easy, but we should choose to serve only God too. He is able to help us! Talk with the students about times when they might need to stand up and make a choice for God, even when it is hard to do.

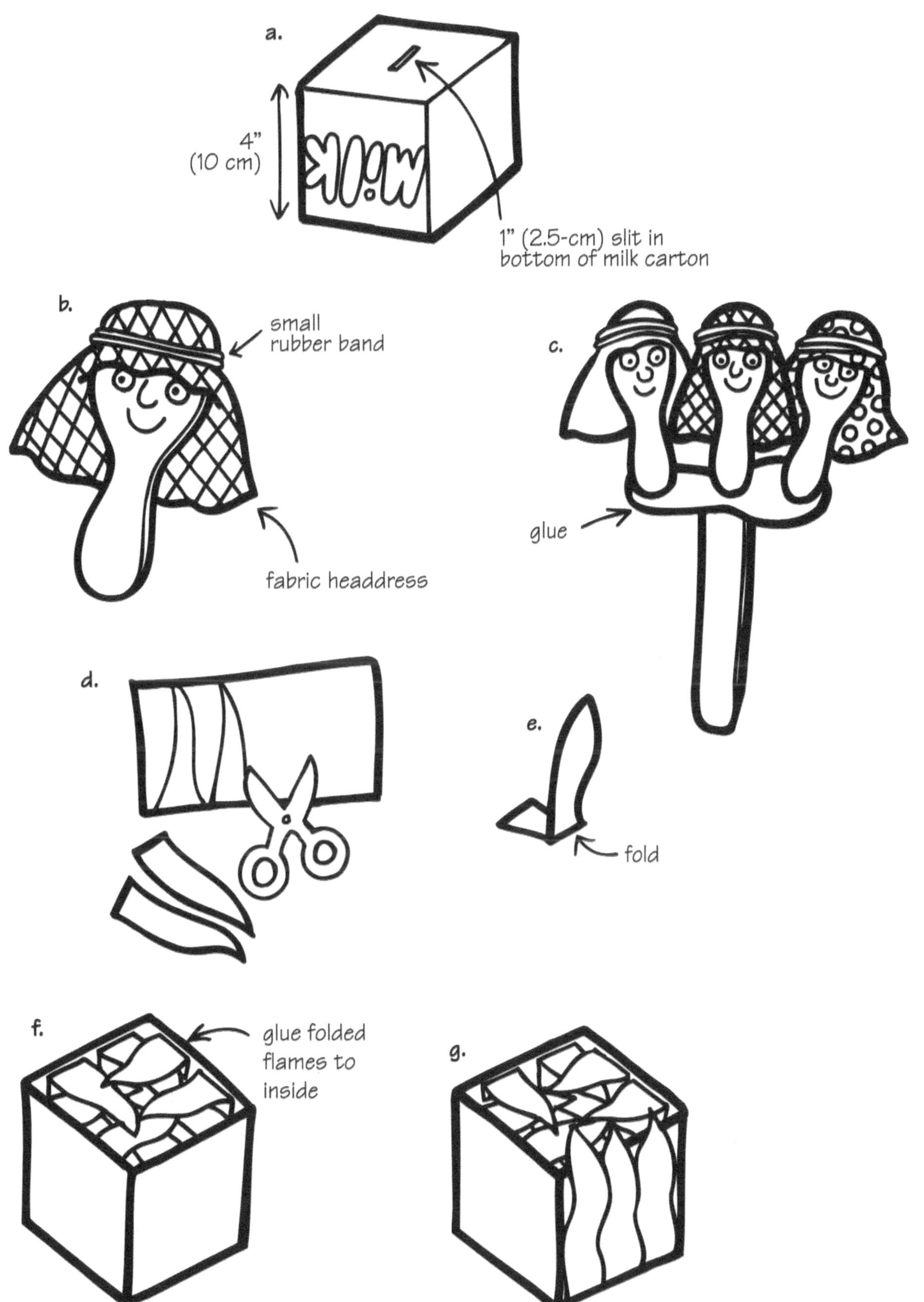
a.
4"
(10 cm)
1" (2.5-cm) slit in
bottom of milk carton
b.
small
rubber band
fabric headdress
c.
glue
d.
e.
fold
f.
glue folded
flames to
inside
g.

Fiery Furnace Candle

Materials

- candlewick
- scissors
- ruler
- table salt
- shallow containers (4 per kid)
- dry tempera paints (black, red, orange, and yellow)
- measuring cup and teaspoon
- empty coffee can
- paraffin wax
- saucepan
- water
- stove (or hot plate)
- oven mitt
- clean baby food jars (1 per kid)
- spoons
- bamboo skewers

Before Class

Cut the candlewick into 3" lengths. Pour one cup of salt into each shallow container. Mix one teaspoon of dry tempera paint into each container of salt to make four colors. (Add more tempera for greater color intensity.) Melt the wax in an empty can that is set in a saucepan of water on a stove. Set the burner on low heat. (Watch closely, as the wax will melt quickly.)

Instructions for Kids

- Spoon layers of red, orange, and yellow salt into a jar.
- Add a final layer of black salt, stopping 1" from the top of the jar (sketch a).
- Press a skewer against the inside of the jar side and push the skewer down through all the salt layers. Carefully pull the skewer out and repeat the procedure around the sides of the jar to make "flames" (sketch b).
- Push a piece of wick down through the middle of the salt (sketch c).
- With adult supervision, carefully pour hot wax into the jar, filling it to the top (sketch c). Allow the wax to harden. Trim the wick if necessary.

Talk About

The fiery furnace that Shadrach, Meshach, and Abednego were thrown into was probably used as a huge kiln for making pottery. Even though they faced death in the fire, Shadrach, Meshach, and Abednego showed their faith in God by obeying Him. What are some ways we show our faith in God? What can you tell your friends about God? Lead in a discussion. Assure students that God will be with them, even when it is hard to stand up for their belief in God.

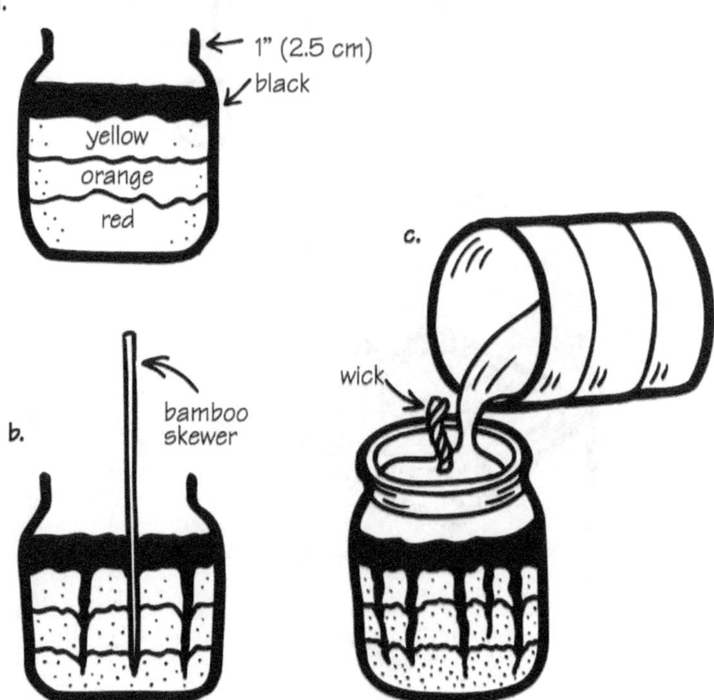

Pom-Pom Lion

Materials

- brown bump chenille wires
- yellow chenille wires
- ruler
- scissors
- 1" yellow pom-poms (2 per kid)
- ½" yellow pom-poms (5 per kid)
- ¼" yellow pom-poms (2 per kid)
- 1" yellow tinsel pom-poms (1 per kid)
- ½" brown pom-poms (1 per kid)
- small wiggle eyes
- craft glue
- small shallow containers
- cotton swabs

Before Class

Cut apart the bumps in the brown chenille wires, one bump for each student. Cut yellow chenille wire into 3" lengths, one for each student. Pour glue into shallow containers.

Instructions for Kids

- Use a cotton swab to dip into the glue. Glue two large (1") yellow pom-poms together to make a lion's body.
- Glue four medium-size (½") yellow pom-poms to the body to make feet.
- Make a tail by bending one end of a piece of yellow chenille wire around the middle of the brown chenille bump (sketch a). Twist the chenille bump ends together. Then glue the tail to the lion's body.
- To make a head with ears, glue two small (¼") yellow pom-poms onto a tinsel pom-pom. Glue wiggle eyes onto the tinsel pom-pom. For the snout, glue the remaining medium-size (½") yellow pom-pom onto the tinsel pom-pom, just below the eyes. Glue on a brown pom-pom to make a nose (sketch b).
- Glue the head onto the lion's body. Allow the glue to dry.

Talk About

How often do you pray to God? What do you pray about? Encourage the students to share. **Daniel was a trusted helper to the king. When some jealous men plotted to get rid of Daniel, the only way they could trap Daniel was through his faithfulness in praying to God. Even though Daniel was thrown into a lions' den, the king hoped that Daniel's God would save him—and God did! Use your pom-pom lion as a reminder to pray often—even when it is hard to do so.**

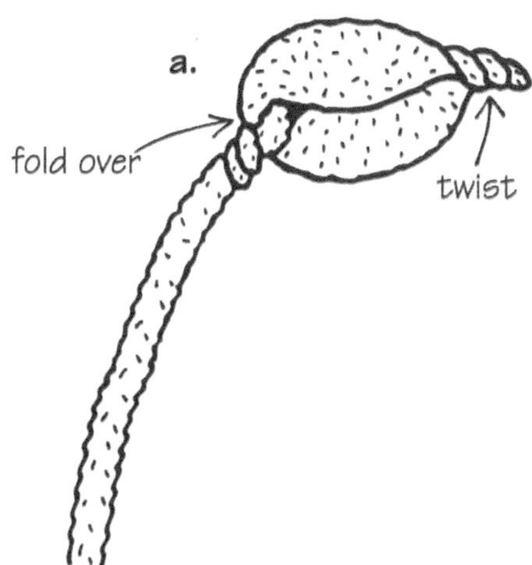

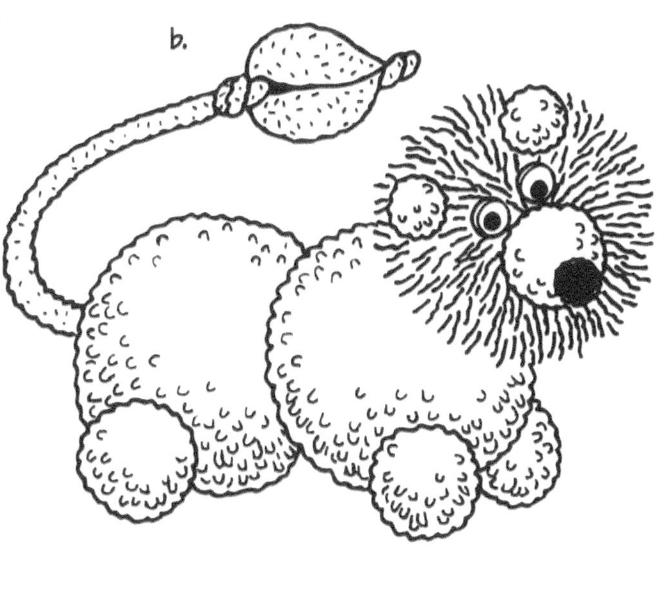

Jonah and the Big Fish Shadow Box

Materials

- big fish pattern (p. 157)
- blue card stock
- construction paper
- empty cereal boxes (approx. 8" x 11", 1 per kid)
- ruler
- scissors
- utility knife
- tissue paper scraps
- wood craft spoons (available at craft supply stores, 1 per kid)
- black markers
- fabric scraps
- small wiggle eyes (2 per kid)
- glue

Before Class

Copy the big fish pattern onto the card stock and cut out the fish, one for each student. On each fish, cut the fin where indicated by the heavy black line on the pattern. With a utility knife, cut out an opening in the center section of each box, leaving about 1" on each side of the opening (sketch a).

Instructions for Kids

- Imagine what Jonah saw inside the belly of the big fish. Use markers, construction paper, tissue paper scraps, and glue to create inside the box a scene that looks like rib bones, seaweed, and small fish (sketch a).
- With markers, draw hair, beard, and facial features on a wood spoon to make a Jonah figure. Glue on wiggle eyes (sketch b).
- Cut and glue a piece of fabric onto the spoon for clothing.
- Cut out a speech balloon from construction paper. Print on the balloon something that Jonah might have said while inside the big fish (sketch c).
- Glue the Jonah figure and speech balloon onto the scenery background you have created inside the box.
- Apply glue to the 1" areas on either side of the box opening. Glue the box behind the fish, centering the Jonah figure and speech balloon behind the fin (sketch d). Fold back the fin to see Jonah inside the fish.

Talk About

Have you ever ignored or tried to get out of doing something that your parents or a teacher told you to do? What happened? Allow the kids to share. **Jonah didn't want to tell God's message to the people in Nineveh. Jonah tried to run away from God, and he ended up in the belly of a big fish! God wants us to obey His Word, and God wants us to share the good news of His great love with everyone.**

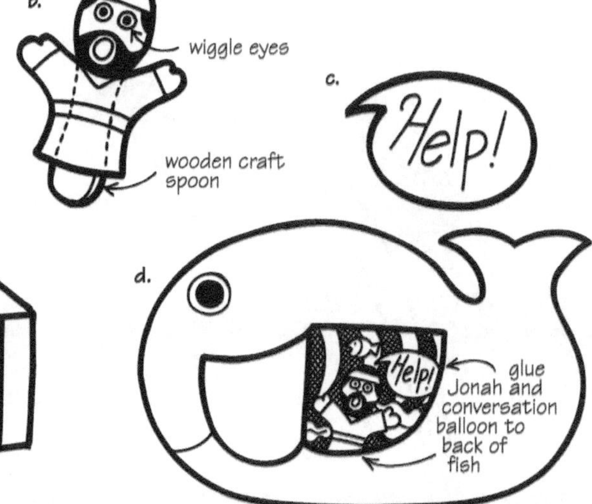

cut fin on heavy black line

Paper-Bag Angel

Materials

- angel and wing patterns (p. 160)
- lightweight cardboard
- paper lunch bags
- narrow ribbon
- ruler
- scissors
- pencils
- paper clips
- pinking shears (or decorative edge craft scissors)
- markers
- tissues
- glitter markers (or glitter crayons)
- small buttons
- sequins
- craft glue
- tape

Before Class

Copy and cut out the angel and wing patterns. Trace the patterns onto cardboard and cut them out. Make several of each pattern piece for kids to share. Cut open paper lunch bags and lay them flat, three bags for each student. Cut ribbon into 4" and 8" lengths, one of each length for each student.

Simplification Idea

Before class, trace and cut out for each student two identical paper-bag angel pieces and a paper-bag wing piece.

Instructions for Kids

- Fold a paper bag in half and paper clip an angel pattern to the fold of the paper bag. Trace around the shape, and then remove the cardboard pattern. With the bag still folded, cut out the angel.

- Open the folded angel. Apply a line of glue along the outline of the head, arms, and sides of the angel. Do not put glue along the bottom edge (sketch a). Press the glued side of the angel onto another paper bag piece.

- Use pinking shears to cut along the edges of first angel, cutting away any excess paper from the second bag. Now you should have a two-sided angel, with an opening at the bottom.

- Use markers to draw facial features and hair on the angel.

- For a tie around the neck, center a 4" length of ribbon across the back of the neck and cross the ribbon in front. Glue the ribbon in place (sketch b).

- Decorate the angel's robe with glitter markers. Glue on buttons and sequins, as desired.

- After the angel has completely dried, gently stuff a couple of tissues inside the angel to fill the angel's body. Then glue the bottom edges of the angel pieces together.

- Trace the wing pattern onto a third paper bag. Use pinking shears to cut out the wings. Decorate the wings with glitter markers. Glue the wings to the back of the angel (sketch c).

- Tape a paper clip to the back of the head, with one end of the paper clip extending above the head (sketch d). Thread an 8" length of ribbon through the top loop of the paper clip. Tie the ribbon ends together to form a hanger (sketch e).

Talk About

An angel told Mary she was going to give birth to the Son of God. And angels announced the birth of Jesus to a group of shepherds. What would you have thought if you had been Mary or one of the shepherds? Encourage students to share their thoughts. **Why is it such good news that Jesus came to earth?** (Jesus came to tell about God's love for us. Jesus died and rose again so we can be with God forever.)

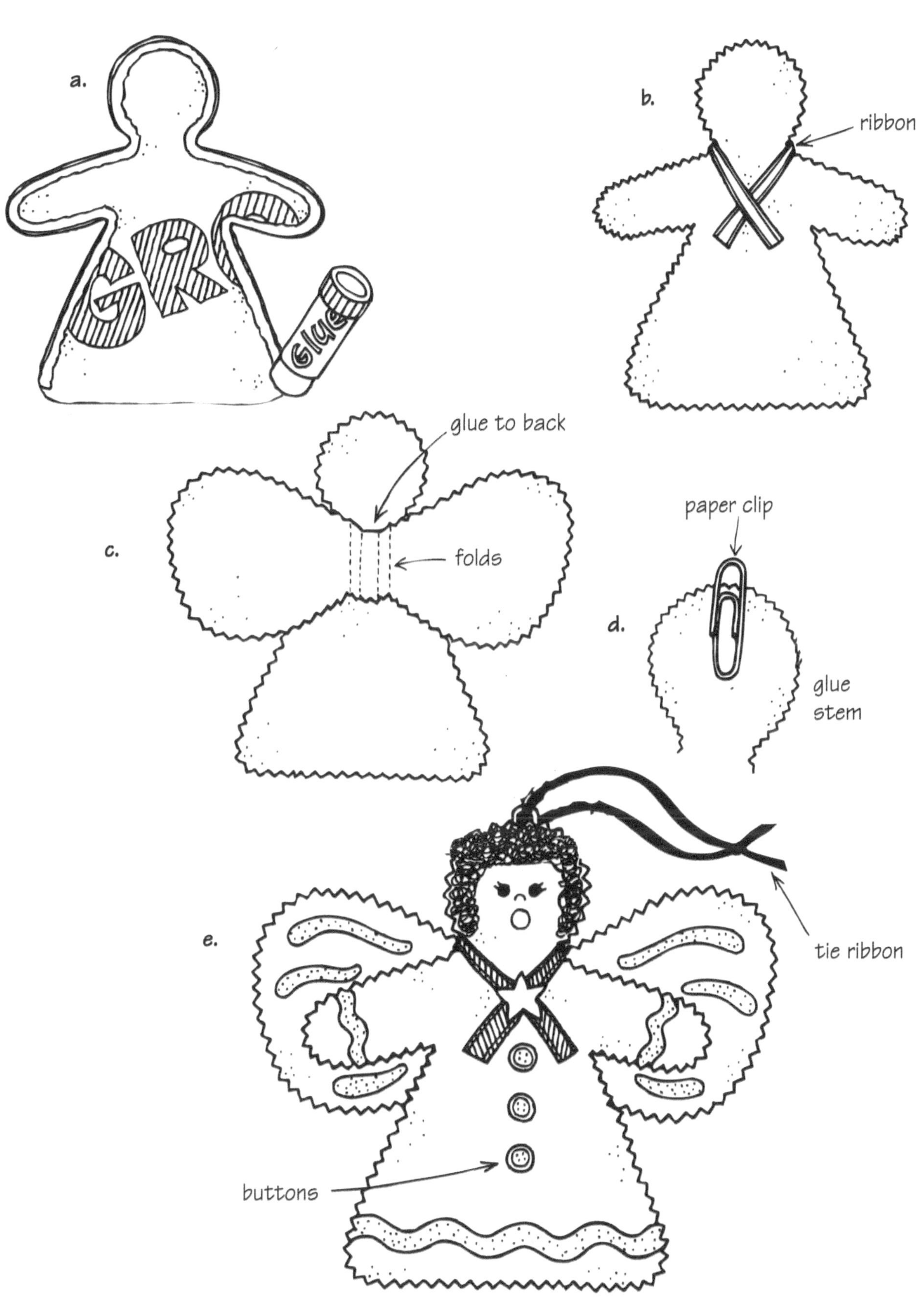
a.
glue
b.
ribbon
glue to back
c.
folds
paper clip
d.
glue
stem
e.
tie ribbon
buttons

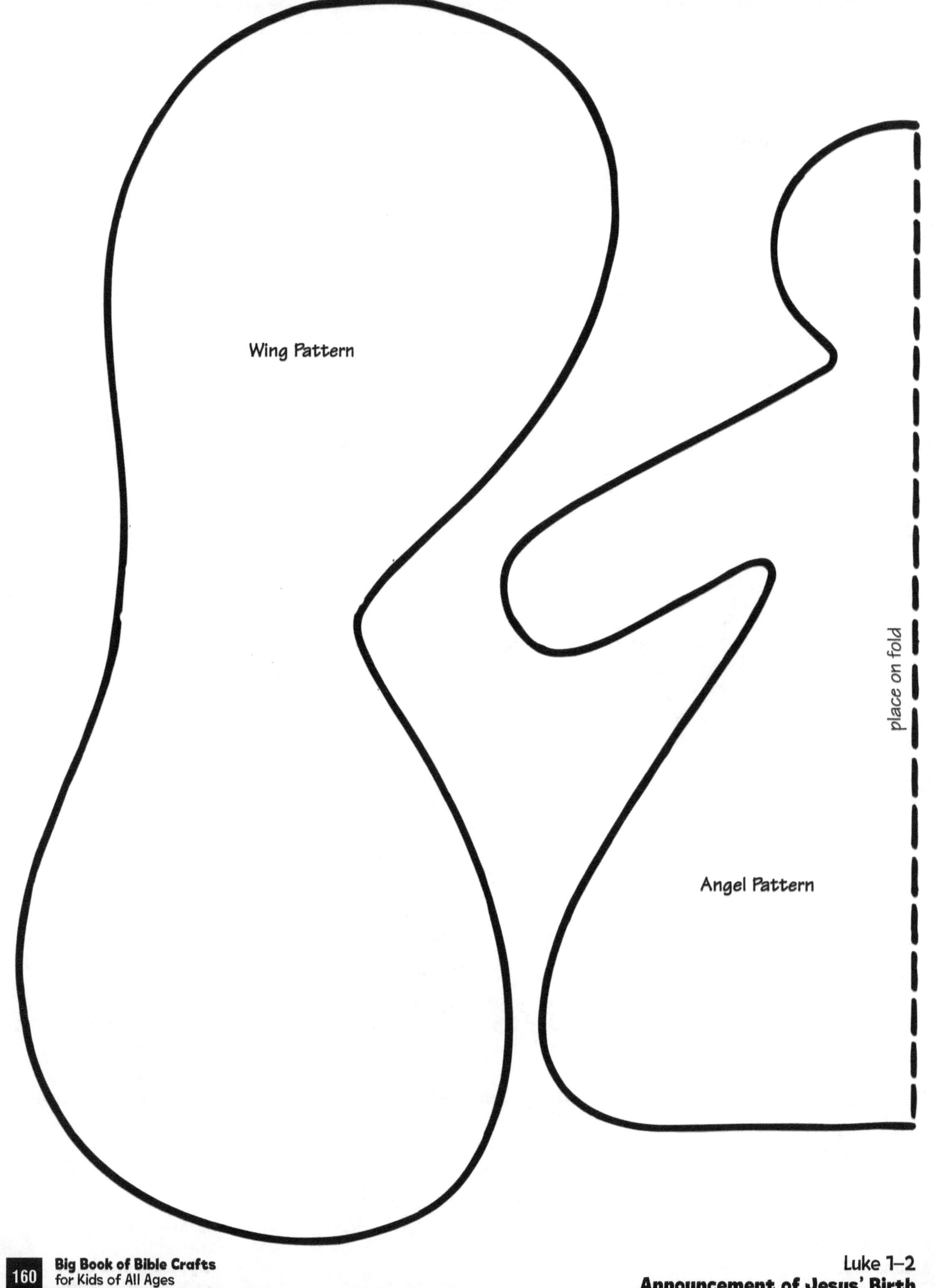
Wing Pattern
Angel Pattern
place on fold

Seashell Angel Ornament

Materials

- ½"-wide satin ribbon
- curly doll hair
- scissors
- ruler
- black and red fine-tip permanent markers
- medium- or large-size fan-shaped shells (1 per kid)
- small bowl-shaped shells (such as clamshells, 1 per kid)
- 16 mm fake pearls (1 per kid)
- hot-glue gun and hot-glue sticks
- craft glue
- tiny shells

Before Class

Cut ribbon into 12" lengths, two for each student. Plug in a glue gun out of reach of the students.

Simplification Idea

A teacher can draw the facial features on the pearls for students.

Instructions for Kids

- With a teacher's help, apply a couple of drops of hot glue to the inside edge of the pointed end of a small bowl-shaped shell. With the inside edges facing each other, attach the small shell to the pointed edge of a fan-shaped shell (sketch a).
- Wrap a ribbon around the neck of the shell angel and tie the ribbon in a knot or bow (sketch a). Trim the ends as needed.
- Slide a second length of ribbon through the neck ribbon at the back of the angel. Tie this ribbon to the neck ribbon and then knot the ends of the second ribbon together to make a hanging loop (sketch b). With a teacher's help, use a drop of hot glue to attach the ribbon loop to the back of the small shell so the angel will hang upright.
- On a large pearl, use a black marker to draw eyes and eyebrows. Use red markers to draw a mouth and cheeks (sketch c). With a teacher's help, hot-glue the pearl to the inside of the small shell.
- Cut a small amount of doll hair and glue it around the pearl for hair.
- Glue tiny shells onto the angel's robe to decorate it. Allow the glue to dry.

Talk About

When Jesus was born, an angel brought very good news to both Mary and a group of shepherds. God loves us so much, He sent His Son to earth to live and die so that our sins can be forgiven and we can live with God forever! Who can you share this good news with? The angel ornaments can be given as gifts, or the students can keep their ornaments as reminders to share God's love with others.

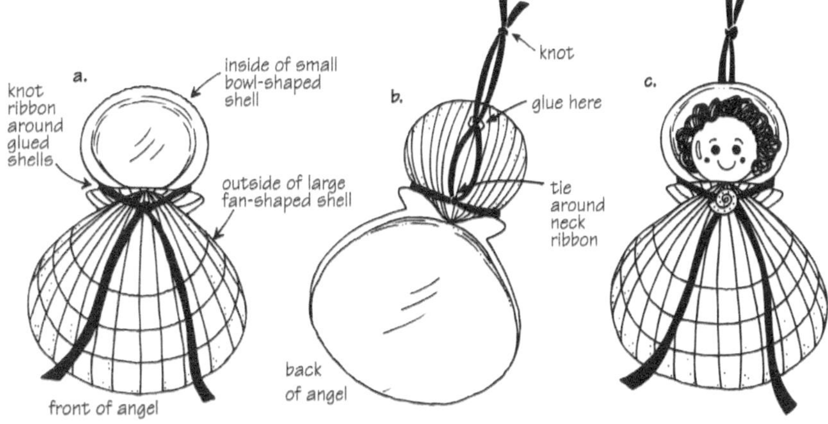

Spool Animals

Materials

- spool animal patterns (p. 163)
- white card stock
- felt (black, pink, and brown)
- yarn
- scissors
- ruler
- empty plastic thread spools (or toilet paper tubes cut in half)
- crayons (or markers)
- fine-tip black markers
- cotton balls
- yarn
- craft glue

Before Class

Copy the spool animal patterns onto the card stock, one sheet for each student. For a donkey or pig, cut brown or pink felt into 1½" x 4" strips, one felt strip for each animal to be made. Cut yarn into 2" lengths for donkey or pig tails.

Instructions for Kids

- Choose an animal to make. Color that animal's front and back. Cut out all the animal's pieces, including the ear patterns.
- Using a fine-tip marker, trace the ear patterns onto felt. Use black felt for a sheep, brown felt for a donkey, and pink felt for a pig. Cut out the ears and glue them onto the animal's head.
- Onto the back piece, glue a cotton ball for a sheep tail or a piece of yarn for a donkey or pig tail.
- For a sheep, pull off a small piece of cotton from a cotton ball and glue it between the ears (sketch a).
- Coat the cylinder of a spool with glue. For a sheep, press cotton balls onto the glue. For a donkey or pig, wrap a strip of brown or pink felt around the cylinder (sketch b).
- Apply glue to both ends of the spool. Then press the front and back body pieces onto the spool (sketch b), keeping the legs even so the animal will stand up.

Talk About

Where were you born? In a hospital? At home? Let the kids share. **The night Jesus was born, Bethlehem was very crowded. There were no rooms where Joseph and Mary could stay, so they found a place where animals lived. Mary laid baby Jesus in a manger, a feeding box for animals. Your spool animals can remind you of the place where Jesus was born. Jesus wasn't born in a palace, but He was, and is, the King of Kings!**

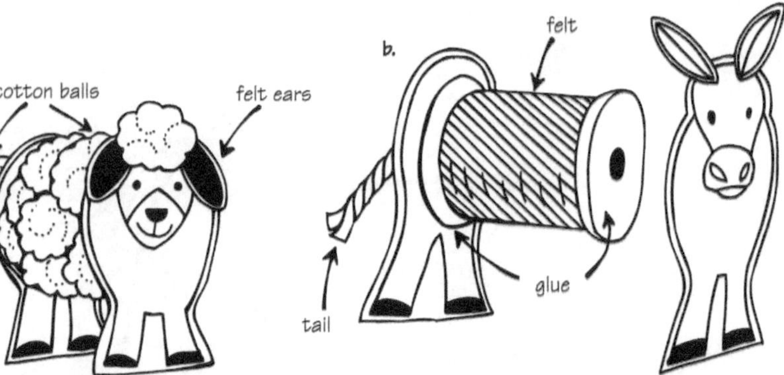

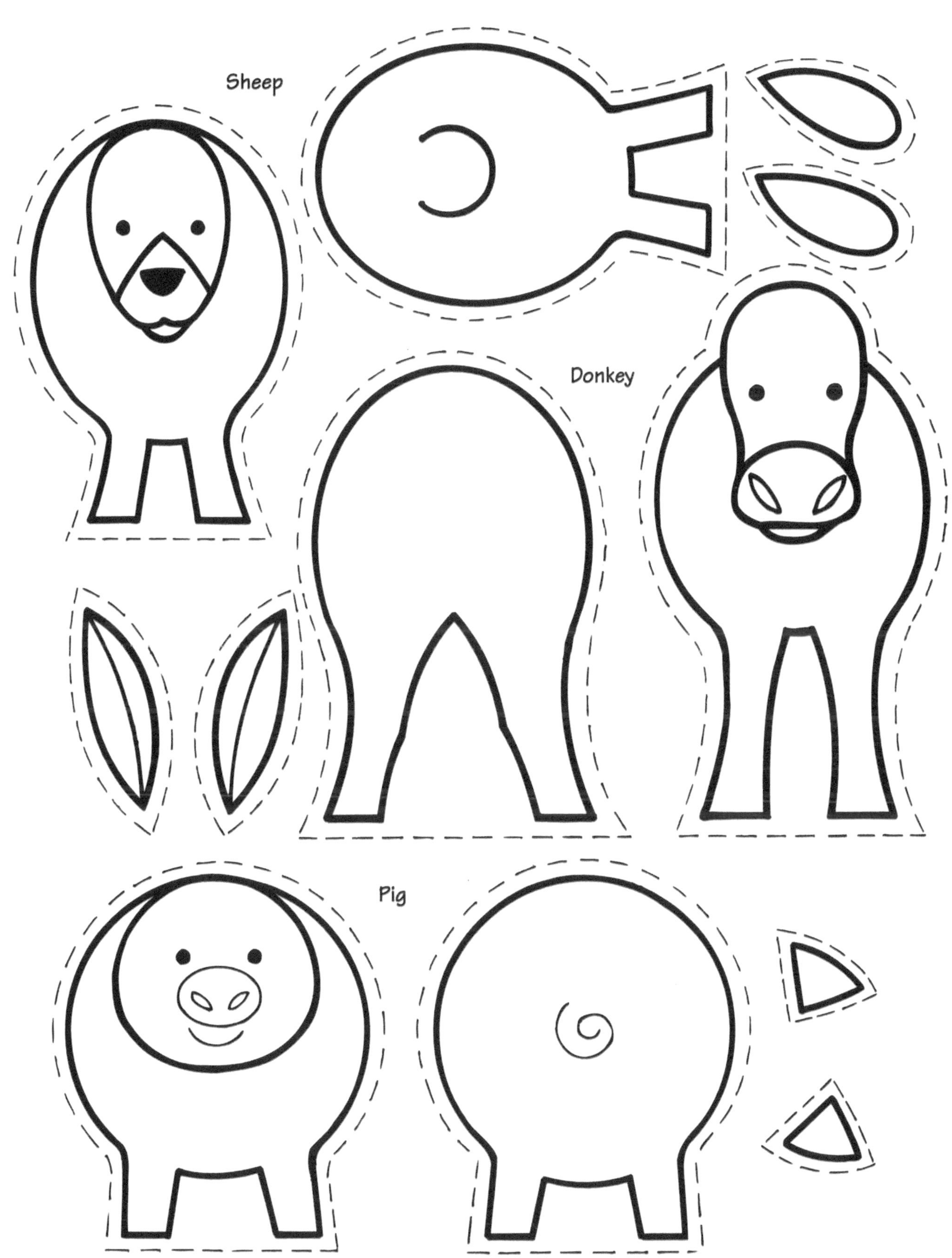
Sheep
Donkey
Pig

Wise Men and Star Puppets

Materials

- ¼"-round wood dowels
- saw
- wood craft spoons (or jumbo craft sticks, 6 per kid)
- craft glue
- wrapping paper (or fabric) in metallic and various colors
- ruler
- scissors
- pencil
- gold star garland
- poster board (silver, gold, or yellow)
- markers in flesh tones
- brown or tan chenille wires
- yarn in various colors (including gray, black, and brown)
- sequins
- acrylic jewels
- black fine-tip permanent markers
- 5 mm wiggle eyes
- duct tape

Before Class

Use a saw to cut wood dowels into 12" lengths. Glue two wood spoons together, end to end, for a puppet body (sketch a). Prepare two or three spoon bodies for each student. Cut wrapping paper into 4" x 8" pieces, two or three pieces for each student. Cut gold star garland into 20" lengths, one for each student. Prepare a 6" star pattern and trace stars onto poster board, one for each student. Cut out the stars. Save the poster-board scraps.

Instructions for Kids

- Decide how many puppets you will make. Choose a flesh-tone marker and color each puppet body.

- To create arms, wrap a chenille wire around a wood spoon one time, below the head. Then twist the ends of the wire together in the back (sketch b). To make hands, bend each wire end back ½".

- For a robe, fold one piece of wrapping paper in half and cut a 1" slit in the center of the fold (sketch c). Slip the head of the puppet through the slit.

- For belts, cut lengths of yarn. Wrap and tie a piece of yarn around each puppet's waist.

- For hair and beards, cut gray, black, or brown yarn into small pieces. Glue the pieces onto the heads of the puppets (sketch d).

- Cut small pieces of metallic gift wrap for crowns. The tops of the crowns can be rounded or cut into points and decorated with sequins or jewels. Glue a crown onto each puppet's head.

- Glue on wiggle eyes. Use markers to draw other facial features as desired.

- For gifts, cut poster-board scraps into 1" squares. Glue on yarn, sequins, or jewels to decorate the gifts. Fold the chenille-wire arms to look like they are holding the gifts. Glue the gifts and arms in place (sketch d).

- To make a star prop, glue a gold star garland around the outside edge of a poster-board star (sketch e). For a handle, use a piece of duct tape to attach a wood dowel onto the back side of the star.

Enrichment Idea

Have the kids use their puppets to act out the Bible story found in Matthew 2.

Talk About

The wise men followed the star a long time and for many miles before they finally got to see Jesus. They were willing to do this because they knew Jesus was the promised king of the Jews, and they wanted to present gifts to Him and worship Him. What can we give to Jesus? How can we worship Him now? Encourage discussion. Then worship Jesus together.

Matthew 2
Wise Men Visit Young Jesus

Punch-by-Punch Ornament

Materials

- disposable aluminum pans (or sheet metal)
- heavy-duty scissors to cut aluminum
- paper
- pencils
- pens
- metal-tooling items of varying sizes (nails, bulletin board pushpins, etc.)
- old phone books (or thick pads of newspaper or corrugated cardboard)
- masking tape
- manila envelopes
- jute string (or ribbon)

Before Class

Cut the sides off the disposable pans. Beware of any sharp edges! Tear old phone books into ½" sections for padding (or use stacks of newspaper for the kids to place under the metal). Cut jute string into 12" lengths. Supply manila envelopes to take home the finished projects.

Instructions for Kids

- Draw on a piece of paper a simple shape (star, crown, gift box) that reminds you of the story of the wise men visiting young Jesus.

- Place a sheet of aluminum on a section of phone book pages. Lay the paper shape on the aluminum. Pushing firmly with the point of a pen, trace the shape to imprint the outline into the aluminum.

- With a teacher's help, cut out the aluminum shape. Cover the edges with masking tape.

- Use nails, pushpins, and other items for tooling metal to create designs on the aluminum shape. Note: Holding an edge of the aluminum with one hand near the area being punched, while using a punch tool with the other hand, is the easiest way to get the punch tool through the aluminum.

- Punch a hole at the top of the project. Thread a string through the hole and tie the ends together, making a loop for hanging the ornament.

Talk About

The wise men came looking for Jesus because they knew He was the promised king of the Jews and His coming to earth would make a difference for all the people. They wanted to worship and give gifts to the new king. These ornaments can remind you it is wise to look for and worship Jesus! How can we let Jesus know that His life, death, and resurrection make a difference in our lives? Students will have a variety of answers.

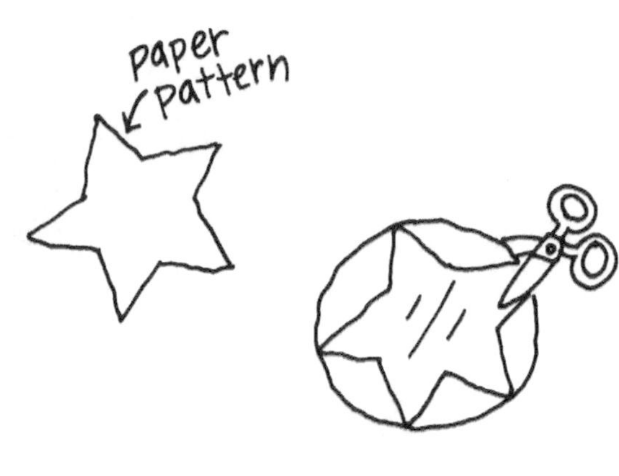

Dove Light-Switch Cover

Materials

- Bible
- dove light-switch cover pattern (p. 168)
- white craft foam
- pen
- scissors
- ruler
- utility knife
- fabric paints (neon colors) in squeeze bottles
- glitter markers
- newspaper
- double-sided mounting tape

Before Class

Cut the craft foam into 8" squares, one for each student. Trace the dove light-switch cover pattern onto each square. Use a utility knife to cut out the switch opening on each dove. Cut 1½" strips of double-sided mounting tape, two for each student. Cover the work area with newspaper.

Instructions for Kids

- Cut out a craft foam dove. Lay the dove on the table in front of you.

- Remove the paper from one side of a mounting strip and place the strip to the left of the switch opening. Repeat this process with another mounting strip, placing it to the right of the switch opening. Do not remove the paper from the top of the strips.

- Turn the dove over. Decorate the front of the dove with fabric paint and glitter markers as desired. Make dots for the dove's eyes and squiggles for feathers.

- Allow the dove switch cover to dry overnight. Ask an adult to help you mount the cover over a light-switch plate.

Talk About

When Jesus was baptized, God showed everyone Jesus was His Son by sending the Holy Spirit in the form of a dove. What did a voice from heaven say? ("You are my Son, whom I love; with you I am well pleased" [Luke 3:22].) **When you turn on the light with the dove light-switch cover, remember that Jesus, God's Son, came to show God's love to everyone. When you turn off the light, your dove will glow in the dark, reminding you that God is always with you.**

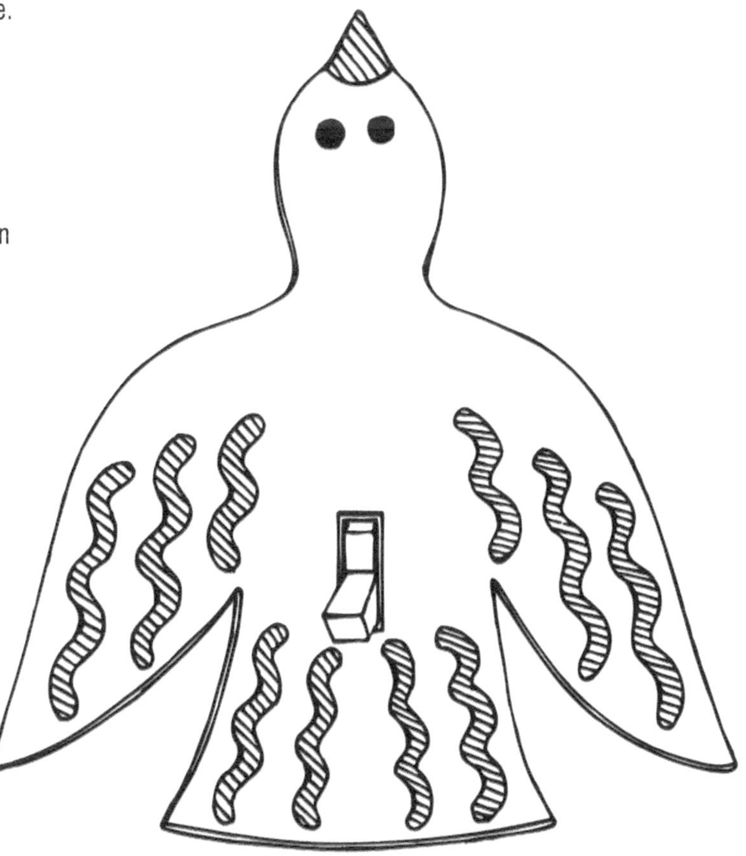

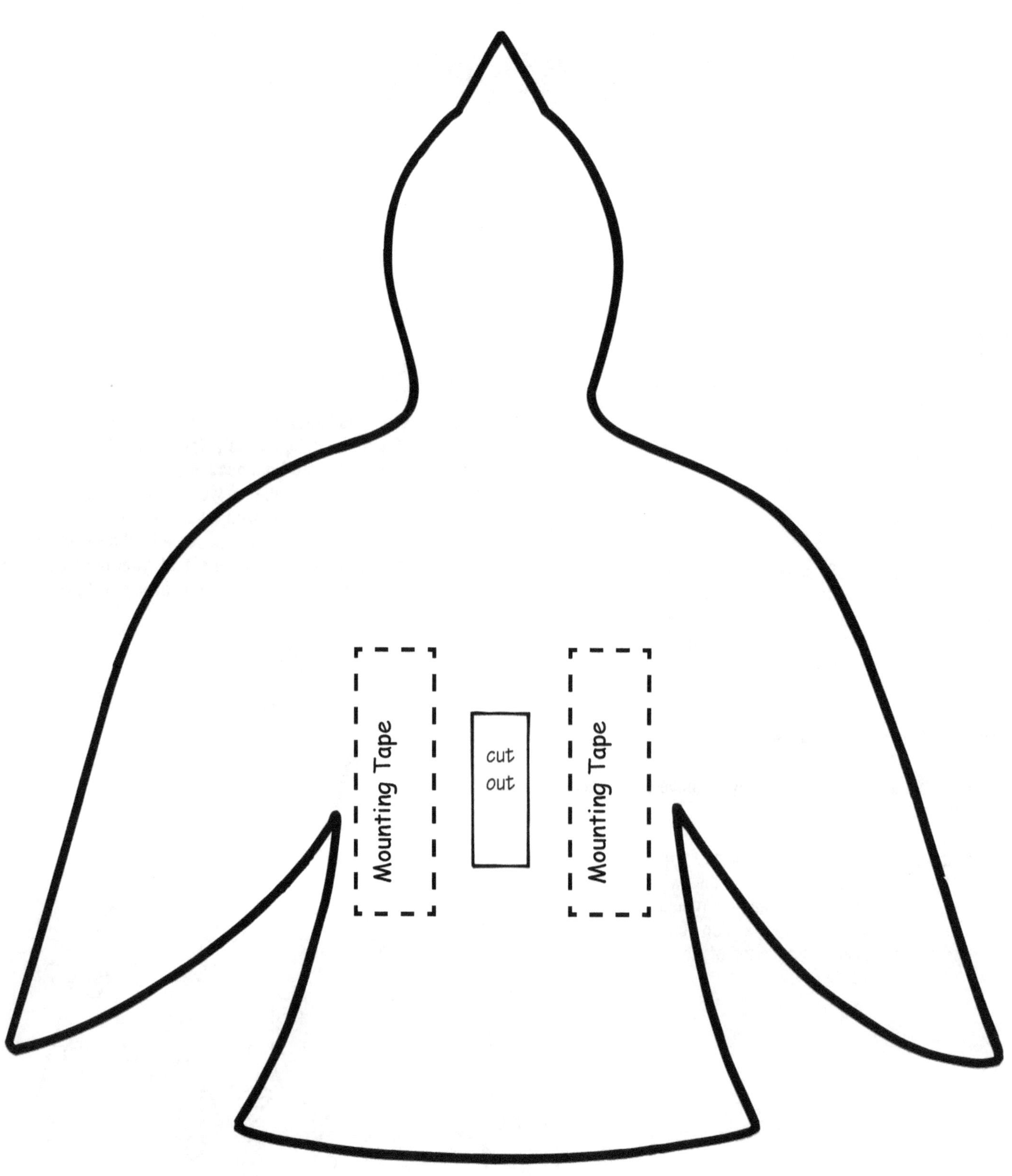
Mounting Tape
cut
out
Mounting Tape

Identity Icon

Materials

- Bible
- poster board (or cardboard) for each kid
- scissors
- assorted markers (metallic, gel, etc.)
- glitter glue
- glue
- rulers
- variety of crafting papers (comics, wallpaper, gift wrap, etc.)

Before Class

Make a coat of arms that represents you and your family to show as a sample as you explain how clans or families in past times created a coat of arms to show their identity.

Simplification Idea

To save time, cut out a shield for each student ahead of time.

Instructions for Kids

- Cut a shield from poster board.
- Use the materials to decorate and illustrate a shield that identifies your family heritage, faith, talents, hobbies, interests, etc. You might draw horizontal, vertical, or diagonal lines on your shield to create sections for each identifying aspect. Include any emblems or symbols that help reflect your identity.

Enrichment Idea

Create a coat of arms that identifies the members of your class as part of God's family. You might include symbols such as a cross (have faith in God), an open hand (welcome and help each other), a heart (love one another), etc.

Talk About

Ask volunteers to show their coat of arms. Have other kids guess what the symbols stand for. **The coat of arms each of you made has symbols that can help others know about you and your family, even without your speaking a word. When Jesus was baptized, God sent a symbol that identified Jesus as the Son of God.** Read Matthew 3:16 aloud. **God's symbol was a dove. What symbols do people use today to show they are followers of Jesus and part of God's family?** (fish symbol, cross) **What does it mean to belong to the family of God?** Be prepared to share what being part of God's family means to you.

Light Décor

Materials

- plastic switch plates and screws (1 set per kid)
- paper
- pencils
- acrylic paint in various neon colors
- paintbrushes (or cotton swabs)
- small paper plates
- resealable sandwich bags
- clear spray sealant, newspaper *(optional)*

Before Class

Purchase inexpensive switch plates at a dollar store or discount shop.

Instructions for Kids

- On a piece of paper, sketch an abstract, geometric, or realistic art idea you want to paint on a switch plate. Try to incorporate into the design something from the Bible story of Jesus talking to Nicodemus. (Examples: stars, moon, a speech balloon with the words "born again")
- Squeeze a small amount of paint onto a paper plate and dip a paintbrush into the paint. Paint your design on the switch plate. Allow the paint to dry completely.
- Place your painted switch plate in a resealable bag, along with the screws that came with the plate.
- Ask an adult to help you mount the switch plate over a light switch.

Enrichment Idea

Outdoors or in a well-ventilated area, lay the painted switch plates on newspapers. Spray the switch plates with clear sealant so the design will last longer.

Talk About

What are some questions you would ask Jesus? Accept all genuine questions from the kids. **Nicodemus wanted to know more about the kingdom of God, so he went to talk to Jesus at night. Jesus told Nicodemus he needed to be born again. Jesus meant that we need to be born spiritually, not just physically. We need to have God's Holy Spirit in our lives to help us live for God. For Nicodemus, Jesus' teaching turned on a "light" to help him understand more about God and His kingdom. Whenever you flick the light on or off, remember God really loves you, and He wants you to be a light to the world for Jesus.**

Spool Cross

Materials

- Bible
- small empty thread spools (5 per kid)
- 12" chenille wires (1 per kid)
- narrow ribbon
- scissors
- ruler
- permanent markers in various colors

Before Class

Purchase spools at a craft or department store. Cut chenille wires in half, two halves for each student. Cut ribbon into 6" lengths, one for each student.

Instructions for Kids

- Use markers to decorate five spools.

- Thread three spools onto one piece of chenille wire, leaving about a 1" gap between the top two spools. (To make sure you are leaving the right size gap, lay another spool head in the gap.) Bend each end of the wire and tuck it into the top hole of the top spool and the bottom hole of the bottom spool, making a small loop at each end to secure the spools (sketch a).

- Twist a second wire horizontally to the vertical wire, between the top two spools (sketch b). Thread one spool onto each end of the second wire. Push these spools toward the center of the cross until they nearly touch. Then bend and tuck each end of the second wire into the end of a spool, making a loop on each end to secure the spools.

- Thread a piece of ribbon through the wire loop at the top of the cross. Tie the ends of the ribbon together to make a hanger (sketch c). Trim the ends as needed. Twist the top wire loop to secure the ribbon.

Talk About

God had a specific purpose for sending His only Son, Jesus, into the world. Read John 3:16 aloud. **Your spool cross can remind you Jesus loved you so much He died on a cross. He did it so you can be part of God's family and have eternal life! What can we do to express our thanks to God for giving up His Son so that we could have our sins forgiven?** (believe in Jesus, obey and be baptized in Jesus' name, live lives that are pleasing to God) Have the kids repeat John 3:16 with you.

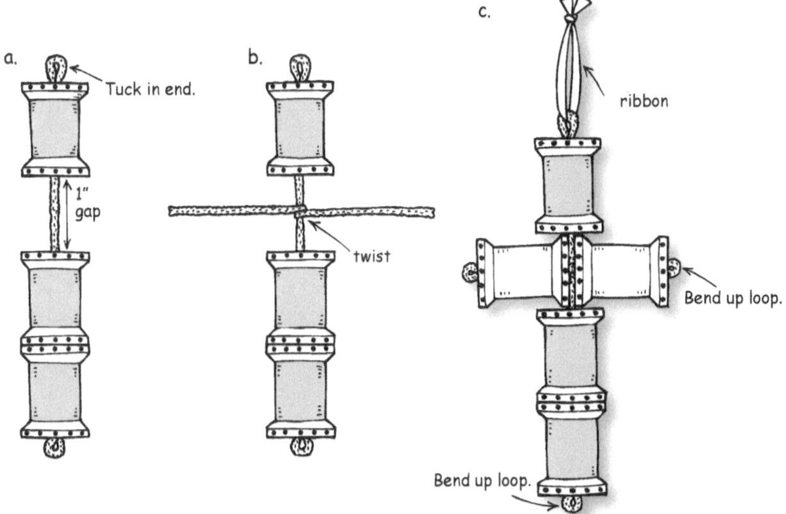

Instant Water Cup

Materials

- sheets of copy paper
- pencils
- pitcher of water

Before Class

Cut sheets of paper into 8" x 8" squares. Make a folded cup before class so you're familiar with the folds.

Instructions for Kids

- Place a paper square on the table so the corners point up and down, diamond style (sketch a).
- Fold the bottom corner up to the top corner (sketch b).
- Fold down the top corner you just folded, so the top corner tip touches the center fold at the bottom (sketch c). Fold the top corner back up and use a pencil to make a small mark at the right edge where the fold is (sketch d).
- Fold up the left corner so that the tip of the corner touches the mark and reaches just to the edge of the paper (sketch e).
- Fold the right bottom corner so it touches the same place on the opposite side (sketch f).
- Fold down the top triangle in front, and then fold down the back triangle in the back (sketch g). Now you can open the cup and try drinking from it.

Talk About

Pour some water into each student's cup. **Did you think you could make a real drinking cup out of a piece of paper? What else do you think could happen with some simple materials, a touch of creativity, and a little time?** Encourage the kids to think creatively. **One day Jesus asked a woman from Samaria for something simple—a drink of water. The woman's life was changed when she took the time to ask questions and talk to Jesus. Now that you've seen even a simple thing can be used by God, what do you plan to do this week to share God's love with others?** Be prepared to share something you can do, as a prompt for getting kids to think about ways they can let God use their abilities, possessions, and time.

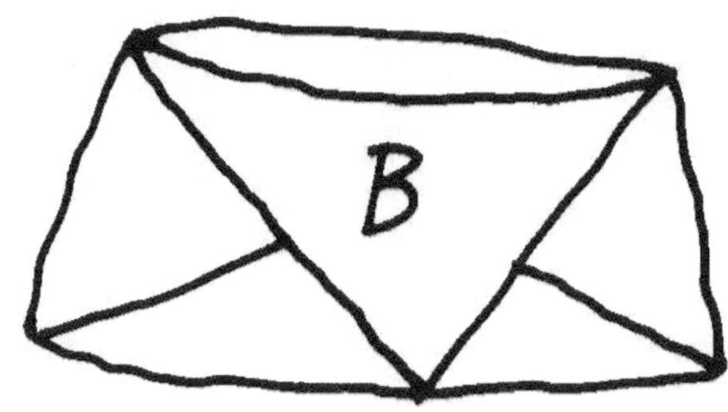

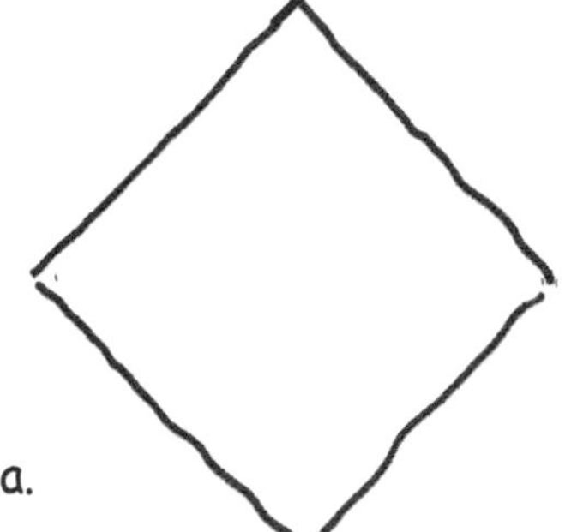

a.

b. fold up

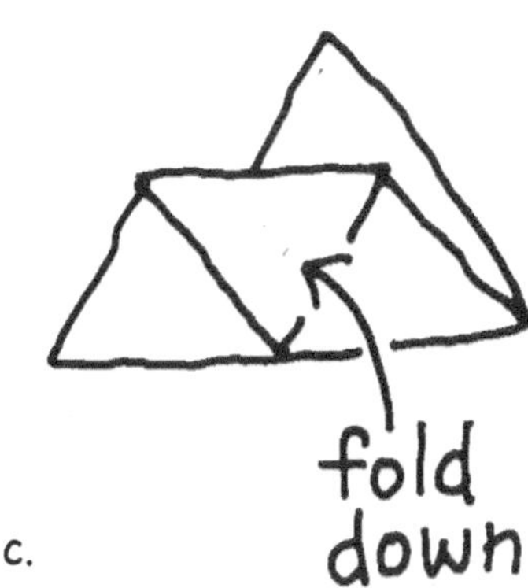

c.

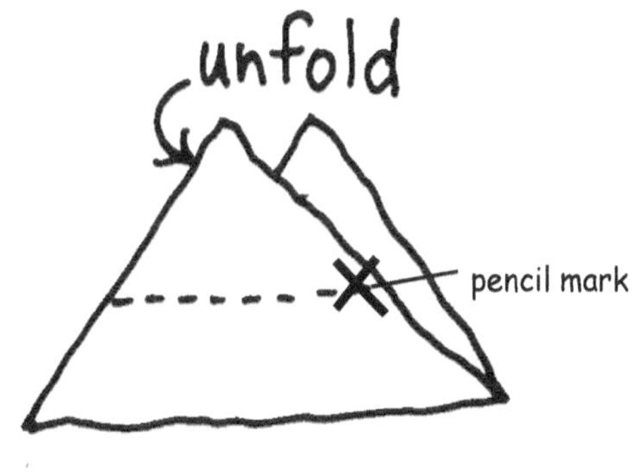

d.

e. fold left corner up to mark on opposite side

f. fold right corner the same way in opposite direction

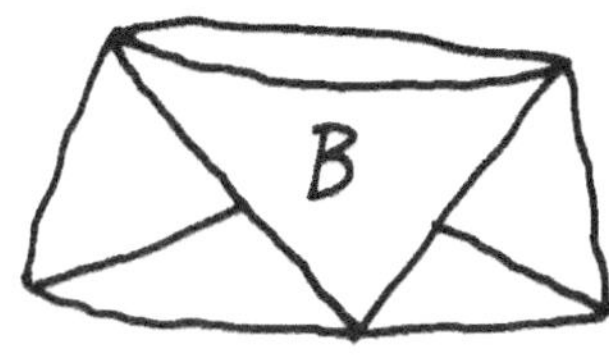

g. fold down triangles

Disciples Museum

Materials

- burlap and fabric scraps
- white poster board
- scissors
- ruler
- round-head wood clothespins (1 per kid)
- chenille wire in various colors (including tan)
- fine-tip and broad-tip markers
- glue
- yarn
- modeling clay
- assorted decorating materials (twigs, netting, fish-shaped crackers, etc.)

Before Class

Cut the burlap and other fabric scraps into 3" x 6" rectangles for robes and 1½" x 3½" rectangles for headpieces, one each for each student. Cut the poster board into 6" x 12" rectangles and 1" x 3" strips, one each for each student.

Instructions for Kids

- Choose one of Jesus' first disciples (Peter, Andrew, James, or John) and make a clothespin figure of that disciple.

- Center and wrap a tan chenille wire below the head of a clothespin for arms.

- Choose a 3" x 6" piece of burlap or fabric for a robe. Fold the fabric in half. Cut a slit in the fold large enough for a clothespin head to fit through. Slip the robe over the head (sketch a).

- Squeeze a little glue onto the clothespin body to secure the robe to the clothespin. Tie a length of yarn around the robe at the waist as a belt.

- Use markers to draw the disciple's face on the head of the clothespin. Glue small pieces of yarn on the head of the clothespin to make hair and/or a beard (sketch b).

- To make a headpiece, glue a 1½" x 3½" piece of burlap or fabric to the top of the head and tie it in place with yarn around the forehead (sketch c).

- Roll a piece of clay to form a ball. Stick the bottom of the clothespin into the ball and set it on a table. Flatten the bottom of the clay slightly to make the disciple stand (sketch c).

- Fold the large poster-board piece in half. On the front half, draw and color a scene where your disciple could be (at a lake fishing, walking down a road, etc.).

- If desired, glue materials onto your scene, such as netting for a fishnet, small fish-shaped crackers for fish, twigs for branches of trees, and so on.

- Bend up ½" at each end of a poster-board strip to make tabs. Glue the tabs inside the poster-board backdrop to make the backdrop stand (sketch d).

- Set your disciple in front of the scene.

Enrichment Idea

Have the students display their backdrops and disciple figures on a table. Each student can explain where the disciple is and how that disciple followed Jesus.

Talk About

What is fun about games like Follow the Leader or Simon Says? What can be hard about those games? Encourage the kids to share. **When Jesus invited four fishermen to leave their nets and follow Him, they did so willingly. It wasn't always easy for the disciples to follow Jesus, and it isn't always easy for us to follow Him. When might it be hard for you to follow Jesus?** Accept all genuine responses. **Knowing Jesus is the Son of God makes following Him worth any problems we might face along the way.**

cut slit
a.
chenille wire arms
b.
fabric
c.
yarn
yarn
clay
d.
tab

Peter's Boat Bookmark

Materials

- boat and fish patterns
- white card stock
- yarn
- scissors
- ruler
- washable markers
- craft glue

Before Class

Copy the boat and fish patterns onto card stock, two of each for each student. Cut the yarn into 10" lengths, one for each student.

Instructions for Kids

- Using markers, color the two boats and two fish. Cut out the pieces.
- Glue the two boats together, back to back, with the colored sides out and one end of the yarn between the two pieces.
- Glue the two fish together, back to back, with the other end of the yarn between the pieces. Allow the glue to dry before using your bookmark.

Talk About

When Jesus told Peter to put out his fishing net again, Peter said, "Because you say so, I will let down the nets" (Luke 5:5). **Then Peter and the other fishermen caught so many fish, their nets began to break! Sometimes it might not make sense to others when we follow and obey Jesus, but Jesus' way is always the best way! What is something you can do to follow and obey Jesus this week?** Encourage the students to think beyond the common responses of "Pray" and "Read the Bible."

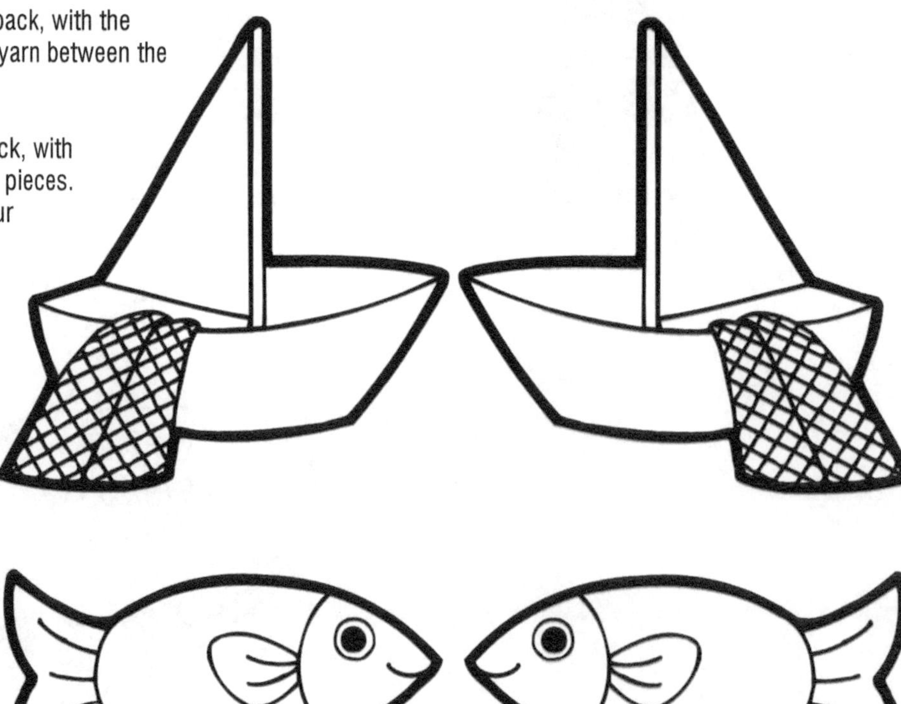

Ready Red-Cross Kit

Materials

- travel containers for bar soap
- medical-themed stickers (stethoscopes, bandages, etc.)
- permanent markers
- first-aid supplies that fit in soap boxes (cotton swabs, adhesive bandages, single-pack antiseptic wipes, gauze squares)
- basic first-aid instructions
- heavy-duty resealable quart-size bags *(optional)*

Before Class

Look for medical-themed stickers in the scrapbooking section at a craft store. Basic first-aid instructions may be obtained through the Internet and public agencies in many communities. You might want to reproduce some of this information onto cards that will fit inside the plastic soap containers.

Simplification Idea

If you can't purchase travel containers for bar soap, use heavy-duty resealable quart-size bags for the first-aid kits.

Instructions for Kids

- Use permanent markers, stickers, and adhesive bandages to decorate the outside of a soap container.

- Select items from the first-aid supplies to fill the first-aid kit.

Talk About

People who lived in Bible times avoided people who had a disease called leprosy. What might keep us from helping someone who needs our help? (fear, uncertainty about what to do) **But when a man with leprosy came and asked Jesus to heal him, Jesus didn't avoid the man. In fact, the Bible says Jesus reached out His hand and touched the man—and the man was healed! Today there are plenty of people who, like the man with leprosy, need someone to help them. We can be like Jesus and be willing to help others. The first-aid kits you made might come in handy when you need to help others!**

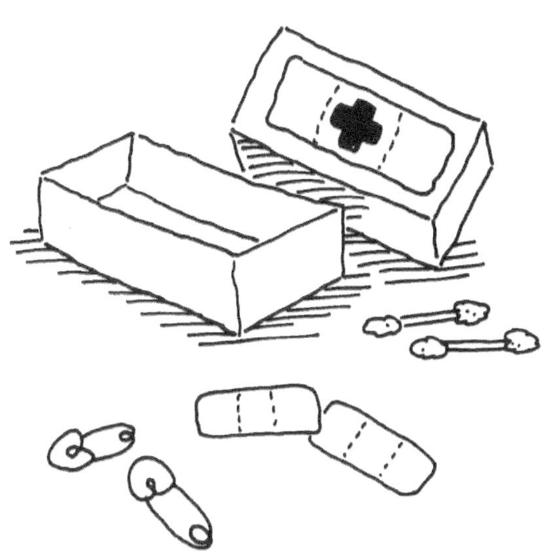

Bouncing Back

Materials

- white glue
- borax
- cornstarch
- water
- electric teakettle (or microwave and glass bowl for heating water)
- plastic cups (2 per kid)
- wood stirring sticks (2 per kid)
- timer
- resealable plastic sandwich bags
- measuring spoons
- wet wipes
- food coloring *(optional)*

Before Class

Make a sample ball so you can give tips about stirring the various ingredients and handling the mixture.

Simplification Idea

Have the students do this project in pairs. Set out each person's two cups, then assign each student a task. One student can measure the glue, another can measure the borax, and so on.

Instructions for Kids

- With a teacher's help, heat the water until warm to the touch.
- Place one tablespoon of glue into a plastic cup. Add a few drops of food coloring (if desired) and mix with a wood stick.
- In another cup, combine two tablespoons warm water and ½ teaspoon borax. Mix the ingredients with a wood stick until the borax is dissolved.
- Add one tablespoon cornstarch to the borax and water mixture. Combine this mixture with the glue and let it stand for 15 seconds.
- When the time is up, stir the mixture with a wood stick until the ingredients are completely mixed. When the mixture is too thick to stir, knead the mixture with the stick, keeping it moving as you begin to form it into a ball.
- Mold the mixture with your hands into a ball. It will be sticky, but it will become more solid as you work with it.
- Place the ball in a resealable bag to take it home.

Talk About

How well your ball bounces depends on how well mixed your ingredients are and how round the ball is. Have fun no matter how zanily the ball bounces. Jesus healed a man who was paralyzed and could not walk. Just like your ball comes up from the floor, the man came up onto his feet when Jesus healed his legs. How do you think the paralyzed man felt when he first stood up after Jesus healed him? Allow the kids to share. **Your needs—in your body, your mind, and your spirit—are just as important to Jesus. He can help you with every need.**

Lofty Hovercraft

Materials

- Bible
- hovercraft sketches (p. 180)
- index cards
- markers
- scissors
- tape
- rulers
- whiteboard and dry-erase marker

Before Class

Make copies of the hovercraft sketches, one page for each student.

Instructions for Kids

- Decorate both sides of an index card with markers.
- Cut the index card lengthwise 1¾" down the center. This creates tabs 1 and 2 (sketch a).
- Make two cuts on each of the long sides of the card approximately ½" below where the first cut ends. The cuts should only go in 1" of the way. They create tabs 3 and 4.
- Fold tabs 1 and 2 in opposite directions. They should remain raised above horizontal (forming a shape somewhere between a T and Y).
- Fold tabs 3 and 4 over each other and tape closed (sketch b).
- Throw the hovercraft into the air above your head and watch it spin as it comes down.

Enrichment Idea

Allow time for kids to practice flying the hovercrafts. Explain that tilting the wings a little can make the hovercrafts move in different directions. Try creating targets for the hovercrafts to hit or timing them to see whose stays in the air the longest.

Talk About

Jesus went up on a mountainside and called 12 specific men to come to Him. These men would travel with Jesus, and He would send them out to preach about the kingdom of God. What are the names of Jesus' 12 apostles? Have the kids list from memory as many as they can. Write the names on a whiteboard. Then read Mark 3:16–19 aloud to check or complete the list. **So what does a hovercraft have to do with the 12 apostles? Well, the apostles couldn't accomplish their mission without looking upward and praying to God. They needed God's wisdom and His Holy Spirit to help them as they taught about God and Jesus and healed people. When you twirl your hovercraft and it rises upward, it's a reminder that you too are called to take God's message to others. We all need to pray and look up to God, even though we know God is actually always near us. God can give us the wisdom we need when we ask Him to do so.**

cut
fold back
fold forward
TAB 1
TAB 2
fold
cut
cut
TAB 3
TAB 4
a.
fold
fold

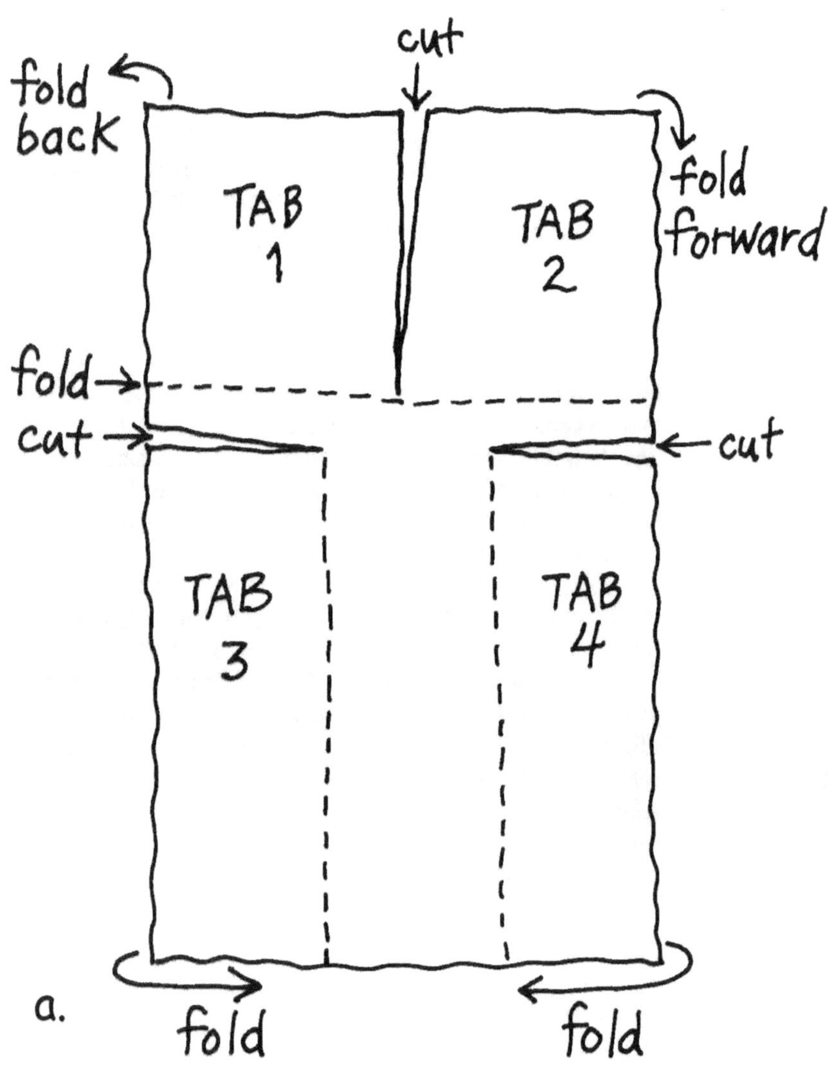

tape
tape
b.

Mason Jar Candle

Materials

- Bible
- 18-gauge wire
- wire cutters
- needle-nose pliers
- raffia ribbon
- scissors
- ruler
- pint-size mason jars with lids (1 per kid)
- sand
- plastic scoops
- votive candles (or battery-operated tealight candles; 1 per kid)
- gold glitter

Before Class

Cut wire into 20" lengths, two for each student. Cut raffia ribbon into 18" lengths, several strands for each student. You may also want to wrap the first wire onto each jar for students.

Instructions for Kids

- Curl one end of a wire length into a small loop. Use pliers to make the loop tighter.

- Starting a third of the way up from the bottom of the jar, use your thumb to hold the looped end of the wire against the jar and wrap the wire halfway around the width of the jar. Bend the wire down and wrap the wire under the jar until it meets the starting loop (sketch a).

- Hook the wire through the starting loop and wrap the remaining wire around the other side of the jar (sketch b). Wrap the end of the wire under the intersecting wire and curl the end into a loop.

- Make a handle with the second wire by threading the ends through the loops of the first wire (sketch c). Curl the ends.

- Wrap raffia ribbon tightly around the neck of the jar to hold the handle in place. Tie the ends in a bow and trim off any excess.

- Use a scoop to fill the jar halfway with sand. Sprinkle gold glitter over the sand. Push the bottom of a votive candle into the sand (sketch d). Screw on the lid.

Talk About

The Bible often refers to our faith in Jesus as a light that shines to others. Read aloud Matthew 5:14–16. What does that mean? What are some ways we can show God's love to our families, friends, and neighbors? Encourage discussion. Lead the kids in saying Matthew 5:16 from memory. Explain that kids should use their candles under adult supervision. After removing the lid, an adult can use a long matchstick to light the candle inside the jar. Kids should not touch the wire handle or place the lid on the jar until the candle is extinguished and the jar is cool.

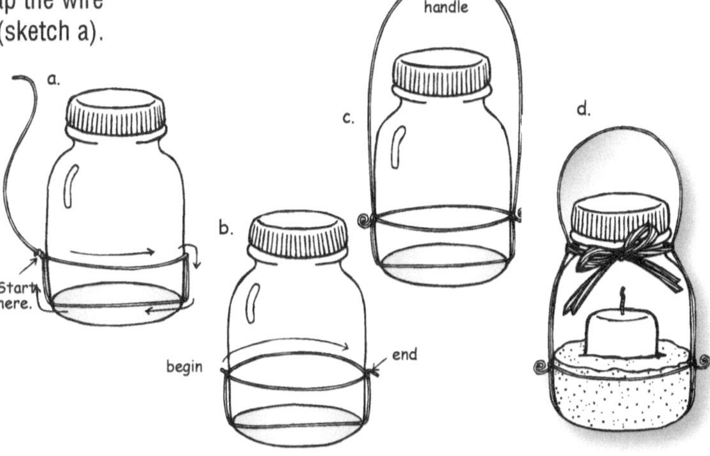

Lord's Prayer Place Mat

Materials

- Lord's Prayer place mat patterns (pp. 183–184)
- brown packaging paper (or large paper grocery bags)
- clear adhesive covering
- scissors
- ruler
- colored copy paper
- tempera paints
- objects to stamp with (such as cut vegetables or pieces of sponge)
- knife
- glue
- shallow containers
- newspapers

Before Class

Cut the packaging paper into 11" x 15" rectangles, one for each student. Cut the clear adhesive covering into 12" x 16" rectangles, two for each student. Copy the "Lord's Prayer" pattern onto colored paper, one for each student. (Note: The pattern is provided in both *King James Versio*n and *New International Version*.) Cover the work area with newspaper. Pour the paint into shallow containers. Cut vegetables, if using.

Instructions for Kids

- Crumple a rectangle of packaging paper into a small wad, and then carefully smooth out the paper. Repeat this process until the paper is as soft as a piece of cloth.

- Cut out a copy of the Lord's Prayer and glue it in the center of the paper rectangle (see sketch).

- Use the paints and objects provided to stamp and decorate the place mat. Allow the paint to dry.

- Lay one piece of clear adhesive covering on the table, sticky side up. Gently pull off backing.

- Place the paper rectangle, prayer side down, on top of the clear adhesive covering and smooth out the air bubbles. (Work with a partner on this step.)

- Partially pull the backing off the second piece of clear adhesive covering. Position the sticky portion onto the back of the place mat and continue peeling off the backing as you smooth out any air bubbles. (Work with a partner on this step also.)

- Trim the edges of the clear adhesive covering.

Talk About

Who can say the Lord's Prayer from memory? Allow those who know it to recite it together. **What is your favorite part of this prayer?** Allow responses and discuss why. **Jesus taught His disciples how to pray, using this prayer as an example. What can you learn about prayer from Jesus' example?** Guide the students as they discuss various aspects of the prayer—how to address God, what to include, and what to ask for in prayer.

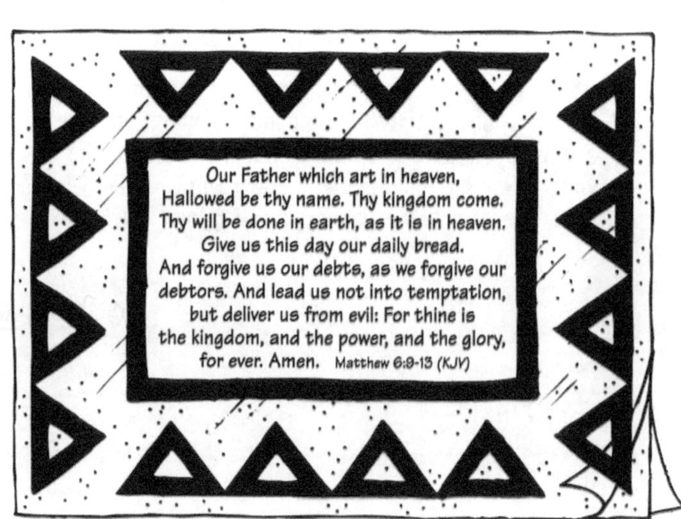

Our Father which art in heaven,
Hallowed be thy name. Thy kingdom come.
Thy will be done in earth, as it is in heaven.
Give us this day our daily bread.
And forgive us our debts, as we forgive our
debtors. And lead us not into temptation,
but deliver us from evil: For thine is
the kingdom, and the power, and the glory,
for ever. Amen. Matthew 6:9-13 (KJV)

Our Father in heaven, hallowed be your name, your kingdom come, your will be done, on earth as it is in heaven. Give us today our daily bread. And forgive us our debts, as we also have forgiven our debtors. And lead us not into temptation, but deliver us from the evil one, for yours is the kingdom and the power and the glory forever. Amen. Matthew 6:9–13 (NIV)

Daily Bread Magnet

Materials

- bread and ribbon patterns
- white card stock
- mini toast (found in cracker or deli sections of most grocery stores; 1 slice per kid)
- clear acrylic spray
- newspapers
- black yarn
- scissors
- ruler
- wiggle eyes (2 per kid)
- colored pencils (or markers or crayons)
- ½" round magnets (or magnet strip cut into 1" pieces; 1 per kid)
- craft glue

Before Class

Copy the bread and ribbon patterns onto card stock, one set for each student. Cut the yarn into 1" pieces, one for each student. On newspaper, spray the slices of toast with clear acrylic spray.

Instructions for Kids

- Glue wiggle eyes onto a piece of toast. Then glue a piece of yarn onto the toast to make a smile.
- Cut out a slice of bread from card stock. If desired, color the bread a light brown to look like wheat bread. Glue the toast onto the bread cutout (sketch a).
- Color the ribbon pattern backgrounds; then cut out.
- Glue a magnet to the back of the bread cutout. (Make sure the glue is applied to the repellent side of the magnet, not the magnetic side.)
- Glue the ribbons to the back of the bread cutout (sketch b).

Talk About

The Bible says God will give us the things we need. We can pray to God and say, "Give us today our daily bread." What other things do you *need* each day? Lead kids in a discussion that helps them understand the difference between wants and needs. **Your magnet can remind you to thank God for the people who care for you and the things He has given you.**

Ribbon Patterns

daily bread.

Bread Pattern

Flowers of the Field

Materials

- Bible
- flower and leaf patterns (p. 187)
- construction paper
- white card stock
- scissors
- ruler
- small rocks (or sand)
- floral moss
- salt
- small vegetable or soup cans (1 per kid)
- green chenille wires (3 per kid)
- chenille wires in any color (2 per kid)
- markers (pink, yellow, green)
- glue

Before Class

Copy the flower and leaf patterns onto card stock, one sheet of flowers and leaves for each student. Cut construction paper into rectangles that fit around the cans.

Instructions for Kids

- Color and cut out three flowers and three leaves. The flowers should be white, pink, or yellow. The leaves should be green.
- Apply glue to one side of each flower to make designs (sketch a). Sprinkle salt over the glue. Shake off any excess salt and set the flowers aside to dry.
- Glue a construction-paper rectangle around a can.
- Glue colored chenille wires around the top and bottom of the can; trim the wires if necessary.
- Glue a green chenille wire onto the center of each flower on the side with the salt.
- Wrap the lower edges of the flower together around the stem to look like a calla lily, and glue the edges together. Hold the edges in place a few seconds to let the glue dry (sketch b). Repeat this procedure for each flower.
- Fill the can one-half full of rocks. Then push the flower stems and leaves down into the filled can.
- Place moss around the flowers until it reaches the top of the can (sketch c).

Talk About

What do you worry about? Allow kids to share. **Jesus taught that we don't need to worry because God knows what we need.** Read aloud Matthew 6:28–30. **God will provide our needs when we trust Him. Use your flower arrangement as a paperweight or give it as a gift to remind someone that God cares for them.**

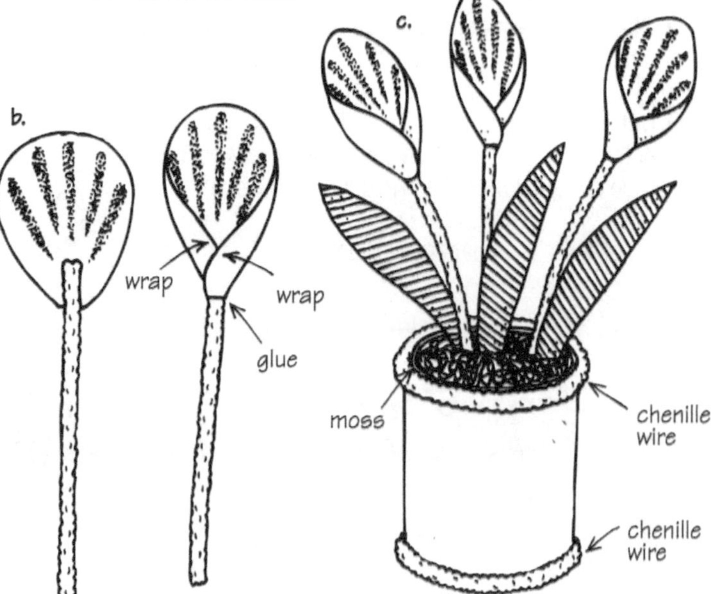

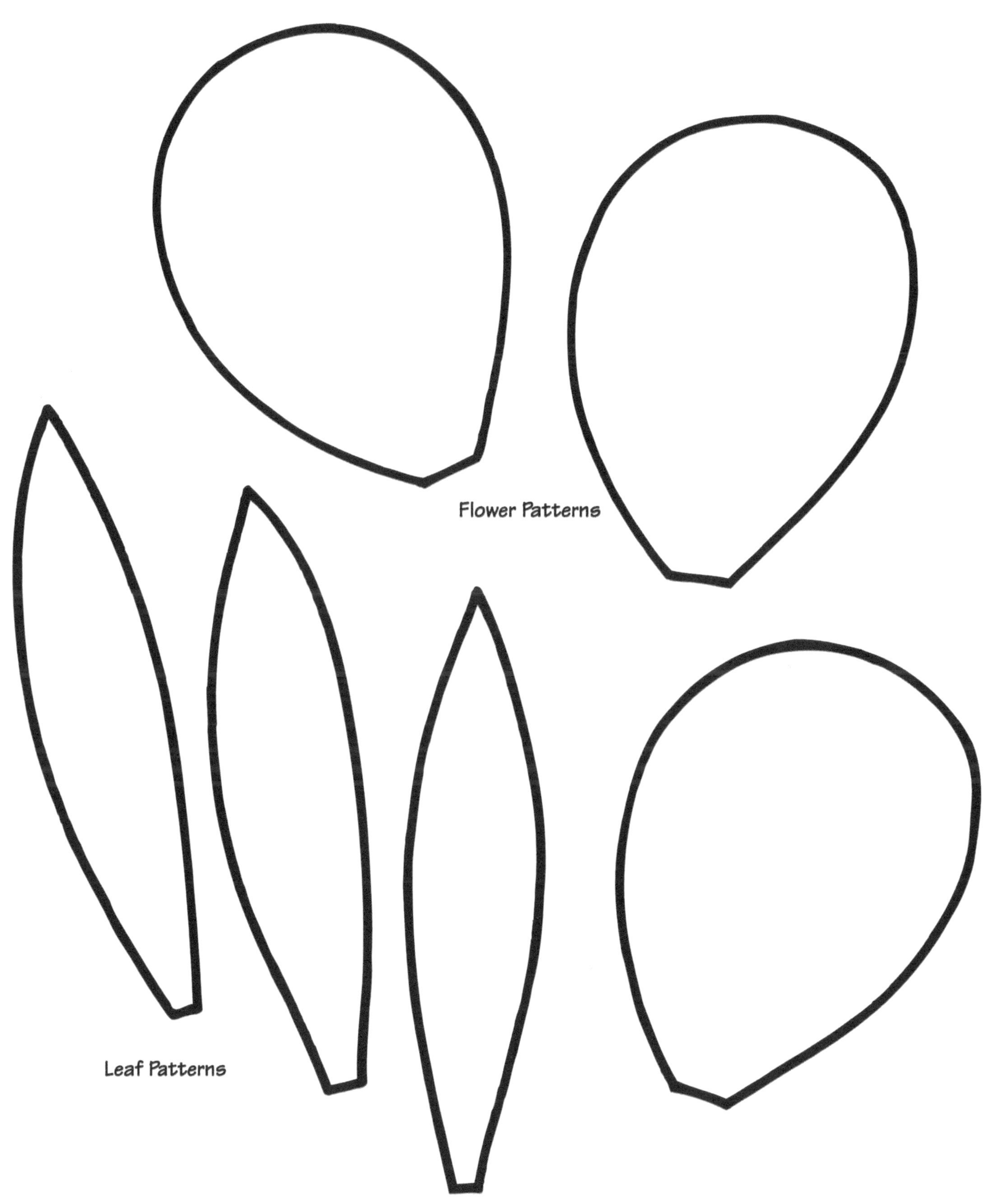
Flower Patterns
Leaf Patterns

Loaves and Fishes Basket

Materials

- Bibles
- basket pattern (p. 189)
- brightly colored poster board
- raffia ribbon
- construction paper
- scissors
- ruler
- pencil
- spring clothespins
- markers
- glue
- whiteboard and dry-erase marker
- thick craft yarn or rug yarn *(optional)*

Before Class

Trace the basket pattern onto poster board, one basket for each student. Cut out the baskets. With the point of a pair of scissors, score along the dotted lines and bend the flaps up to make the sides of the basket (sketch a). Cut the raffia ribbon into 3' lengths, several for each student. Cut the construction paper into 1" x 3" strips, five for each student. Print "Jesus Cares for Me" on the whiteboard.

Simplification Idea

Use thick craft yarn or rug yarn instead of raffia.

Instructions for Kids

- Print "Jesus Cares for Me" in the center of a basket.
- Glue one end of a length of raffia inside the basket (sketch b). Weave the raffia around the inside of one flap of the basket and outside the next flap (sketch b). When one raffia length is completed, glue the end to the basket and glue on a new length of raffia.
- Continue weaving until the raffia is ½" from top of the basket. Cut the raffia and fasten the end inside the basket with glue.
- Finish off the top of the basket by gluing on folded strips of construction paper (sketch c).
- Use clothespins to hold the paper in place until the glue dries (sketch c).

Talk About

The miracle of Jesus feeding over 5,000 people with only two fish and five loaves of bread can be found in all four gospel books in the New Testament. Have four volunteers find where the miracle is recorded in Matthew 14, Mark 6, Luke 9, and John 6. **Why do you think this miracle was so important? What does the miracle teach us about Jesus?** Encourage the students to share their ideas.

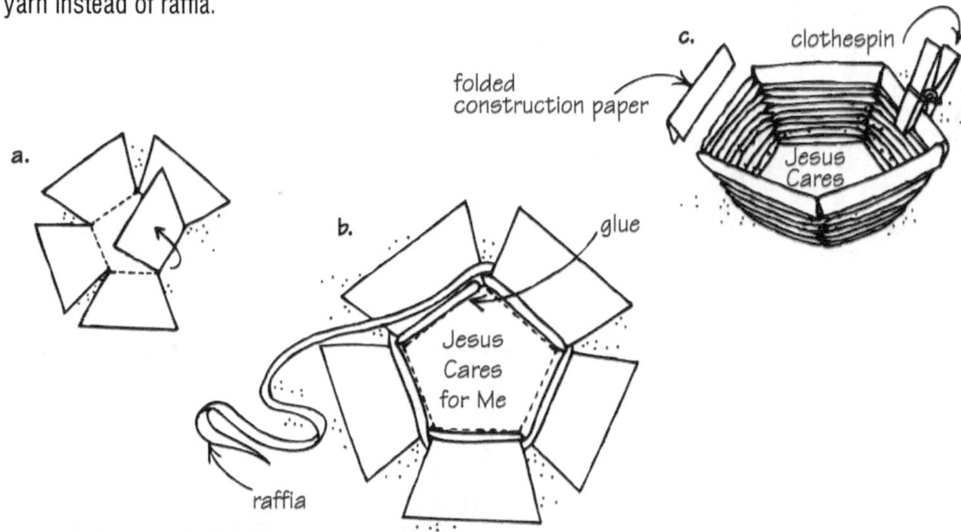

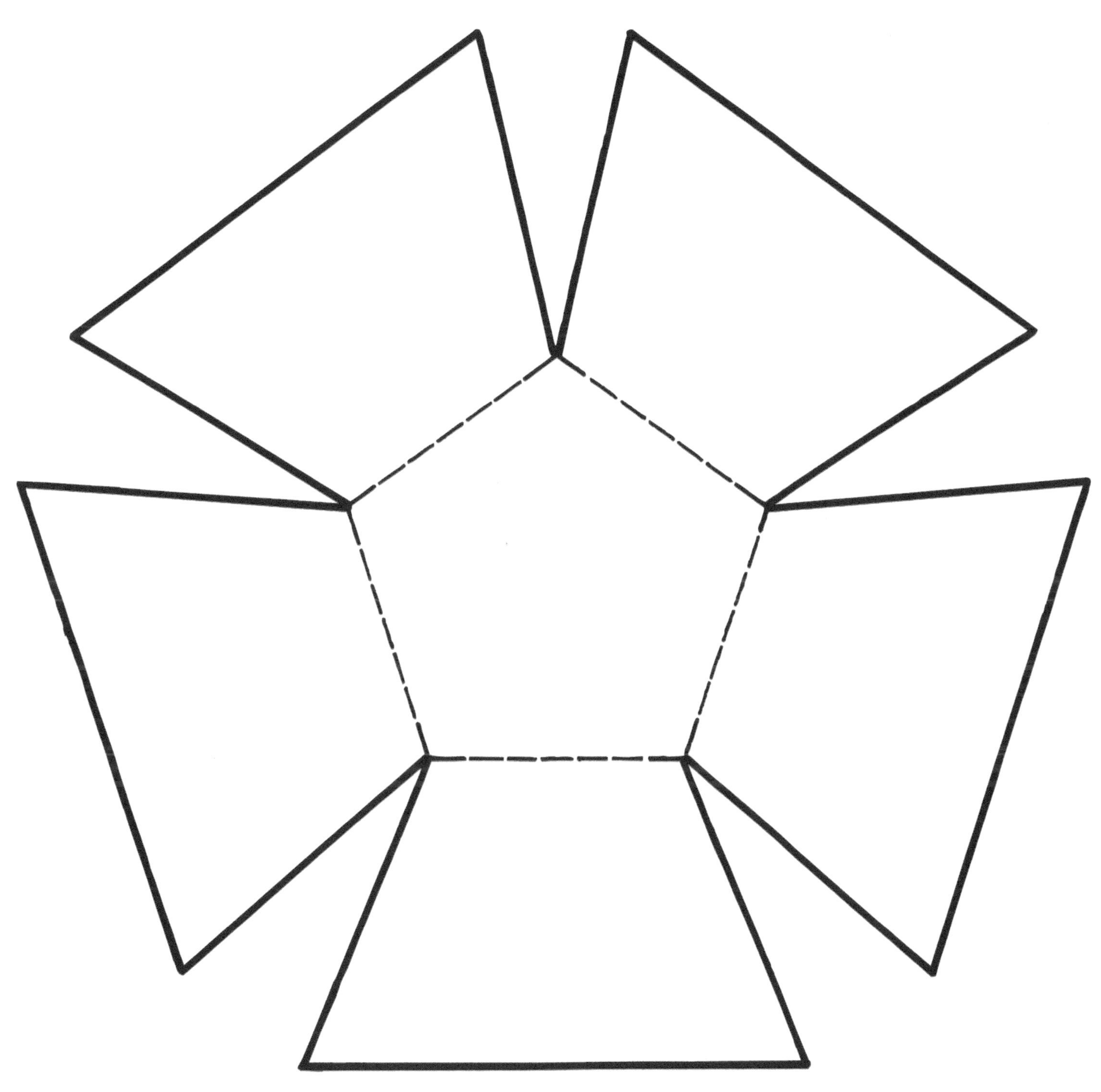

Scratch Art

Materials

- half sheets of card stock (or index cards)
- crayons (all colors, including several extra black crayons)
- paper clips
- toothpicks
- newspapers

Before Class

Cover the work area with newspaper so students can color off the edges of the card stock.

Simplification Idea

This project is easy, but can be more or less labor-intensive depending on the size of card stock or index card that you select.

Instructions for Kids

- Cover a half sheet of card stock with a strong and colorful crayon design. Be sure to completely cover the entire area, from edge to edge.
- Firmly color a thick layer of black crayon over the entire colored design.
- Use a toothpick or straightened paper clip to scratch a message or design in the black crayon so the colors underneath show through.

Talk About

How do you feel when you want to be forgiven but the other person won't forgive you? What makes you choose not to forgive someone sometimes? Encourage the students to share honest answers. **When you don't forgive others, life can feel ugly and dark, like the black color covering your scratch art design. Jesus told His disciples they should always be willing to forgive others. When you choose to forgive the way God forgives, you change from a dark life to one filled with beautiful colors. God wants us to live in color, not under a cloud of darkness.**

Feed the Pig

Materials

- pig face patterns
- lightweight cardboard
- pink chenille wires
- scissors
- white and pink craft foam (or construction paper)
- pink tissue paper
- white foam take-out boxes (1 per kid)
- black fine-tip markers
- pink crayons (or markers)
- craft glue

Before Class

Cut a square portion out of the top of each foam box, one for each student (sketch b). Trace several copies of the pig face patterns onto lightweight cardboard. Label and cut out the pieces. Cut the chenille wires in half, one half for each student.

Instructions for Kids

- Using the ear and nose cardboard patterns, trace two ears and one nose onto pink craft foam. Cut out the pieces. Trace two eyes onto white craft foam, using the eye cardboard pattern. Cut out the foam eyes.
- Squeeze a little glue onto the straight edge of each ear piece. Pinch the sides and hold them together until the glue is dry (sketch a).
- Use a black marker to make dots on the eyes and nose (sketch b).
- Color the outside of the take-out box pink. Lightly crumple the tissue paper and place it inside the box. Close the lid.
- Glue the ears, nose, and eyes onto the top portion of the box at the front opening.
- Wrap a piece of chenille wire around your finger to curl a pig's tail. Push the tip on one end of the wire into the foam at the back of the box. Glue the tail in place (sketch b).

Talk About

Jesus told a story about a son who left home and wasted all his father's money on parties. Soon the son had nothing left and had to get a job feeding pigs. When the son finally decided to go home, his father was waiting for him! God loves us like this father loved his son. Even when we do things we know are wrong, God still loves and forgives us.

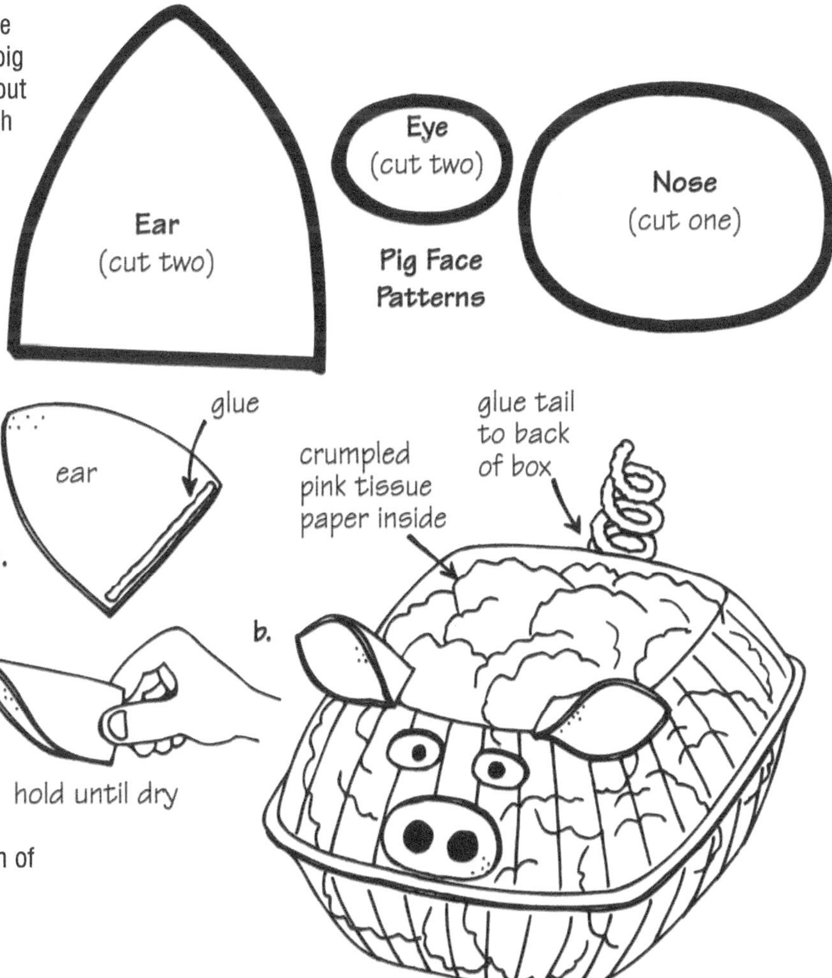

"Zacchaeus, Come Down"

Materials

- Zacchaeus and treetop patterns (p. 194)
- white and brown card stock
- brown yarn
- scissors
- ruler
- utility knife
- markers
- hole punch
- masking tape
- glue
- wood beads (2 per kid)
- green and brown craft foam *(optional)*

Before Class

Copy the Zacchaeus and treetop patterns onto white card stock. Cut out one set for each student. Use a utility knife to cut the slits in the treetop for a doorknob opening (sketch a). Cut yarn into 4' lengths, one for each student. Cut the brown card stock into tree-trunk shapes, 2" x 11", one for each student.

Instructions for Kids

- Use markers to draw and color Zacchaeus's face, hair, and clothes.

- Use markers to draw birds or leaves on the treetop. Then color the treetop.

- Punch the holes where indicated in the Zacchaeus figure and treetop.

- Wrap a small piece of masking tape around one end of a piece of yarn to make a sewing tip. Tie a double knot at the opposite end of the yarn.

- Thread one bead onto the yarn and pull the bead to the knotted end of the yarn. Make sure the knot is big enough to hold the bead in place.

- Lay the cutouts on a table with Zacchaeus below the treetop. Thread the yarn tip up through Zacchaeus's foot, hand, and the treetop holes on one side, and then down through the treetop holes and Zacchaeus's hand and foot on the other side (sketch b).

- Thread the second bead onto the yarn end. Cut off the masking tape tip and tie a double knot to secure the bead.

- Glue the tree trunk to the back of treetop, below the doorknob cutout. Allow the glue to dry.

Talk About

Show how to place the treetop opening over a doorknob. Slide Zacchaeus up to the treetop. Alternately pull down on each side of yarn to watch Zacchaeus climb down, or gently pull the yarn out to the sides to watch Zacchaeus climb up (sketch c). **Zacchaeus collected taxes. Sometimes he made the people pay more tax money than they had to. But after Zacchaeus met Jesus, Zacchaeus wanted to give back the money he had wrongfully taken—and give back more! When people learn about Jesus, their lives often change. What are some ways your life is different because you know and love Jesus?** Share a way Jesus makes a difference in your life. Encourage the kids to share their ideas.

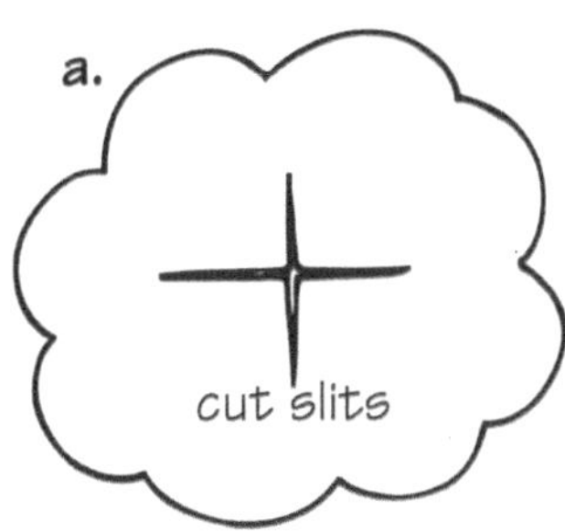
a.
cut slits

punched holes
b.
start threading here
double knot
bead
masking-tape tip

c.
glue tree trunk to back of treetop
pull down alternately

Greatest Commandment Hearts

Materials

- Bibles
- parchment paper
- markers
- ingredients for sugar dough (water, sugar, flour)
- measuring cup
- mixing bowl
- red food coloring
- peppermint extract
- various heart-shaped cookie cutters
- scissors
- ribbon
- ruler
- skewers
- oven
- baking sheets
- oven mitt
- cooling rack
- sprinkles, edible glitter, sugar pearls, etc. *(optional)*

Before Class

For each batch of sugar dough, knead together 1 c. water, 2 c. sugar, and 3 c. flour. Then add red food coloring to make red or pink dough. Add a few drops of peppermint extract to make the dough smell nice. Cut the ribbon into 8" lengths, several for each student.

Instructions for Kids

- Cover your work area with a piece of parchment paper. Use a marker to write your name on a corner of the paper.
- Pat a lump of dough out to flatten it, about 1/8" thick. Then use cookie cutters to cut heart shapes out of the dough. Prepare two or three hearts. Use a skewer to make a small hole in the top of each heart.
- Place your parchment paper with the dough on it onto a baking sheet. With a teacher's supervision, place the baking sheet in an oven that has been preheated to 300°. Bake the hearts until the dough is hard, but not burned, approximately one hour. Ask a teacher to use an oven mitt to remove the baking sheet from the oven. Set the tray on a cooling rack.
- When the hearts have cooled, string a length of ribbon through the hole in each heart. Tie the ends of the ribbon together to form a loop for hanging.

Enrichment Idea

Have the kids mix the ingredients and prepare the dough. They can press decorations into the dough before baking the hearts.

Talk About

When some teachers asked Jesus about the greatest commandment in the law, Jesus' reply included two commandments. Have the students find and read Matthew 22:37–40. **In what ways can we show love to God? How can we show love to others? Why do you think Jesus said that "all the Law and the Prophets hang on these two commandments"?** Encourage the students to think creatively about ways they can show love to God and others. Point out that if they obey these two commands, they will also be obeying other commands, such as honoring parents or not stealing.

Master's Money Bag

Materials

- muslin fabric (or faux leather)
- a variety of coins
- 1-mm leather-like cording
- awl (or hole punch)
- crayons in a variety of colors
- fabric scissors
- tape
- ruler
- pencil
- chocolate coins or play coins *(optional)*

Before Class

Use a compass to draw 9" circles on the muslin, then cut out, one for each student. Cut cording into 24" lengths and wrap tape around one end of each cord, one for each student. Use an awl to make 20 evenly spaced holes around the circle, about 1" from the edge (sketch a). Make sure the holes are large enough for students to thread the cording through.

Instructions for Kids

- Choose a coin and a crayon. Wrap a piece of muslin cloth tightly around the coin and rub the crayon across the top of the covered coin, making an imprint of the coin on the cloth (sketch b).
- Continue the crayon rubbing process all over the muslin circle, using different-size coins and different-colored crayons.
- Tie a knot in the untaped end of cord. Beginning on the side of the fabric you have colored, weave the taped end of the cord in and out of the holes (sketch c).
- Pull the ends of the cording together, gathering the muslin to form a pouch (sketch d).
- Wrap and tie the ends of the cording together.

Enrichment Idea

Give the kids some chocolate or play coins to take home in their pouches.

Talk About

Jesus told a story about a master who called three servants together and gave them his money to take care of while he was on a trip. Two of the servants used the money to make even more money for their master. The other servant buried his master's money in the ground and didn't do anything with it. Jesus told this story to teach us that He wants us to use the abilities and talents He has given to us to do good for others. Your money bag can remind you that God wants you to use the abilities He has given to you. Plan a class service project that allows the kids to use their talents and abilities to help others.

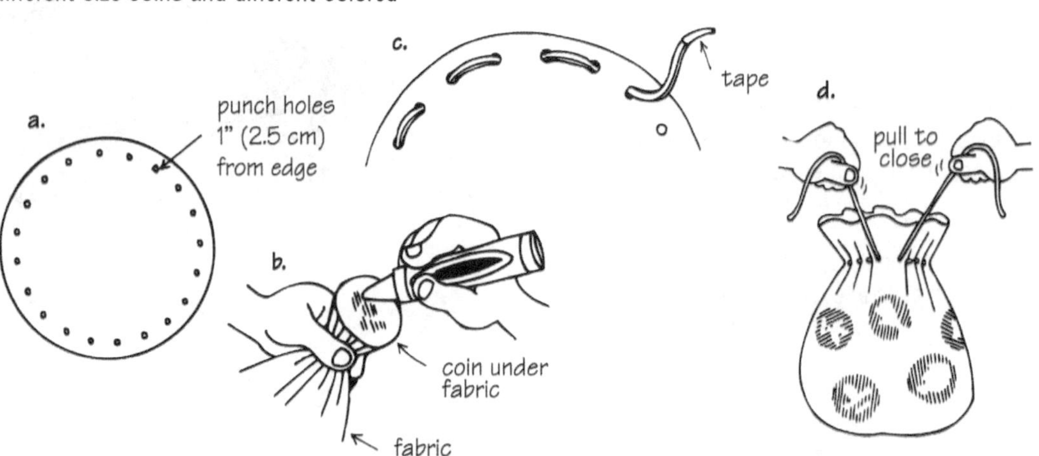

Easter Cross

Materials

- 3" x 1" green floral foam discs (1 per kid)
- felt
- red satin fabric
- pen
- fabric scissors
- heavy-duty scissors
- ruler
- jumbo craft sticks (1 per kid)
- regular craft sticks (2 per kid)
- red thread
- small artificial flowers on wire stems
- craft glue
- green modeling dough *(optional)*

Before Class

Use a green floral foam disc as a pattern and trace circles onto felt, one circle for each student. Cut out the circles. Cut red fabric into 1½" x 7" and 3" x 8" strips, one of each for each student. Use heavy-duty scissors to cut a blunt point in one end of the jumbo craft sticks, one for each student (sketch a).

Simplification Ideas

Prepare a swag for each student before class. Use lumps of green modeling dough for bases if foam discs are not available.

Instructions for Kids

- For a swag, use your fingers to gather one end of 3" x 8" fabric strip. Wrap and knot a piece of thread around the gathers. Cut off the ends of the thread. Repeat on the other end of the fabric strip. Tip: Working with a partner can make it easier to wrap and knot the thread.
- Glue the gathered ends of the fabric onto opposite ends of one regular craft stick (sketch b).
- To make a crossbeam, horizontally glue the craft stick with the swag onto the front of a jumbo stick, about ¾" from the top rounded end of the stick (sketch c). Be sure the ends of the fabric swag are facing the backside of the cross.
- Glue a second regular craft stick behind the crossbeam onto the back of the jumbo stick and over the gathered ends of the fabric swag (sketch d).
- To finish the banner, fold the long edges of the remaining fabric strip to the center to hide the raw edges. Fold the strip in half over one end of the swag and crossbeam (sketch e). Glue this piece of fabric in place.
- Glue a felt circle to the bottom of a foam circle.
- Push the assembled cross into the center of the foam circle (sketch e).
- Push stemmed flowers into the foam base around the bottom of the cross.

Talk About

The Bible tells us that when Jesus was arrested and put on trial, soldiers put a scarlet robe on Him and mocked Him, saying, "Hail, king of the Jews." They spit on Jesus and mistreated Him. The soldiers didn't realize that Jesus is the king of the Jews—and of all people! Jesus died on the cross to forgive the sins of all people. When you look at your cross, remember how Jesus was mistreated. Then think of a way you can honor Jesus for what He did for you. Lead the students in naming some ways they can honor Jesus.

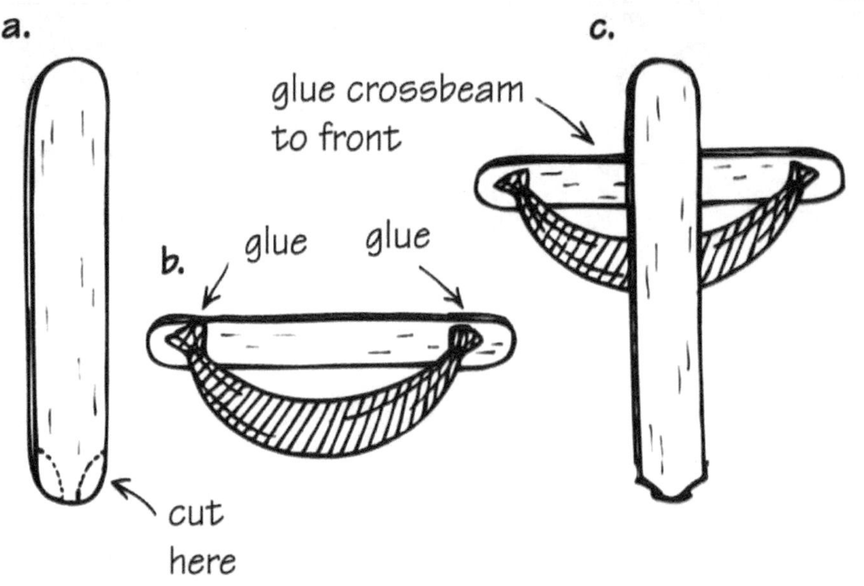
a.
b.
c.
glue
glue
glue crossbeam
to front
cut
here

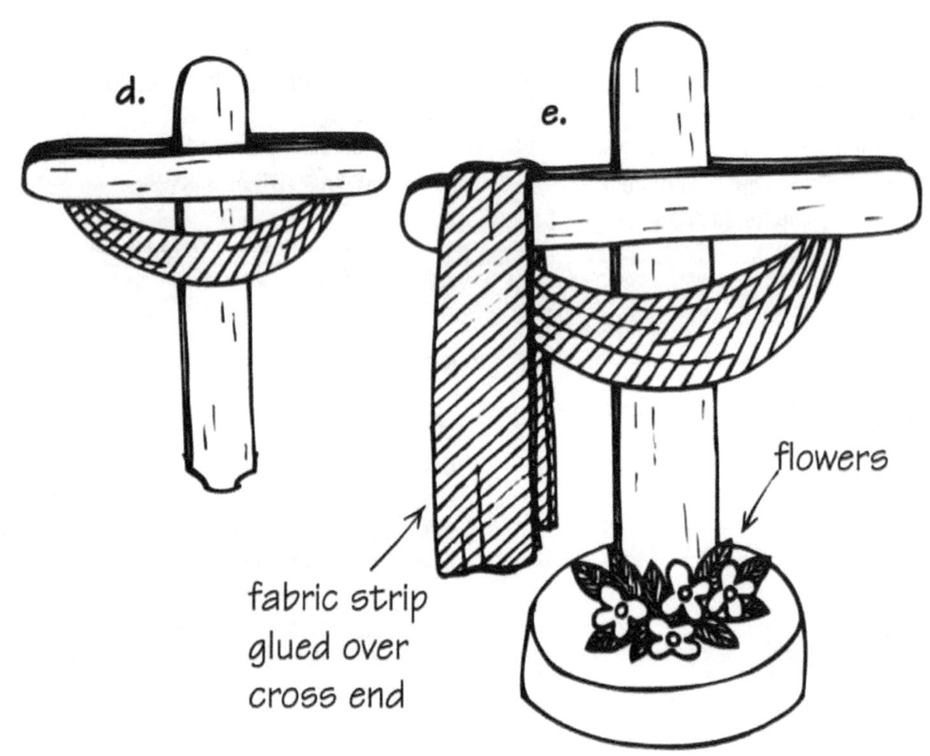
d.
e.
flowers
fabric strip
glued over
cross end

Clothespin Cross

Materials

- metallic gold thread
- 1½"-wide ribbon
- scissors
- ruler
- spring wood clothespins (5 per kid)
- craft glue
- washable markers

Before Class

Remove the springs from the clothespins. Cut the ribbon into 15" and 9" lengths, one of each for each student. Cut the metallic thread into 4" lengths, one for each student.

Instructions for Kids

- Fold 1" of a 15" piece of ribbon to the back and crease it. Then tie and knot together the ends of a piece of metallic thread.
- To form a hanger, place the tied metallic thread inside the fold of the ribbon and glue the folded portion to the back of ribbon (sketch a).
- Fold a 9" piece of ribbon in half lengthwise to find the midpoint. Glue the midpoint of the shorter ribbon across the longer ribbon about 5" from the top, forming a cross (sketch b).
- Use markers to color the clothespins, if desired. Glue four clothespin pieces (two pieces side by side with the flat sides down) onto the horizontal bar of the ribbon. Repeat this procedure on the vertical bar of the ribbon, using six clothespin pieces (sketch c).

Talk About

Why do you think Jesus died on a cross? Why do you think He rose again from the dead? Accepting the students' honest answers will give insight into what they understand about Jesus' death and resurrection. **Jesus' death and resurrection were part of God's loving plan to forgive our sins and give us eternal life. What can we do to show our thanks to God for the gift of salvation through Jesus?** Encourage the kids to name ways they can show thanks to God through their worship and in their daily lives.

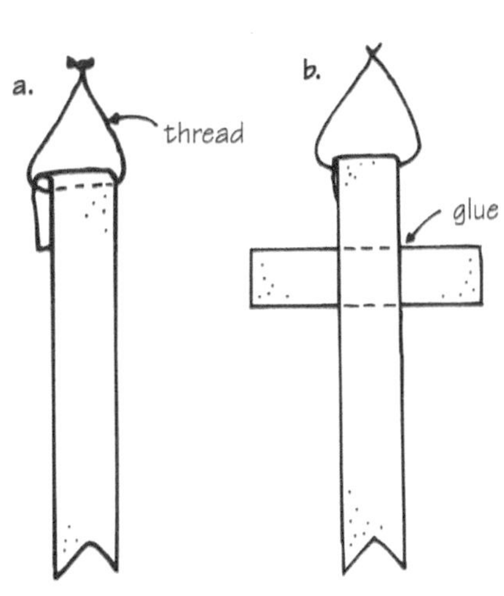

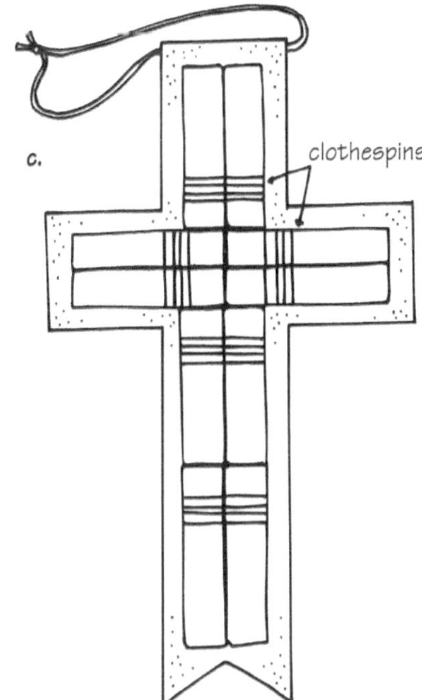

Top Secret Certainty

Materials

- white paper
- lemon juice
- measuring spoons
- water
- baking soda
- blue food coloring
- small cups
- cotton swabs
- newspapers
- small paintbrushes *(optional)*

Before Class

Measure lemon juice into small containers, four teaspoons in each cup. Prepare a cup for each student. Cover the work area with newspaper to absorb excess liquid.

Instructions for Kids

- Decide on a message you want to write on a sheet of paper. You might write "Jesus is alive" or "I believe!" Don't tell anyone else what you are writing.

- Lay a sheet of paper on the table. Dip a cotton swab into the lemon juice and then write the first letter of your phrase. Re-dip after every one or two letters, until you have written the entire message (sketch a). Don't get too much liquid on the paper. Keep the paper lying flat so the liquid doesn't run and make the letters unreadable.

- When finished writing, keep the paper flat until the liquid is completely dry.

- In another cup, mix four tablespoons water and two teaspoons baking soda. Add six to eight drops of food coloring (sketch b).

- To reveal the message, after the lemon juice is completely dry, dip a cotton swab (or paintbrush) into the baking soda, water, and food coloring mixture and paint it over the page (sketch c). You will need to dip into the mixture several times to cover most of the page.

Enrichment Idea

Students might have fun swapping papers to discover a message that someone else has written.

Talk About

It can be fun to prove something to a person who doubts you. You can try that with your secret messages. Once you reveal your writing, no one can doubt that you really did write something invisible. The disciples had some doubts about Jesus' resurrection—until Jesus appeared to them! Imagine you are one of the disciples after the resurrection. What proof would you need that Jesus was really alive again? (Possible answers: touch Him, see Him, hear Him talk, ask Him questions, etc.) **What truth about Jesus, God, or the Bible do you have a hard time believing?** Students will have a variety of responses. Acknowledge their honest questions. Assure them that it is okay to have these questions, but they should know that God's Word is true. They can believe and trust God and Jesus with every aspect of their lives.

lemon juice
Believe
a.

blue food coloring
baking soda
water
b.

Believe
baking soda, blue food coloring and water mixture
c.

Happy Healed Man

Materials

- Happy Healed Man patterns (p. 203)
- yarn (brown, black, or gray)
- scissors
- ruler
- white card stock
- large rubber bands (4 per kid)
- crayons
- markers
- glue
- stapler and staples
- scissors
- ruler
- hole punch

Before Class

Copy the body, feet, and hands patterns onto card stock, one set for each student. Cut the yarn into 2' lengths, one for each student.

Instructions for Kids

- Use crayons or markers to color the face, clothes, hands, and feet. You may want to add details, such as stripes or designs on the clothes, fingers on the hands, or sandals on the feet.
- Cut out the Happy Healed Man's body, feet, and hands.
- Cut short pieces of yarn and glue them onto the face to make hair and/or a beard.
- Cut open four rubber bands. With a teacher's help, staple a rubber band to each hand and foot (sketch a). Then staple the opposite end of each rubber band to the appropriate part of the body (sketch b).
- Use a hole punch to punch a hole in the top center of the head.
- Cut a length of yarn and thread it through the hole. Tie the ends together to make a hanging loop (sketch b).

Talk About

When Peter and John went to the temple at the time of prayer, a man who could not walk asked them for money. Peter gave the man something much better than money—Peter healed the man through the name and power of Jesus! The Bible tells us in Acts 3:9 that the man went with Peter and John "walking and jumping and praising God." When has God done something special for you or someone you know? What can we do or say to tell others about God's great love and power? Encourage students to share. Help the kids understand that God might not heal a disability or illness, but He will give us what we need to live joyfully each day.

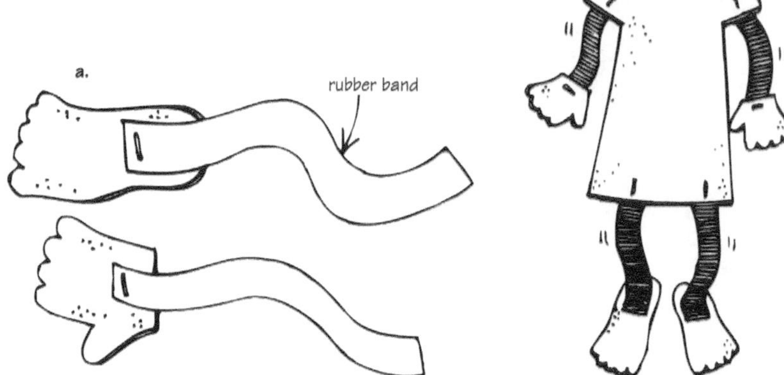

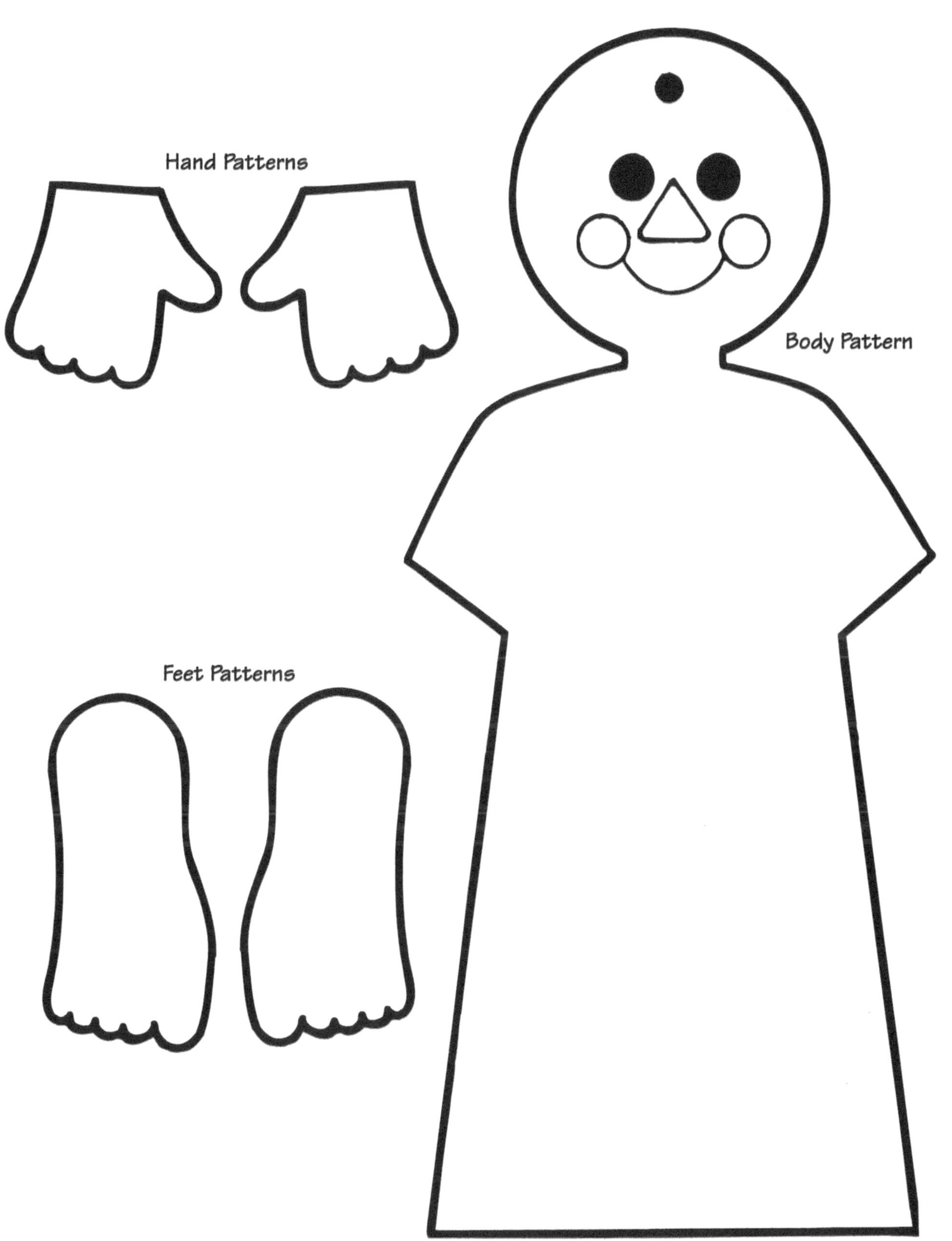
Hand Patterns
Body Pattern
Feet Patterns

Good News Message Carrier

Materials

- yarn
- leather-like cording
- fringe fabric trim
- scissors
- ruler
- paper towel tubes (1 per kid)
- construction paper in various colors
- tape
- faux jewels
- masking tape
- hole punch
- paper
- colored pencils

Before Class

Cut the yarn into 6" lengths, several for each student. Cut the cording into 2' lengths, one for each student. Cut the fringe into 6" lengths, one for each student.

Instructions for Kids

- Cut a sheet of construction paper to cover a tube, and then tape the paper in place.
- Place two pieces of masking tape crisscross over one end of the tube (sketch a). Glue a piece of fringe around the taped end, hiding the ends of the tape (sketch b).
- Punch two holes at the top of the message carrier (sketch c). Thread an end of the leather cording through each hole and knot the ends.
- Glue yarn pieces and jewels onto the tube to decorate it (sketch d).
- With paper and colored pencils, write a message about Jesus or draw a picture to give to someone. Roll up the paper and carry it in the message carrier.

Talk About

Have you ever sent or received an important message? How did you receive the message—by phone, mail, or another way? Allow kids to share. **In Bible times, people often carried important papers by rolling them up and placing them inside special containers. In Acts 8 we read about Philip, a disciple of Jesus, who traveled around taking a message of good news to people. Philip told people the good news about Jesus! What good news about Jesus can we share with others? How can we share that good news?**

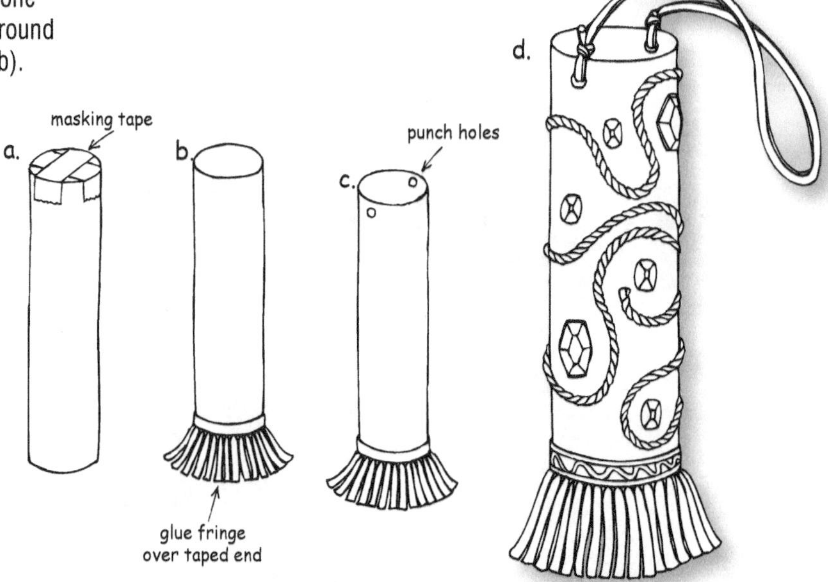

Peter's Storybook

Materials

- Peter's Storybook pictures (p. 206)
- letter-size manila file folders
- string
- scissors
- ruler
- pencil
- hole punch
- white copy paper
- crayons (or markers or colored pencils)
- glue
- craft sticks (5 per kid)
- paper fasteners (1 per kid)
- old keys (1 per kid)

Before Class

Cut 1" off the tabbed side of each file folder and discard it. Then cut the folders in half to make small books, one half for each student (sketch a). Punch a hole through the back page of each book, near the edge of the right side (sketch b). Copy the Peter's Storybook pictures onto white paper, one set for each student. Cut the string into 8" lengths, one for each student.

Instructions for Kids

- Color the Peter's Storybook pictures and cut them out along the bold lines.
- Glue the picture of Peter onto the front center of the book (sketch b).
- Open up the book and glue the verse on the inside left-hand page. Glue the picture of Peter and Rhoda on the right-hand page (sketch c).
- Draw and color blocks of stone around the picture on the front of the book (sketch d).
- Use black or gray crayons to color one side of five craft sticks. With the colored side up, glue the craft sticks vertically across the front picture to make prison bars (sketch d).
- Push a paper fastener through the front page of the book, near the right edge. Spread the ends of the paper fastener apart on the inside left-hand page.
- Tie one end of a length of string to the hole on the back page of the book. Tie the other end of the string to a key. To keep the storybook closed, coil the string around the paper fastener (sketch e).

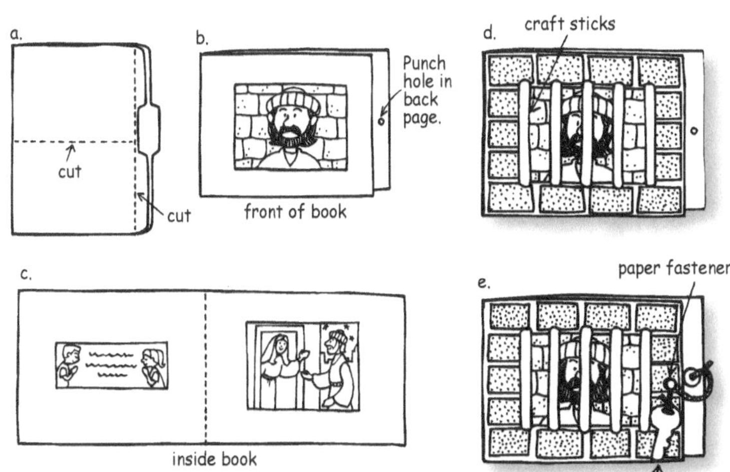

Talk About

Peter had been put into prison because of his faith in Jesus. Peter may have felt lonely or sad or afraid. What can we do when we're lonely, sad, or afraid? (Talk to a friend or an adult who you trust. Pray to God.) **God heard the prayers of Peter's friends and sent an angel to lead Peter out of the prison. You can pray for others too. God hears your prayers.**

"The Lord
will hear when
I call to him."
Psalm 4:3

"God Bless Our Home" Banner

Materials

- navy (or black) felt
- fabric scraps and ribbons in a variety of colors
- white (or silver) satin fabric
- fabric scissors
- ruler
- pencil
- silver or gold sequins
- ½" wood dowels
- saw
- sewing machine (or needle) and thread
- yarn
- fine-tip permanent markers
- craft glue

Before Class

Cut felt into 9" x 11" rectangles, one for each student. Fold over about 1" at the top of each felt rectangle and stitch close to the edge to make a casing (sketch a). Cut the ribbon into 5" lengths, three for each student. Saw dowels into 1' lengths, one for each student. Draw 3" to 4" stars onto white fabric. Cut out one for each student.

Simplification Idea

Cut fabric scraps into a variety of geometric shapes ahead of time.

Instructions for Kids

- Cut and lay out fabric scraps onto a felt banner to look like your home (sketch b). Glue the pieces in place.

- Use markers to print a message on a fabric star, such as "God bless our home."

- Choose three ribbons. Glue the star at the top corner of the banner, attaching the ends of the ribbons underneath the star (sketch b). Glue sequins onto the banner for additional stars.

- Slide a dowel through the casing at the top of the banner. Cut a piece of yarn to the desired length for a banner hanger. Tie the ends of the yarn onto the ends of the dowel to make the hanger.

Talk About

It was nighttime. An earthquake shook the jail and the chains fell off the prisoners, but none of the prisoners left. When the jailer asked Paul and Silas what he needed to do to be saved, Paul told the jailer about Jesus. The jailer invited Paul and Silas to his house. The jailer and his family were baptized and became followers of Jesus! What can you tell your family about Jesus? How can you show God's love to your family? Allow the students to share their ideas. Remind the kids that God is always with them. They can ask God to help their families and to keep their families safe.

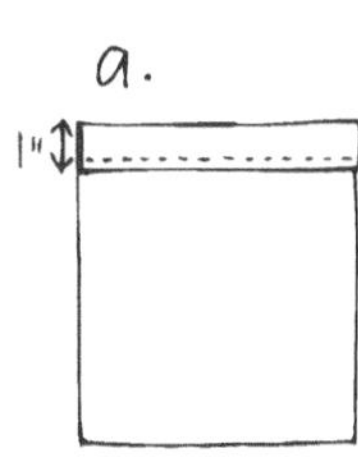

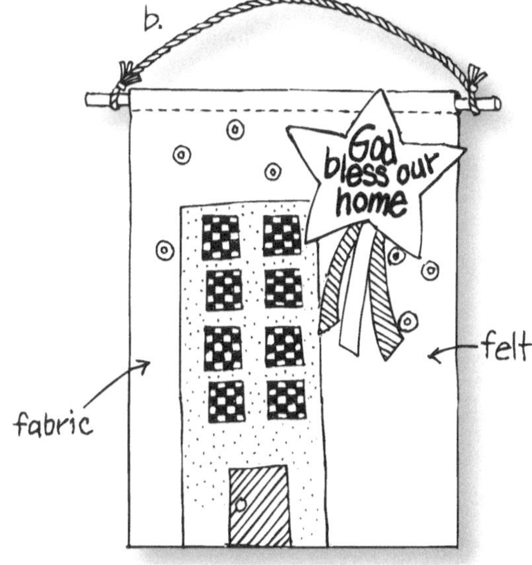

Feather Pen and Message

Materials

- Bible
- envelope pattern (p. 209)
- white electrical tape
- large feathers (1 per kid)
- ballpoint pens (or markers, 1 per kid)
- ivory-colored copy paper (or parchment paper)
- scissors
- colored candles
- matches
- embossed metal buttons with shanks
- newspapers

Before Class

Copy the envelope pattern onto the copy paper, one for each student. Cover the work area with newspaper.

Instructions for Kids

- Cut a length of white tape approximately 12". Holding the pen next to the feather, start at the bottom of the pen and wrap the tape up and around the pen and feather quill to fasten them together securely. Make sure you don't cover the tip of the pen (sketch a).
- Halfway up the pen, stop wrapping both the feather and pen together, but continue to wrap only the pen until it is covered (sketch b). Cut more tape if needed.
- Cut out a paper envelope. Inside the dotted-line area on the envelope, use your feather pen to write a message of encouragement or draw a picture to give to someone.
- Fold the envelope along the dotted lines, with the lines and message showing inside of the envelope. Fold the bottom flap up and the two side flaps in. Then fold the top flap down to close the envelope (sketch c).
- Turn the envelope over and write, in the blank area, the name of the person who will receive the letter.
- Turn the envelope back over. With a teacher's help, light a candle and hold it over where the flaps meet. Allow the candle wax to drip and form a circle. Let the wax cool slightly and then press a metal button into the wax to make a seal. Carefully lift off the button to see the impression (sketch d).

Talk About

What are some ways we send or share messages? (email, phone, mail, text, etc.) **The apostle Paul wrote letters to people who were part of the church. Paul often told the people that he thanked God for them.** Read 1 Corinthians 1:4. **The letters taught the people about God, Jesus, and the Holy Spirit. Paul liked to sign the letters himself.** Read 1 Corinthians 16:21. **Paul may have used a feather quill pen and ink to sign his letters.** Pray and thank God for the people who will receive the messages written by the students. Encourage students to deliver their messages.

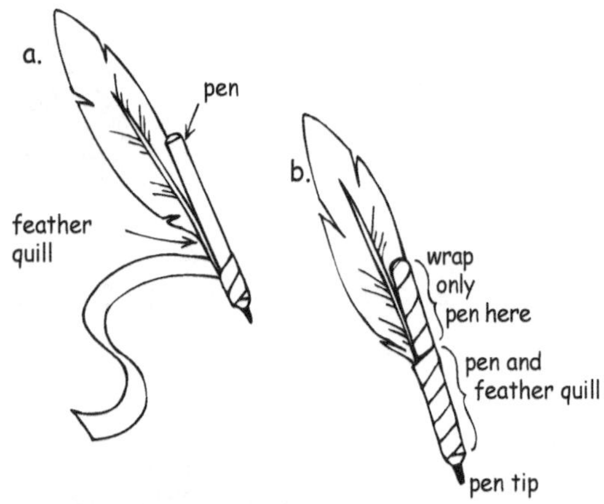

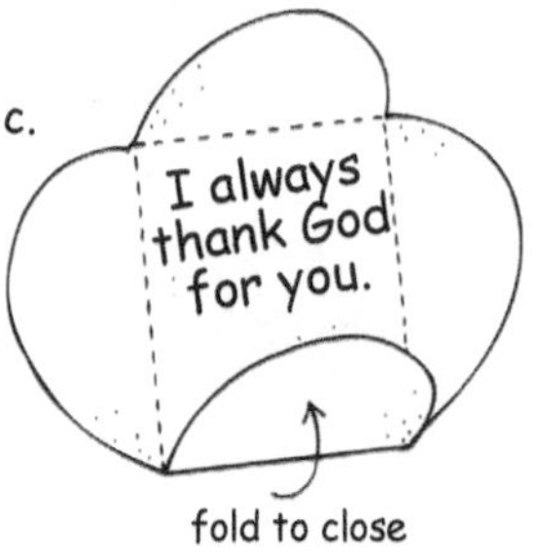

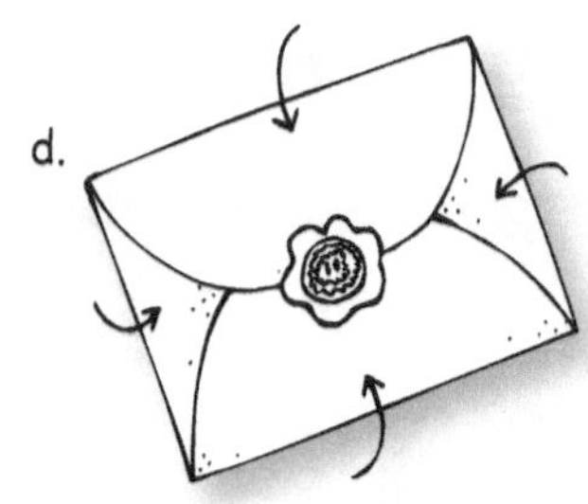

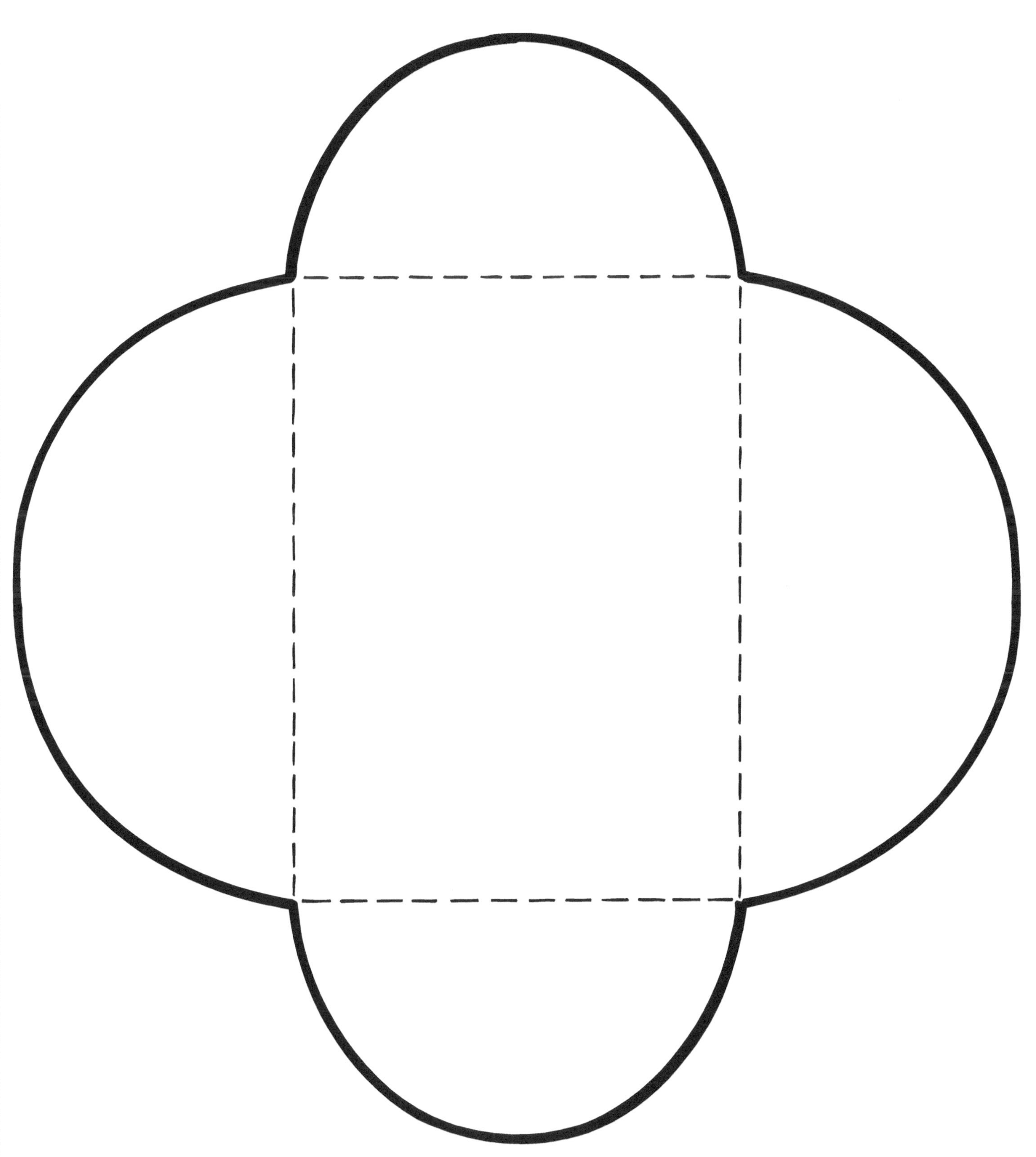

New Creation Butterfly

Materials

- Bibles
- tissue paper in a variety of bright colors
- scissors
- ruler
- chenille wires
- large round-head wood clothespins (1 per kid)
- fine-tip permanent markers
- glue

Before Class

Cut tissue paper into pieces the following sizes: 4" x 6", 5" x 6", 6" x 6", and 6" x 7", one of each for each student. If possible, provide a variety of colors, so students can choose their own color combinations and each person's butterfly will be unique.

Instructions for Kids

- Use a marker to print "2 Corinthians 5:17" along the front prong of a clothespin. Draw eyes and a mouth on the head of the clothespin.

- Select four different-size sheets of tissue paper to use for the butterfly's wings. Lay the tissue sheets one on top of the other, with the largest on the bottom and the smallest on top (sketch a).

- Slide the tissue sheets between the prongs of the clothespin. Gather the tissue so it is about 1" from the bottom of the clothespin (sketch b). Add a drop of glue at the bottom of the tissue to hold it in place.

- Bend a chenille wire in half. Place the center at the front "neck" of the butterfly, and wrap the wire around the neck. Twist the wire at the back of the neck, extending the ends evenly upward behind the head of the butterfly. Curl the ends of the wire to make antennae.

Talk About

Who can tell me what is special about a butterfly? Lead students to tell the process a caterpillar goes through to become a butterfly. **The Bible says when we believe in Jesus, we change into something new! We don't look different on the outside, but we are different inside because God's Spirit comes into our lives and helps us become more like Him.** Have the students find 2 Corinthians 5:17 in their Bibles. Repeat the verse several times and encourage the kids to keep the butterflies where they can serve as reminders of this Bible truth.

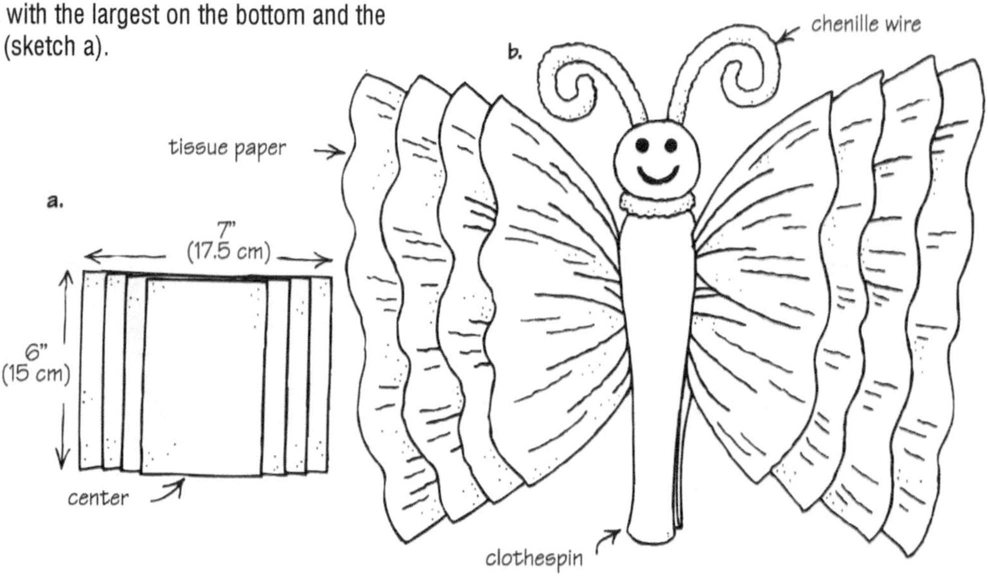

Seed Packet Bookmark

Materials

- Bibles
- unlined index cards (5 per kid)
- narrow ribbons in five colors
- scissors
- ruler
- empty seed packets (1 per kid)
- washable markers
- crayons (or colored pencils)
- tape
- whiteboard and dry-erase marker

Before Class

Cut the index cards to fit inside the seed packets. Cut the ribbon into 15" lengths, one of each color for each student. Write on a whiteboard the qualities of the fruit of the Spirit and any Scripture references that kids will be finding in their Bibles.

Instructions for Kids

- On individual index cards, print the first five qualities of the fruit of the Spirit listed in Galatians 5:22: love, joy, peace, forbearance (patience), and kindness (sketch a). Draw a simple picture to illustrate the quality named on each card.
- Tie the ends of five ribbons together, leaving 1" below the knot (sketch b). Tape the ribbons onto the back of a seed packet, 2" above the knot (sketch c).
- Place the index cards inside the seed packet, and then place the bookmark inside your Bible to mark Galatians 5:22–23.
- Use the ribbons to mark a verse for the first five qualities of the fruit of the Spirit. (love—Philippians 1:9; joy—1 Peter 1:8; peace—Hebrews 12:14; patience—Ephesians 4:2; kindness—Ephesians 4:32)

Talk About

What are the first five qualities of the fruit of the Spirit? (love, joy, peace, patience [forbearance], kindness) **Which of these qualities are the hardest for you to show?** Accept kids' answers. **When God's Holy Spirit lives inside us, He helps us grow in these qualities. Every time you open your Bible and see the seed packet bookmark, try to name the fruit of the Spirit. Look inside the seed packet to check that you are correct. Pray and ask God to help you show these qualities at home, school, or wherever you go.**

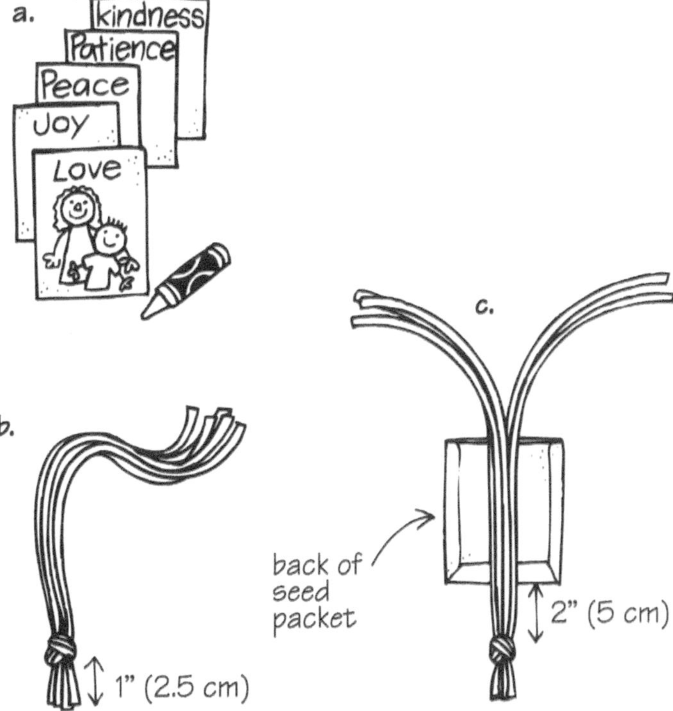

"Put It into Practice" Catch Can

Materials

- Bibles
- large frozen juice cans (1 per kid)
- construction paper in various colors
- string (or yarn)
- scissors
- ruler
- ¾" wood beads (1 per kid)
- tape
- markers
- hole punch
- decorative stickers
- whiteboard and dry-erase marker

Before Class

Cut 2¾" off the top of each juice can; discard the cutoff portion (sketch a). Cut construction paper into rectangles that will wrap around the cans, one for each student. Cut the string into 14" lengths, one for each student. Wrap a piece of tape around one end of each length of string and tie a knot at the other end. Print "Philippians 4:9" on the whiteboard.

Instructions for Kids

- Print "Philippians 4:9" on a construction paper rectangle. Use markers and stickers to decorate around the Scripture reference. Then wrap the decorated paper around a can and tape it in place.
- With a teacher's help, punch a hole near the top edge of the can.
- Thread a bead onto a length of string and slide the bead just above the knot. With a teacher's help, tie a knot to secure the bead in place at the end of the string (sketch b).
- Thread the opposite end of the string through the hole you made in the can and tie a knot in the string, attaching it to the can (sketch c).

Talk About

Holding the can in one hand, flip the bead up and try to catch it inside can. Allow the kids to do so. **Catching the bead in the can looks simple, but it takes practice. The more you practice, the easier it gets.** Read aloud Philippians 4:9. **Why is it important to "put into practice" the good qualities and teachings we learn from parents, teachers, or other adults in our lives? What have you learned about the Christian life that you need to put into practice?** Lead the students in a discussion. Challenge them to say the Bible verse from memory as they play with their Catch Cans.

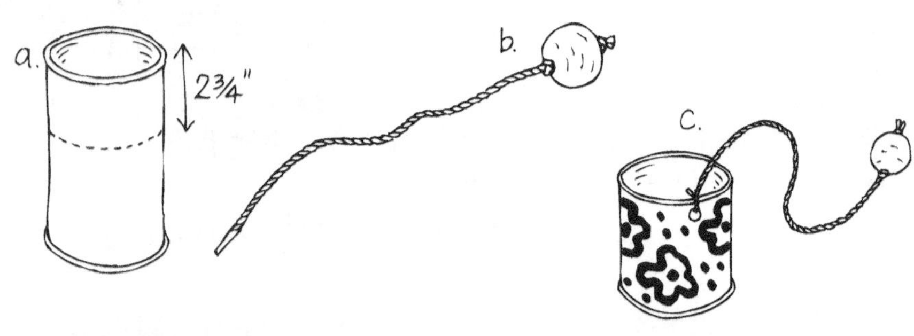

Sculpture of Honor

Materials

- Bible
- shallow boxes (or heavy cardboard or plastic bowls, 1 per kid)
- assorted items for construction (foil, bubble wrap, foam packing peanuts, paper tubes, straws, chenille wires, empty spools, fake fur, beads, bottle caps, plastic bottles, small jugs or vases, corks, wire, bolts with nuts and washers, large screws, nails, pinecones, twigs, acorns, shells, driftwood, small stones, artificial flowers, etc.)
- scissors
- craft glue
- hot-glue gun and hot-glue sticks
- newspapers
- unlined index cards
- pens

Before Class

Cover the work area with newspaper. Spread out the construction items on tables so the kids can see what's available to them. Recruit additional adults to operate the hot-glue guns. You will need one adult for every two or three students.

Instructions for Kids

- Position a box or bowl upside down, or use a piece of cardboard as a base to construct a sculpture.

- Choose assorted items that you can twist, wire, or glue together to build a trophy-like sculpture. Start with larger pieces near the bottom for more strength and stability. A teacher will help if the pieces need to be attached with hot glue.

- Use an index card and pen to make a title plaque for your sculpture. Include the name of the leader or person you intend to honor, the date, and a few words of appreciation or respect. Attach the card to the sculpture.

Talk About

In what ways have the leaders in your life helped you learn to follow Jesus? Allow time for the students to think and respond. Read 1 Thessalonians 5:12–13. **The sculptures you made are one-of-a-kind creations that will show appreciation to some of the leaders who have helped you grow in Christ. Besides presenting trophies to them, how can you show honor to these leaders?** Be sure the kids have the opportunity to deliver their trophies.

"Set an Example" Bookmark

Materials

- Bible
- bookmark patterns (pp. 215–216)
- card stock in a variety of colors
- scissors
- gold and silver permanent markers
- sequins
- glue
- colored markers
- pens (or pencils)
- individual photo of each kid *(optional)*

Before Class

Choose from bookmark design 1 or design 2 for your class. Copy those bookmark pieces onto colored card stock. If you are using photos, trim around the outline of each student's photo.

Instructions for Kids

- Choosing contrasting colors, cut out a front and a back bookmark piece.
- In the spaces on the bookmark front piece, complete the information and tell about yourself.
- Lay the back piece of the bookmark on the table, with the printed side down. Draw a picture (or glue on a photo) of yourself at the top of this blank side (sketch a).
- Glue the bookmark front piece onto the blank side of the bookmark back piece, below your picture (sketch b).
- Decorate the bookmark front and back with markers and sequins (sketches c and d).

Talk About

When have you done something just because you saw someone else do it? What did you do? Allow the kids to share. Read aloud 1 Timothy 4:12. **Paul knew people were watching the followers of Jesus. Paul wanted Timothy to know how important it is to set a godly example for others to see—even when we are young. We should be careful of what we say and how we say it. We should act in ways that are pleasing to and honor God. We are to love God and others. What is a way you can set a good example for others to follow at home? At school? At church?** Encourage the kids to memorize the Bible verse printed on their bookmarks.

back bookmark piece · front bookmark piece · finished bookmark · back of bookmark

younger elementary bookmark patterns

bookmark back

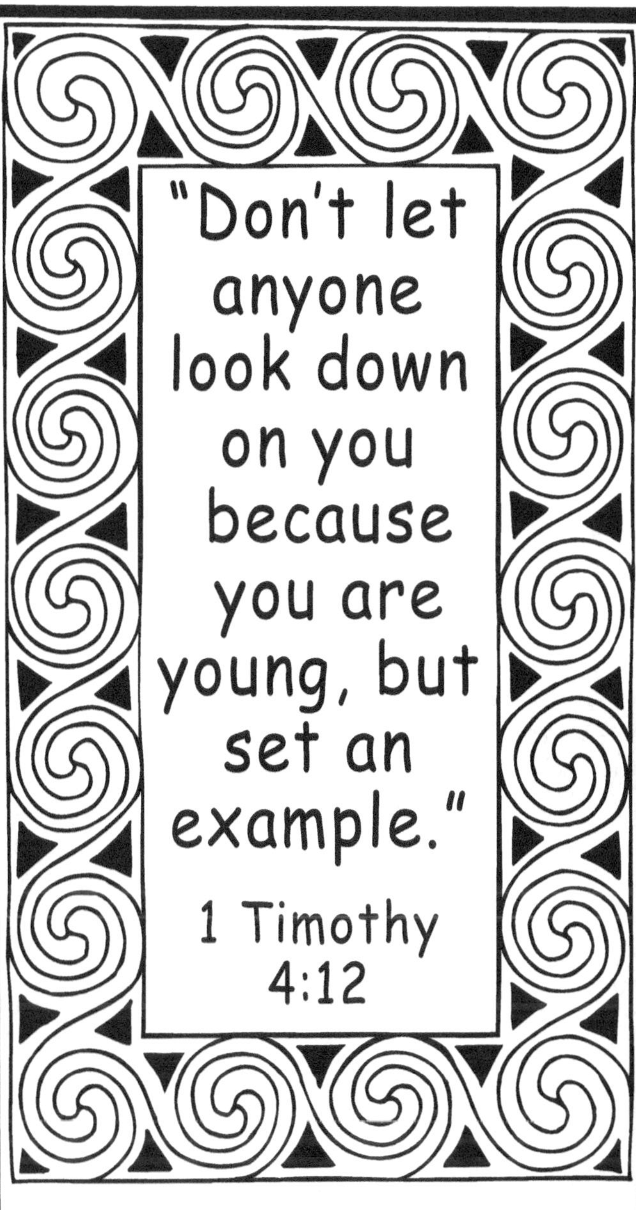

bookmark front

I am ______ years old.

I like to

My favorite food is

God Made Me!

older elementary bookmark patterns

bookmark back

bookmark front

"Don't let anyone look down on you because you are young, but set an example."

1 Timothy 4:12

I am _____ years old.

I like to

My favorite food is

God Made Me!

Fabulous Flipbook

Materials

- 8½" x 11" copy paper (5 sheets per kid)
- scissors (or paper cutter)
- pencils
- markers
- crayons
- pens
- construction paper
- stapler and staples

Before Class

Cut the copy paper into fourths (4¼" x 5½" rectangles). Cut enough so that each student has 20 pages.

Instructions for Kids

- Plan a sequence of up to 20 simple scenes showing minor changes from one to another that will appear to move as animation when flipping rapidly through all the scenes.
- Using a pencil, sketch your first scene on a piece of paper. Once you are satisfied with the drawing, trace over it with a pen or marker so the details show clearly.
- Stack a second paper on top of the first paper, then use the pencil to trace the first scene to make your second scene. Make a change, showing a small, but noticeable difference in the position or location of something in the scene. When you're happy with that page, trace over it with the pen or marker.
- Stack a third paper on top of the second scene and add or change something like you did in the previous step.
- Continue stacking, tracing, and making minor changes until your sequence is complete. Be sure to number the pages as you go, keeping page 1 on the bottom.
- Use construction paper to make front and back covers for the book. Be sure to include the illustrator's name!
- Square up your stack of papers. Be sure the first page is on the bottom and the last page is on top. Staple the edge to bind the pages together as a book.
- Hold the binding and flip rapidly through the pages, back to front, to see your animated story.

Talk About

What did you like or dislike about making a flipbook? Was it hard to trace the pictures and draw exactly what you wanted? Allow the kids to share. Read 2 Timothy 3:16–17. **If you thought making a short book with just pictures was hard work, think about how much time and work the writers of the Bible put in! The Bible was written by the direction of God's Holy Spirit, and it was meant for you and me.** Encourage the kids to read God's Word regularly so they will be ready to share it with others.

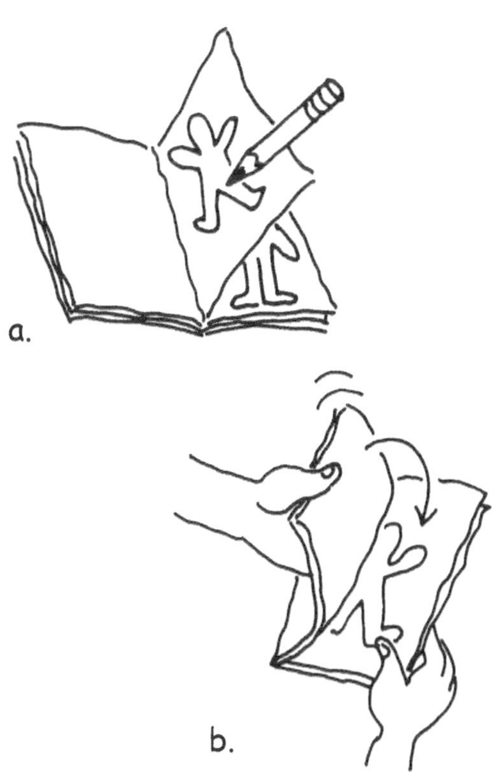

Faith Catcher

Materials

- Bible
- Faith Catcher pattern (p. 220)
- white copy paper
- scissors
- colored markers

Before Class

Copy the pattern onto white paper, one for each student.

Instructions for Kids

- Cut out a Faith Catcher on the solid line. Color each hot air balloon with a different color marker. Lay the paper on a table with the printed side down.
- Fold the Faith Catcher in half on the center dotted line. Open the paper. Then fold the paper in half in the opposite direction. Open the paper (sketch a).
- Fold each corner to the middle of the back side of the paper on the dotted lines (sketch b).
- Turn the folded paper over and fold the corners into the middle of square on dotted lines, covering the Bible verses (sketch c).
- Fold the paper in half. Open and fold it in half in the opposite direction (sketch d). Open it. The faith words should be showing on top.
- Slip your thumbs and pointer fingers into the folded pockets of the game under the balloons (sketch e), folding the points upward to hide the faith words inside. Move your fingers back and forth and side to side to make the game open and close.

To Play the Game

1. Hold up the Faith Catcher and ask a partner to pick a colored balloon.
2. Open the catcher in opposite directions for each letter as you spell that color. Keep the catcher open on the last letter.
3. Have your partner look down into the Faith Catcher and choose one of the four words of faith. Open the catcher in opposite directions as you spell that word.
4. Have your partner choose another word of faith. Take the catcher off your fingers and gently lift the flap that word is printed on to read the verse under the word.
5. Fold the flap back inside the Faith Catcher and play the game again, this time letting your partner move the catcher.

Enrichment Idea

After playing several times, see if the kids can say the verses under the flaps without looking at them!

Talk About

Hebrews 11 tells about some great men and women who had hope and trusted God even when they didn't know how God was going to do what He said He would do. Read Hebrews 11:1. **We can grow to be people of faith as we learn God's Word and trust Him to keep His promises to us.** Give the kids time to play with their Faith Catchers.

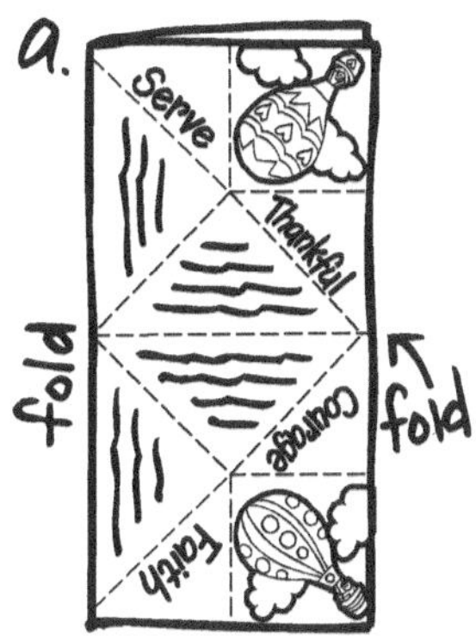
a.
Serve
Thankful
Courage
Faith
fold
fold

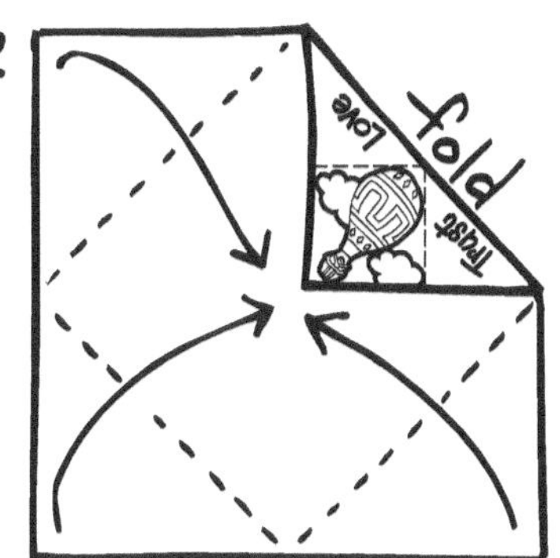
b.
Love
Trust
fold

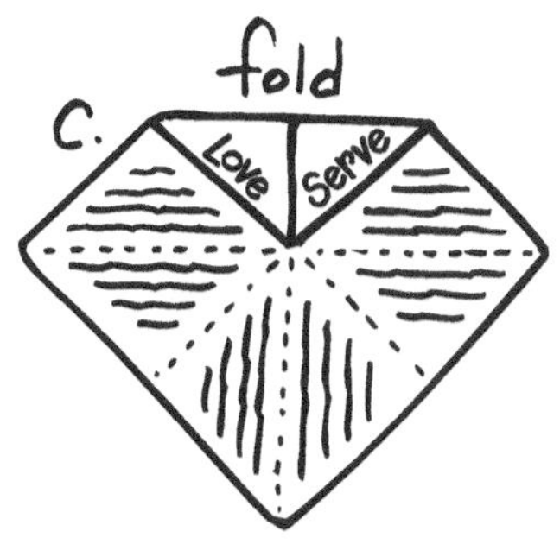
fold
c.
Love
Serve

d.
fold

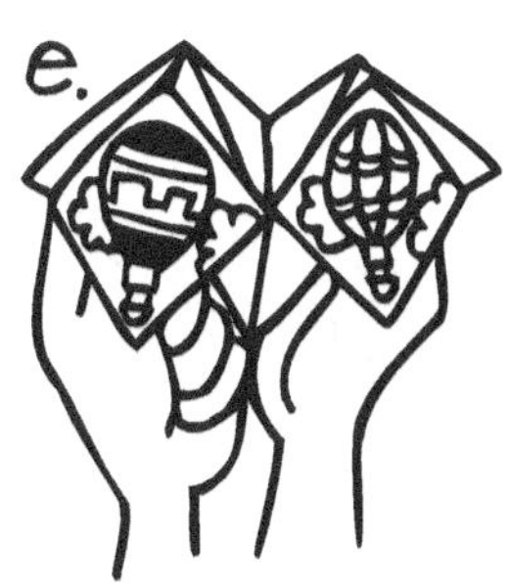
e.

Love
Serve
Trust
Thankful
Do Good
Courage
Believe
Faith
"The only thing that counts is faith expressing itself through love." Galatians 5:6
"Do not be afraid...do not turn away from the Lord, but serve the Lord with all your heart." 1 Samuel 12:20
"And we know that in all things God works for the good of those who love him, who have been called according to his purpose." Romans 8:28
"Just as you received Christ Jesus as Lord, continue to live in him, rooted and built up in him, strengthened in the faith as you were taught, and overflowing with thankfulness." Colossians 2:6–7
"Trust in the Lord and do good. Commit your way to the Lord." Psalm 37:3, 5
"Be strong and courageous. Do not be afraid...for the Lord your God goes with you; he will never leave you nor forsake you." Deuteronomy 31:6
"For God so loved the world that he gave his one and only Son, that whoever believes in him shall not perish but have eternal life." John 3:16
"Now faith is being sure of what we hope for and certain of what we do not see." Hebrews 11:1

Prayer Journal

Materials

- Bible
- white poster board
- utility knife
- ruler
- pointed scissors
- hole punch
- white copy paper
- glue
- paper fasteners (2 per kid)

Before Class

Cut some of the poster board into 9" x 13" rectangles, one for each student. Use a utility knife to score two lines ½" apart on each piece of poster board. Use pointed scissors to make two holes 3" from the outside edges and ½" below second scored line (sketch a). Punch two holes at the top of the sheets of paper (the same distance apart as the holes in the poster board, approximately 15 sheets for each student). Cut the remaining poster board into 9" x 12" rectangles, one for each student.

Instructions for Kids

- Draw a picture or design on the smaller poster-board piece.
- Fold the larger poster-board piece along the score lines.
- Glue the top edge of the small poster board onto the front flap of the larger poster board (sketch b).
- Stack the plain paper inside the journal. Aligning the holes, push paper fasteners up though the holes in the back of the journal and the holes in the paper (sketch c).

Talk About

Read 1 John 5:14. **God wants us to spend time with Him in prayer. He listens to us when we pray out loud. He hears the prayers we think silently. He even knows the prayers we write to Him. God always listens!** Encourage the students to write (or draw pictures) in their prayer journals the names of people they want to pray for or things they want to pray about.

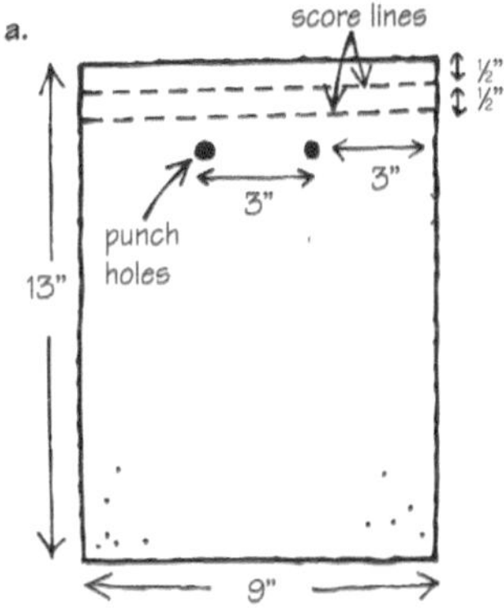

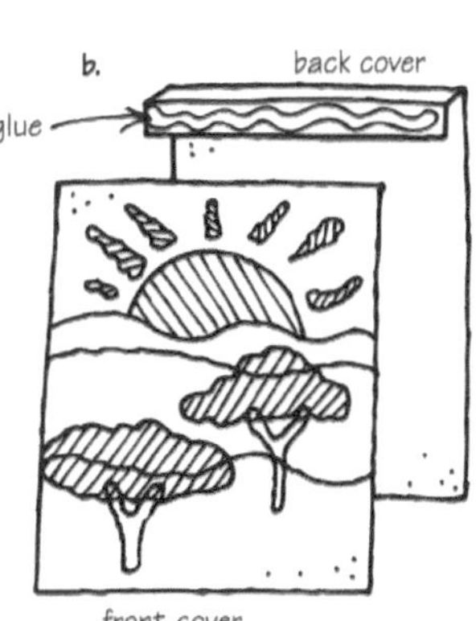

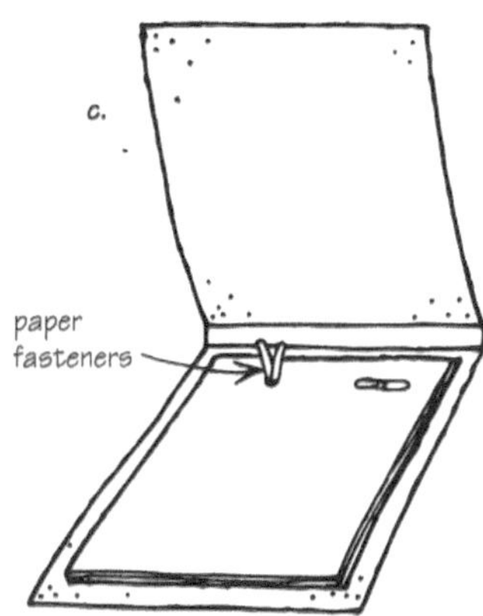

"Look Up!" Kite

Materials

- Bible
- kite pattern (p. 224)
- card stock
- cotton string
- sturdy wrapping paper in a light color (or roll paper)
- wide gift ribbon (or crepe-paper streamers)
- scissors
- ruler
- pencils
- colored markers
- tape
- hole punch
- drinking straws (2 per kid)
- toilet paper tubes (1 per kid)

Before Class

Copy the kite pattern onto card stock and cut out several patterns. Cut the wrapping paper into 8" x 14" rectangles, one for each student. Cut ribbon into 30" lengths, two for each student. Cut string into 40" lengths and 25' lengths, one of each length for each student. (Safety note: Never use metal such as wire, tinsel, or foil to make or decorate a kite.)

Simplification Idea

Prepare kite reels with cotton string before class, one for each student.

Instructions for Kids

- Fold a piece of wrapping paper in half the short way, Place the kite pattern on the fold of the wrapping paper, as shown on sketch a. Trace the pattern and cut out the kite.
- Use a marker to print "Look Up!" on the kite. Draw other decorations on the kite, if desired.
- Place a small strip of tape around each corner of the kite to reinforce the corners (sketch c).
- Attach two straws to the back side of the kite, as shown in sketch b, taping the ends of the straws.
- Punch a hole in each of the two farthest corners (sketch b).
- Tie a 1" loop at the center of a 40" length of string (sketch c). Tie each loose end of this string through the punched holes in the corners of the kite to make a bridle.
- Tape two ribbons onto the bottom edge of the kite to make kite tails (sketch d). Then reinforce the bottom edge of the kite with a long strip of tape.
- Flatten a toilet paper tube and tape one end of a 25' length of string onto the tube. Then wrap the string around the flattened tube to make a kite reel.
- Tie the other end of the flying line to the loop in the bridle on the kite (sketch d).

Talk About

What do you look forward to seeing or doing someday? Encourage the kids to share their ideas. **When Jesus returned to heaven after His resurrection, angels promised the disciples that Jesus would come back someday.** Read Acts 1:10–11. **Revelation 22 says three times that Jesus is coming soon.** Read Revelation 22:7, 12, and 20. **To fly your kite, take the kite outside and hold it up. As the wind begins to carry the kite, slowly release the string so that the kite rises with the wind. As you fly the kite, look up and remember that Jesus is coming back someday. As followers of Jesus, we can look forward to seeing and being with Jesus!**

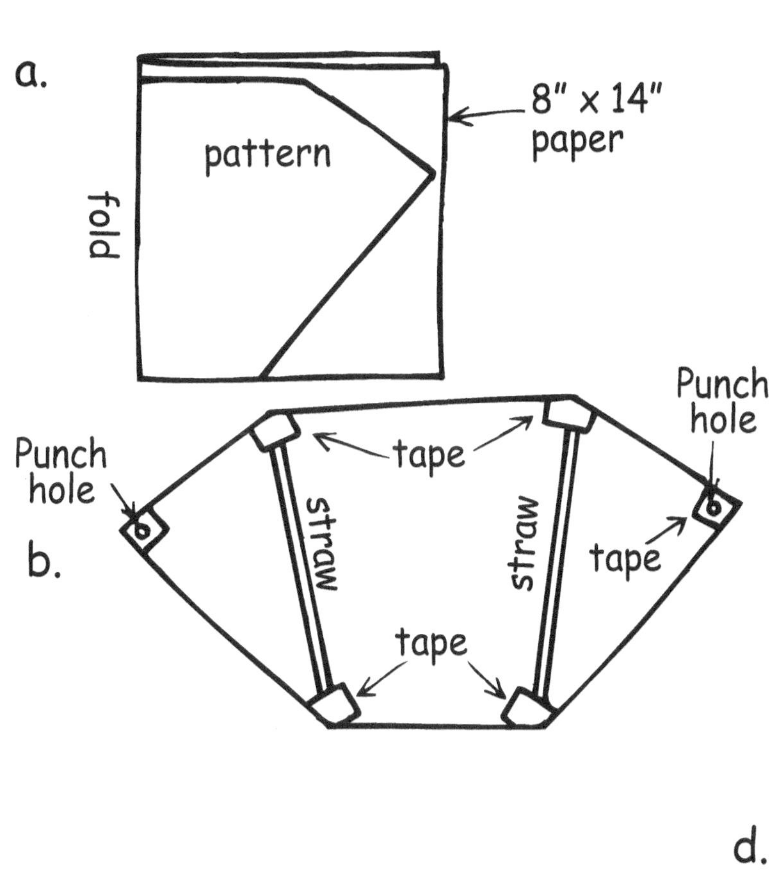

a.
8" x 14"
paper
pattern
fold
b.
Punch
hole
Punch
hole
tape
straw
straw
tape
tape

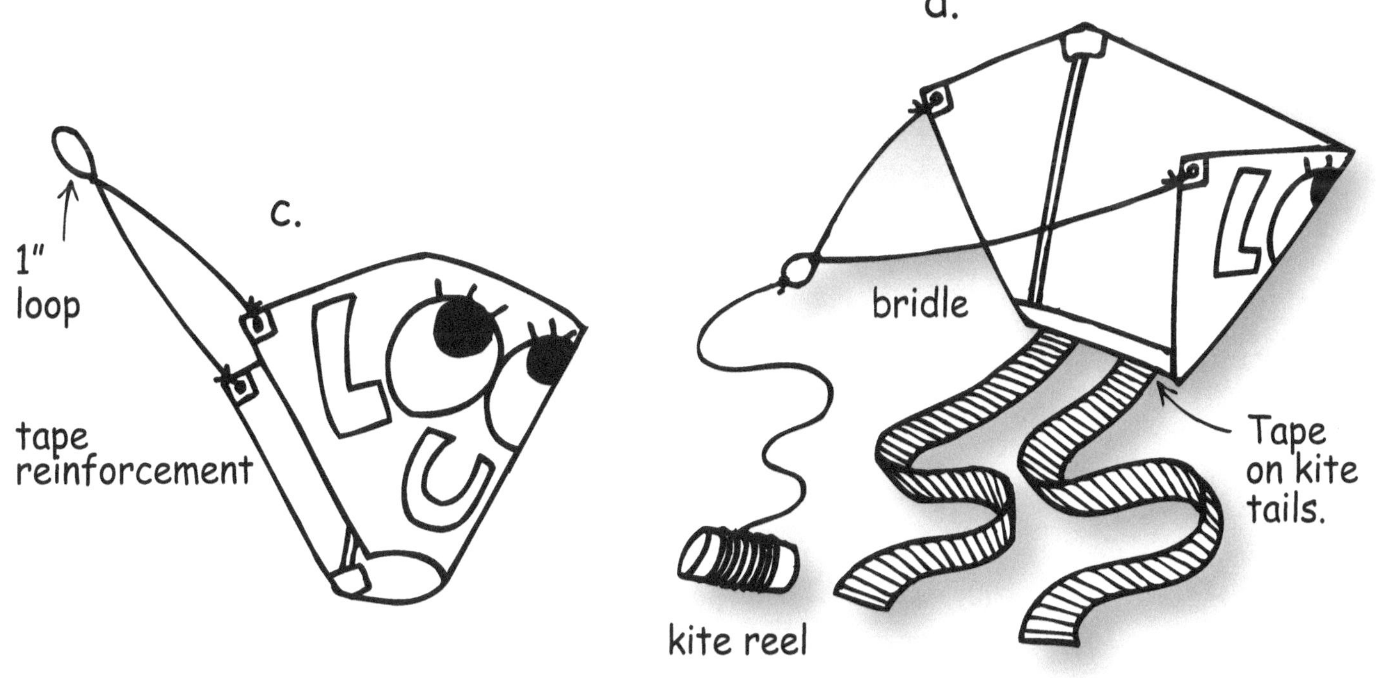

c.
1"
loop
tape
reinforcement
d.
bridle
Tape
on kite
tails.
kite reel

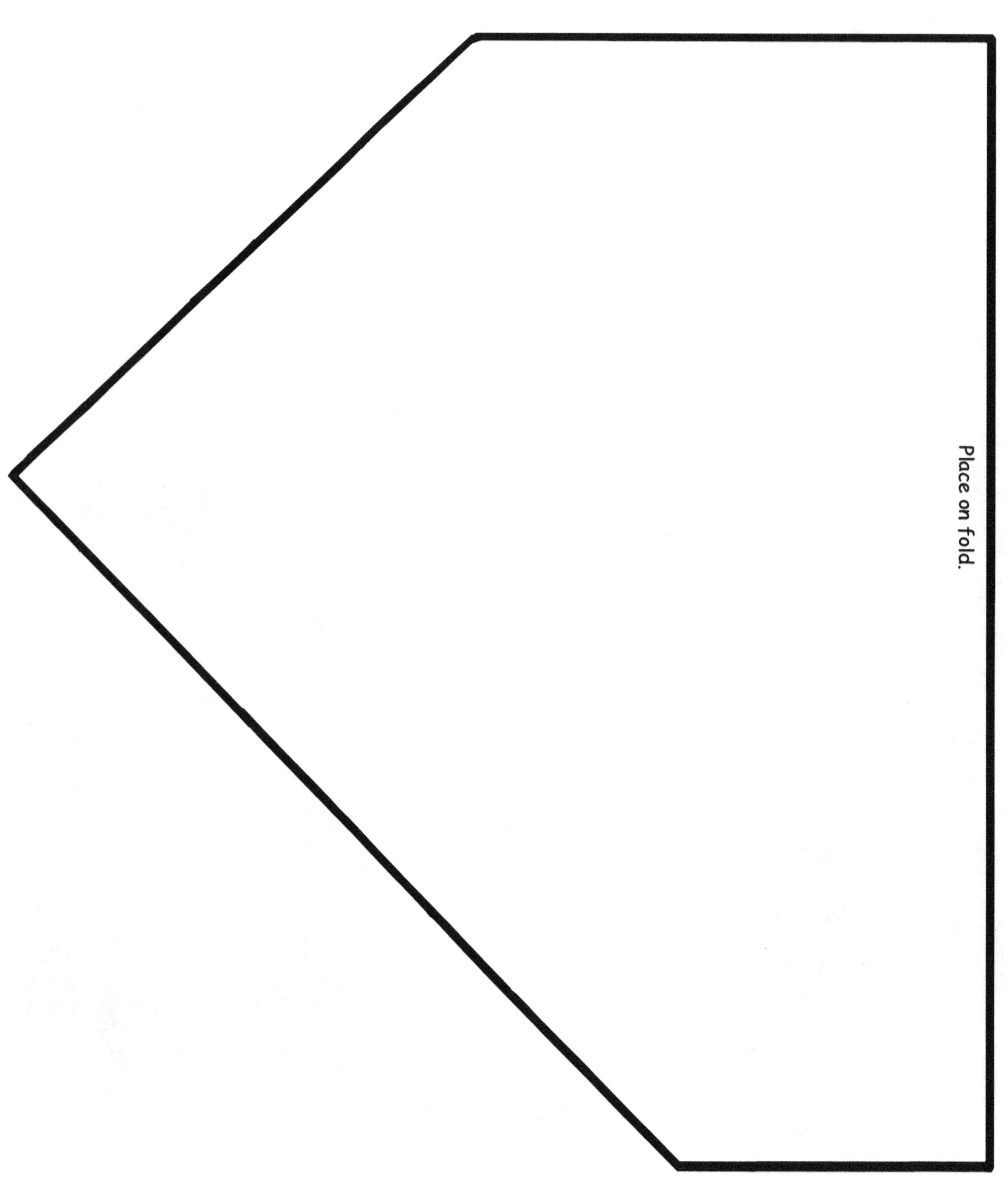
Place on fold.